INSIDE THE
FOREIGN
LEGION

INSIDE THE
FOREIGN
LEGION

THE SENSATIONAL STORY OF THE
WORLD'S TOUGHEST ARMY

JOHN PARKER

PIATKUS

First published in 1998 by
Judy Piatkus (Publishers) Limited
5 Windmill Street
London W1P 1HF

First paperback edition 1999

*A catalogue record for this book is available
from the British Library*

ISBN 0 7499 1856 X (HB)
0 7499 1992 2 (PB)

Edited by John Malam
Designed by Paul Saunders

Typeset by Phoenix Photosetting, Chatham, Kent
Printed and bound in Great Britain by
Mackays of Chatham PLC, Chatham, Kent

CONTENTS

ACKNOWLEDGEMENTS

Many people have contributed to this book by way of long and detailed interviews with the author amounting to some 118 hours on tape, as well as making available their own memorabilia, photographs, personal diaries, private memoirs and archives. Although documentary research provides the basis for the story of the French Foreign Legion in its early years, the author was fortunate to have the benefit of much previously unpublished material provided by Mr Jim Worden, an accredited historian of the Foreign Legion, who was for many years *secretaire général* of the *Association Amicale des Anciens Combattants de la Légion Étrangère de Grande-Bretagne* (the Foreign Legion Association of Great Britain) and who very kindly made available his own archives, notes and accounts written and collated over the last thirty years. Otherwise, principle sources were men who have served between five and twenty-one years in the Legion, and, as will be evident from the text, personal recall was relied upon for the running narrative for the last sixty years of its history, beginning with John Yeowell who joined in 1938 through to those whose service ended in 1997: frank, intriguing and fascinating recollections, encompassing not only the men's service in the Legion, but explanations as to why they joined, and stayed. Thereafter, most became members of the British Veterans Association, of which John Yeowell was a founder member.

The anonymity that the Foreign Legion affords all its volunteers is respected here, and some contributors remain unidentified or have been given fictitious names for the purpose of this account. The author wishes to record his sincere thanks to all of them, and particularly to Brigadier Tony Hunter-Choat OBE, former President and now Secretary General of the Association, who also read this manuscript prior to publication; John Duckmanton who succeeded him as President; John Yeowell, Robert Wilson, Kevin John Maunder, Paul James, Phil Meason, Michael Nisbet and Tadeusz Michniewicz.

FOREWORD
by Brigadier A. Hunter-Choat, OBE

In a speech made in 1981, at the 150th anniversary of the formation of the French Foreign Legion, the speaker remarked that it took the Legion to create Algeria, but it took Algeria to create the Legion. It goes further than that. Legionnaires for the past 167 years have been formed and indelibly marked by their experiences in the Legion, while the Legion has gained its strength and strength of character from the disparate wealth of its individual members. The Legion is, and has always been, unique. Not simply because it is an officially recognized and employed mercenary force, but because of the marvellous and skilful balance of national and individual characteristics, blended together to produce *Monsieur Légionnaire*. Throughout its long, hard, often brutal, always bloody history, the Legion has gathered to it all those of like character and forged them with the hammer of discipline on the anvil of combat into the world's most famous fighting force. This forging and developing is a never-ending process, and the Legion changes with changing times.

The early wars in Algeria, Morocco and Spain, the debilitating soul-destroying Mexican campaign in the late 19th century, the blood and mud of World War I, the Rif campaigns, World War II from Narvik to Alsace, the fearsome battles throughout Indo-China, the drawn-out Algerian 'war' and its demoralizing conclusion, and the plethora of worldwide operations since, many still ongoing, have all been part of the formative process and need to be understood if one is to fathom what is a legionnaire. John Parker describes them well and takes the reader beyond dry history into the battles themselves, and into the legionnaires' reactions to them. Their reactions are usually total disdain! He then leads us into that which the book set out to achieve, and that which I doubted could be achieved – an understanding of what the British and Irish (those the French loosely call *les anglais*) see as the Legion and what it has made of them. And achieve it he does, admirably. Over recent years there have been two outstanding histories of the Legion (Tony Geraghty's *March or Die*, and Douglas Porch's *The French Foreign Legion*) but John Parker breaks new ground with his superb research into long gone legionnaires; and interviews with the living – from John Yeowell who joined in 1938, to Arthur, who has only just left.

Their stories are fascinating, fun and revealing. They reveal that since its formation in 1831, although the Legion has changed and developed, the essential character of the legionnaire remains unchanged. The physical changes to the Legion have been enormous; the size has fluctuated from as high as 34,000 in Indo-China, to 26,000 in Algeria to 8,200 today; from four or five nationalities at the beginning to 121 today. Modernization, rationalization, downsizing, sophistication – it's all there, but ask the legionnaire what he feels about it, what he feels about his 'country' – *Legio Patria Nostra* – and you will get the same answers over the years.

And what do these answers tell the reader? Has the Legion changed in essence? No, of course it hasn't, and it cannot afford to, other than in appearances. All the factors that have given the Legion its strength and made it the fighting force par excellence it undoubtedly is, are still there in abundance. And the factor which has the greatest influence on the character of the Legion is the character of each and every legionnaire.

Tony Hunter-Choat
former 1167798 Sergent Choat
1st Foreign Parachute Regiment

MAPS

FOREIGN LEGION BASES IN FRANCE AND CORSICA

FRANCE

PARIS ●

ORANGE ●
NÎMES ● ● AVIGNON
CASTELNAUDARY ●
MARSEILLE ● ● AUBAGNE

CALVI ●
CORSICA

ML 0   50   100
KM 0 50 100 150

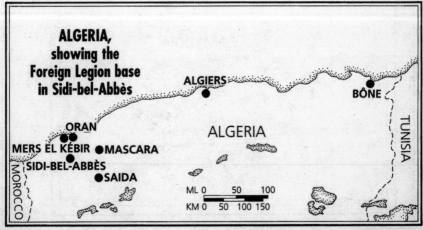

ALGERIA, showing the Foreign Legion base in Sidi-bel-Abbès

ALGIERS ●
BÔNE ●

ALGERIA

TUNISIA

ORAN ●
MERS EL KÉBIR ● ● MASCARA
SIDI-BEL-ABBÈS ●
SAÏDA ●

MOROCCO

ML 0   50   100
KM 0 50 100 150

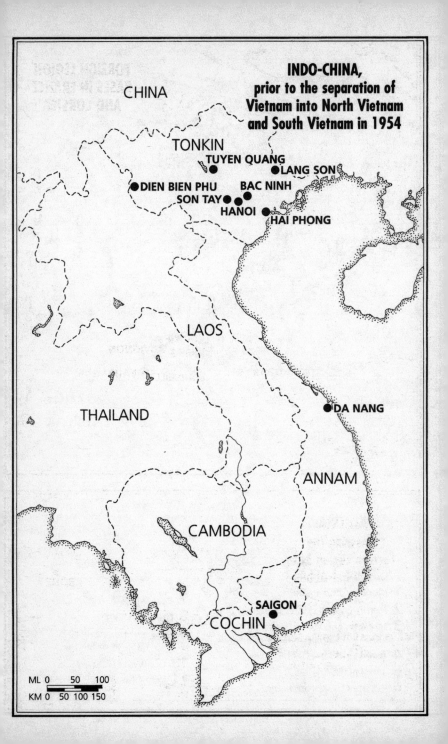

INDO-CHINA,
prior to the separation of
Vietnam into North Vietnam
and South Vietnam in 1954

CHINA

TONKIN

TUYEN QUANG

LANG SON

DIEN BIEN PHU

BAC NINH

SON TAY

HANOI

HAI PHONG

LAOS

THAILAND

DA NANG

ANNAM

CAMBODIA

SAIGON

COCHIN

ML 0   50   100
KM 0   50 100 150

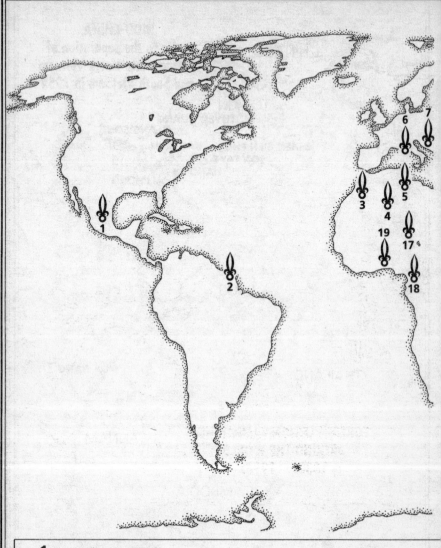

1 Mexico (1863 – 1869)
2 French Guiana (1968, continuing)
3 Morocco and Western Sahara (1904 – 1959)
4 Algeria (1831 – 1971)
5 Tunisia (1884 – 1957)
6 Corsica (1958, continuing)
7 Bosnia (1992, continuing)
8 Crimea (1884)
9 Syria and Lebanon (1919 – 1945, intermittently in Beirut)
10 Gulf War (1990 – 1991)
11 Indo-China (1893 – 1954)

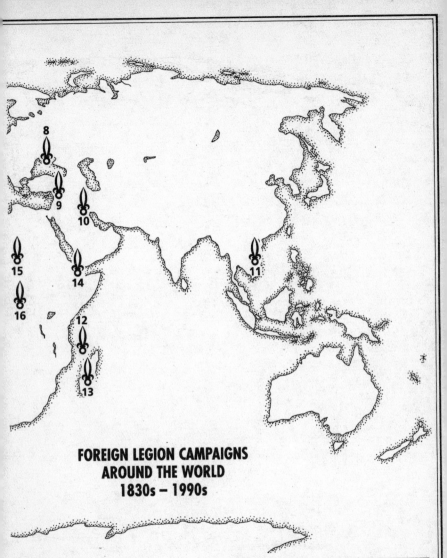

FOREIGN LEGION CAMPAIGNS
AROUND THE WORLD
1830s – 1990s

12 Mayotte, Comoros Islands (1912, continuing)

13 Madagascar (1896 – 1969)

14 Djibouti (1888, continuing)

15 Chad (1910, continuing intermittently)

16 Central African Republic and Zaire (1880s – 1979)

17 Niger (1890 – 1960)

18 Cameroon (1919 – 1960)

19 Benin, formerly Dahomey (1899 – 1960)

Louis-Philippe, Roi des Français,

À tous présens et à venir, Salut :

Les Chambres ont adopté, Nous avons ordonné et ordonnons ce qui suit :

Article 1er

Il pourra être formé dans l'intérieur du Royaume une Légion d'Étrangers, mais elle ne pourra être employée que hors du Territoire continental du Royaume

Article 2e

Les Généraux en chef commandant les pays occupés par les armées françaises hors du territoire continental, pourront être autorisés à former des Corps militaires composés d'indigènes et d'étrangers

Article 3e

Les dépenses de ces divers corps formeront un article séparé au Budget de la guerre

La présente loi, discutée, délibérée et adoptée par la chambre des Pairs et par celle des Députés et sanctionnée par nous ce jourd'hui, sera exécutée comme loi de l'État.

Donnons en Mandement à nos Cours et Tribunaux, Préfets, Corps administratifs et tous autres, que les présentes ils gardent et maintiennent, fassent garder, observer et maintenir, et, pour les rendre plus notoires à tous, ils les fassent publier et enregistrer partout où besoin sera, et afin que ce soit chose ferme et stable à toujours, Nous y avons fait mettre Notre Sceau.

Donné à Paris, au Palais Royal le Neuf Mars, mil huit cent trente un.

Louis Philippe

Par le Roi,

Le Ministre Secrétaire d'État de la Guerre,
Mal Duc de Dalmatie

Vu et Scellé du Grand Sceau :
Le Ministre Secrétaire d'État au Département de la Marine et des Colonies, remplissant par intérim les fonctions de Garde des Sceaux, Ministre de la Justice,

V. d'Argout

Louis Philippe's original document authorizing the formation of the Foreign Legion

INSIDE THE
FOREIGN
LEGION

PROLOGUE

FIRST IMPRESSIONS

'Indoctrination relies heavily on the Legion's history – its most famous battles, its heroes, its passionate music and songs, so that the Legion becomes a kind of Sacred Order.'

IN 1863, a few dozen legionnaires sheltering in a tumbledown hacienda in Mexico held 2,000 heavily equipped Mexican troops at bay for twelve hours, until there were only two of them left standing . . .

Each April, members of the Foreign Legion Association of Great Britain parade before the London memorial to France's great military hero of World War I, Marshal Ferdinand Foch, to commemorate that obscure battle in Mexico more than a century earlier.

The *Récit du Combat*, which describes the Battle of Camerone in detail, is read aloud annually on every Legion parade ground, fort, encampment or post around the globe, and at every veterans' commemoration. It has become the Legion's credo. It is the cornerstone of a tradition with which recruits are indoctrinated; some say it is the key to understanding what the Legion is about. And, more intriguingly, it provides the clue to why men of the world still volunteer for service in an army whose reputation for heroism on the front-line is matched by the harshest of training methods, a tough regime that has been tempered only moderately by the requirements of modern civil and human rights. These two elements – the Legion of France's cannon-fodder and the brutality of its NCOs – have historically remained the most controversial.

The shock of the training routine is often too much for many to bear, even for tough soldiers who have served in other elite forces. One in eight desert, and their stories have made headlines through the ages. And so, as a beginning, the first impressions of a young British legionnaire who joined the modern Foreign Legion – and stayed – give a taster of what any new recruit can expect in an army whose toughness is still moulded by corporal techniques, born in an age when France used the Legion at the forefront of its colonial wars.

Mich, 35, a cool, exceedingly articulate Londoner of Polish extract who joined the Legion's renowned Parachute Regiment, was one of the few in his batch who had more than a passing knowledge of the French language – a distinct advantage but only inasmuch that he was able to understand orders barked at him right from day one, while others stood open-mouthed – thus inviting the fist of a passing NCO.

I was 18 when I joined the Legion. I had tried before, but they discovered my true age when I surrendered my passport and sent me home. My ambition was to get a commission with the British Army after joining the cadets while at school. I had ten O-levels and one A-level at 16 and I was doing three more A-levels. I intended to go for a short service commission in the Royal Marines. I failed the eye test, being short-sighted. My next choice was the Parachute Regiment but there was a two-year waiting list and they suggested I joined the Royal Engineers. I didn't want to do that. So . . . I took a train to Paris and turned up at Fort Nugent. By the end of the week there were ten who had volunteered at Fort Nugent and another nine who came from recruiting centres in Northern France. Out of the Paris ten, there were three other Brits, two of whom were ex-British servicemen who had been discharged for unruly behaviour. They had met in Colchester military prison and had discussed joining the Foreign Legion. They hadn't met since, and both happened to join at the same time.

Everyone looked pathetic; we looked and felt miserable. We took a slow overnight train to Marseille and we were more or less locked up in our compartment. We were picked up by trucks and taken to the Legion headquarters at Aubagne. There, it depended on how fast they managed to process us, usually between two and three weeks, before we knew whether we had been accepted or not. At the beginning of the process, the procedure that has been experienced by new legionnaires down the ages remains much the same – your passport and all other documents, personal belongings and civilian clothes are taken away from you. The documents and other items are put away and given back only when you leave the Legion. But the likelihood is that you will never see your civilian clothes again unless you are discharged during training.

I knew it was going to be tough. Even so, nothing prepared you for the shock of the first days of training. There were corporals and sergeants shouting and screaming at everyone. We were driven to the training camp at Castelnaudary, on the way to Toulouse, north of the Pyrennes. The camp is quite large within what was a small market town, square-shaped and surrounded by high walls. There was only one central gate, the only entry and exit point, with sentry boxes on either side.

Barbed wire rolled all along the tops of the walls for the whole perimeter and though there were no guard towers, searchlights were trained upon the walls at night. At the front of the camp, the first thing you see is the guardhouse and a horseshoe-shaped layout with the parade ground in the middle.

On the first parade there was a thorough inspection going on by a *sergent-chef* named Georges Doulon who later became second-in-command of my unit in the paras. He was a big man. I was quite large myself, but he was taller than me with a face that looked like it was chiseled in granite, apart from his large bulbous nose.

He pushed that nose straight in my face, eyeballs to eyeballs, and said, 'Did you shave this morning?' There was no point in lying. The next thing I knew, I was doubled up in agony. He just punched me in the solar plexus and as my head came down his knee came up straight on to my nose and when I fell to the ground, he kicked me in the ribs. He walked on saying, 'Make sure you shave tomorrow.'

3

'Bastard,' I cursed under my breath. And everyone else, all the other newcomers, were all going, 'O-o-oh . . . shit!'

From the word go, they tell you: you are here, you volunteered into an elite, the only reason this elite exists is to die for France. They try not to mention France that much. The national pride bit is definitely downplayed. You are fighting to uphold the values and the traditions of the Foreign Legion, and great ceremony surrounds that aim, with the rousing songs, the tear-jerking music of the Legion bands, the constant reference to Legion heroes of the past. The sergeants taunt you with it: 'What would the heroes of Dien Bien Phu think of you?', and you hear all those quotes from past leaders about 'You are legionnaires in order to die . . .'

Therefore at the end of basic training, I came out convinced – and I am not joking, it is absolutely true – that the highest honour I could achieve in life was to die in battle for the Foreign Legion.

Recruitment policies have barely changed in more than a century, although today far fewer volunteers are accepted. All who apply are interviewed, but fewer than one in six are taken on. Volunteers have to be between the ages of 17 and 40, physically fit and able to pass a relatively modest intelligence test. Previous military experience is not necessary. They need not even possess a knowledge of the French language which, says its current literature, will be 'acquired' during the contract. There is a somewhat sinister implication in that word.

The first contract is for five years. To enlist, a volunteer must present himself at any recruiting office in France. Travel costs and any other expenses incurred in reaching the Legion's doorstep are borne by the candidate, as he is known until acceptance, and 'no help whatsoever can be accorded by the French Foreign Legion'. After a preliminary medical examination, he is transferred to the selection centre of Legion headquarters, at Aubagne, fifteen kilometres from Marseille, where he begins what is commonly known as 'The Process' – IQ and physical fitness tests and interrogation by the *Bureau des Statistiques de La Légion Étrangère*, unaffectionately known to all as 'The Gestapo'. Those who pass must sign a five-year unconditional contract to serve wherever the French Foreign Legion needs them. The contract is unbreakable, except through injury or illness and it is unlikely that, certainly during the first three years, a legionnaire will be able to return to his own country.

Candidates rejected by the interrogators are immediately given a rail ticket to the frontier in France which is nearest their own country. But even at that stage, acceptance of the selected candidates is not guaranteed. The would-be legionnaire is now confronted by the rigours of the final hurdle, a gruelling and fearsome four-month preliminary training ritual at the 4th Foreign Regiment in Castelnaudary. If he passes that – and up to fifty per cent do not – he is posted to a regiment, depending on his capabilities and the needs of the Legion at the time.

The indoctrination of the candidate now begins in earnest. It relies heavily on the Legion's history – its most famous battles, its heroes, its passionate music and songs which are drummed into them with religious-like fervour, so that the Legion, above all else, becomes a kind of Sacred Order. Most who join it agree that in the end, the way forward in the Legion is in the acceptance of its discipline, learned by painful example by way of fist or boot to a point where the spirit is thrashed but not entirely broken, so that it can be rekindled in the man now to be moulded into a legionnaire.

Progress in what has been described as one of the toughest regimes in military history in the end becomes a question of personal endeavour and sheer bravado among its men, with displays of almost unreal fortitude because that is what is expected, not just by superiors but by comrades. Anyone who cannot withstand the beatings and the harsh realities of Legion life is rejected by both. The specifics are laid down in a Code of Honour, prepared in the early 1900s, which is as poignant today as then:

CODE OF HONOUR

1 Legionnaire: you are a volunteer serving France faithfully and with honour.

2 Every Legionnaire is your brother-at-arms, irrespective of his nationality, race or creed. You will demonstrate this by an unwavering and straightforward solidarity which must always bind together members of the same family.

3 Respectful of the Legion's traditions, honouring your superiors, discipline and comradeship are your strength, courage and loyalty your virtues.

4 Proud of your status as a legionnaire, you will display this pride, by your turnout, always impeccable, your behaviour, ever worthy, though modest, your living-quarters, always tidy.

5 An elite soldier, you will train vigorously, you will maintain your weapons as if they were your most precious possession, you will keep your body in the peak of condition, always fit.

6 A mission once given to you becomes sacred to you, you will accomplish it to the end and at all costs.

7 In combat, you will act without relish of your tasks, or hatred; you will respect the vanquished enemy and will never abandon neither your wounded nor your dead, nor will you under any circumstances surrender your arms.

And so, like gladiators, they are drawn into an arena of death-defying one-upmanship by examples of bravery and courage among their Legion ancestors. The discipline and skills with which they are supposed to be instilled are the platforms on which all else is built. It was always meant to be an army like no other, necessarily controlled, it is said, by iron discipline. Bend to the regime or your life will be hell; bend to it or get out. Many do run away – between 6 and 8 per cent of the annual intake. And beyond the modern route into the French Foreign Legion is a scenario which fluctuates dramatically between hell on earth and the sheer pride of achievement and camerarderie. The latter is best viewed on Bastille Day at the annual grand parade of French military might that makes its way down the Champs Élysées. The armed forces and their hardware pass by to stirring military music and then, for a moment, silence, until the crowds erupt into cheers and a standing ovation as another sound begins – the slower marching music of *Le Boudin* and the legionnaires, perfectly presented, pristine and stern, go on parade in their drawling, arrogant style of eighty-eight paces to the minute (the pace of kings and emperors) instead of the faster 120 rate of the regular armies.

On that day, France cheers the men who have saved thousands of young French lives, simply by being in the front-line of most of France's major conflicts since its formation.

1

1831: LEGIO PATRIA NOSTRA

'Not only has the Legion taken the place of his country,
it becomes his family. He is a member of it and
nothing else.'

THE LEGION *is Our Fatherland.* Legionnaires are familiar with that phrase and in time become comfortable with it. The reason has been no better described than by Major PC Wren in an interview at the time of the publication of his famous book *Beau Geste*, a quotation that is as relevant today as when he made it seventy-five years ago:

Practically no man is there [in the Foreign Legion] under his own name, or what he was. What he is now is a legionnaire and all legionnaires are equal in the sight of God, or at any rate in the sight of the NCO. Before long, under the necessary terrible discipline, a legionnaire becomes a legionnaire and nothing more. The legion is his country and his home. The Legion is his flag; his national pride becomes the pride of the Legion. Not only has the Legion taken the place of his country, it becomes his family. He is a member of it and nothing else. He is more 'apart' than any other man, save perhaps a monk in a monastery. This is shown by the fact that a man who has endured five terrible years, re-enlists to serve another five, and perhaps another.

Legio Patria Nostra.

That's the way it had been since the Foreign Legion came into existence. After the 1830 July Revolution, which sent King Charles X into exile, France was awash with political infighting and intrigue. The new king, Louis-Philippe, was the most bourgeois of monarchs, whose favourite weapon was an umbrella. His bronze bust in the Legion's trophy room at its Aubagne headquarters carries an inscription taken from the decree to form a legion of foreigners who were banned from service within France's continental borders, and who would go to fight largely in its burgeoning colonies.

The Legion was not entirely made up of foreigners. The majority of its officers were, and still are, French and a large number of French volunteers enlisted under false nationalities. When he created the new regiment on 9 March 1831, Louis-Philippe made one or two important stipulations. According to Legion historian Erwan Bergot, the Legion had a dual purpose – to form a fighting force to protect and extend the colonies and 'to remove from France those officers and soldiers . . . who were felt to be awkward, excitable or frankly dangerous subjects for the new monarchy'. They would be sent immediately to take possession of Algeria which France had formally annexed for colonization three years later. It became a natural base for Louis-Philippe's new army, as a springboard to France's other colonial interests across the African continent and to help protect the thousands of *colons* about to come flooding across from France to form the privileged white elite.

They were a pretty sorry sight; a rabble. In the ranks were the flotsam of Europe as well as some very tough and experienced soldiers. The officer corps, on the other hand, was made up of men from disgruntled out-of-favour families or, more likely, men who craved action and excitement and who cared little for the form it took. They were renowned duellists, thrill-seekers, dare-devils and risk-takers who thrived on a permanent air of aggressiveness within the officers' mess.

One of them from that era, Charles Clemmer whose experiences were set down in a book published in France in the late 1890s, joined the Legion in Algeria and found among his colleagues, as with himself, an eagerness for the fight, in whatever form it might take, whether off duty or in battle. From these earliest of descriptions, it will be seen that not a lot has changed in the intervening years. In Clemmer's own words:

> We fought for the pleasure of fighting. Without rhyme or reason, we sought a quarrel with people we did not even know whom we had never met. Anything served as a pretext in the bars and cabarets: a song begun at another table . . . a gesture, even a look was interpreted as requiring a duel.

As Douglas Porch noted, the aggressiveness of Legion officers, and especially the battalion commanders, formed one of the great strengths of the corps. Given this example from the top, NCOs demonstrated their prowess by doing everything, and more, that they would ask of their troops. They also had to be of sufficient physical stature to beat any malcontents into submission. This formation of Legion officers, possessed by reckless fortitude and supported by the NCOs who had to whip virtual jailbait into shape, was its basis for the future and the patterns adopted then undoubtedly permeated down through the ages.

The Arab and Berber tribes of Algeria, more accustomed to 300 years of indirect Ottoman rule which allowed pirates to flourish, mustered fierce resistance to the arrival of the Legion. Their leader was the flamboyant and wealthy 25-year-old Islamic holy man Abd al-Qadir, who claimed descent from Muhammad. He used highly effective hit-and-run tactics and had an army of 50,000 to call upon. The Legion found itself confronted by an elusive enemy and began what would become a battle that was to run, off and on, for 130 years.

Then, an incredible development: having survived the initial sorties with al-Qadir and friends, Louis-Philippe promptly gave away his army of foreigners to Spain. The Foreign Legion was sent en masse to fight in a bloody civil war on behalf of the three-year-old Queen Isabella II against her uncle Don Carlos. The Legion ceased to be part of the French army on 20 June 1835. This, for Louis-Philippe, was an expedient way of assisting the young queen and disposing finally of those 'awkward, excitable and frankly dangerous people' he had exiled to the Legion in the first place. It was also cheaper than the British way of aiding Isabella. They sent 12,000 troops to help quell the Spanish coup.

The Foreign Legion in Spain was supposed to be paid and supplied by the Spanish queen for whom they were fighting, but this fact seemed to have been overlooked by their new employer. A modern Foreign Legion document records contemptuously: 'For good or ill, the officers and men had to accept this. They fought no less fiercely in deplorable conditions . . . without pay, rations or uniform in an adventure which ended three years later. Of the 4,000 legionnaires who took part in this campaign, only 500 returned.'

Statistics of this kind would also become a part of Legion history, repeated over and over again. In the meantime, the French regular army commanders faced a manpower shortage in their clashes with the Arabs. Four months after the first battalion was sent to Spain, Louis-Philippe signed a decree to raise a second French Foreign Legion on 16 December 1835. They were men of the same spirit and background, and it was this unit that is the true ancestor of today's Legion.

The new army picked up where the old one left off, fighting a seemingly unwinable war with guerrillas. Demands on the Legion were such that a second battalion was formed in July 1837, and a third in December that year, bringing their combined strength to 3,000. Spectactular and costly battles continued with al-Qadir, and the sheer weight of the Arab armies, along with disease and sickness, ravaged the Legion's numbers.

Settlements of colonialists they were supposed to protect were wiped out, the *colons* massacred and their villages burned to the ground. The anger of public opinion in France forced the government into action to protect the settlers, and in 1840 the Legion was formed into two regiments, 1st and 2nd *Régiment Étranger* (1RE and 2RE), the first to guard the western areas of the country and the second, stationed at Bone, to defend the Kabylia highlands and south towards Biskra where the Sahara joins the Aures mountains. A new governor general, Thomas Bugeaud de la Piconnerie, was appointed, and he demanded a new military strategy.

Bugeaud wanted a sharper claw and devised methods that were to become the pattern for the Legion of the future. He proposed to operate flying columns of men, racing ahead of the slow-moving military herd, attacking with the element of surprise. They were to carry the minimum of equipment and just enough supplies for survival, living off the land where possible. The legionnaires would have to endure arduous and fast forced marches over tough terrain, attacking enemy villages, killing the menfolk and their horses to preempt attack on the settlers – the kind of warfare in which no prisoners could, or would, be taken.

By the mid 1840s, the Bugeaud tactics began to pay off. Forced from town and village successively, al-Qadir finally surrendered in December 1847. After serving a term of imprisonment in France, he was eventually exiled to Damascus with a pension. There, thirteen years after his own battles with the French ended, and at risk to his own life, he persuaded the Turks to save 12,000 Christians, including many French nationals. The nation that had once imprisoned him as a war criminal now awarded him the *Légion d'Honneur*.

France began to colonize Algeria in earnest. To encourage settlement, the French confiscated or purchased land at low prices from Muslim owners. French schoolchildren grew up with a history lesson that placed Algeria as a province of France, separated by the Mediterranean in the same way that the Seine divided Paris.

The Legion, in preparing swifter lines of communication for its flying columns, built a mass of new roads and in times of peace, busied itself by improving the country's infrastructure further. Like the Romans, they left their architectural mark on the landscape. As numbers grew, they installed themselves in dozens of purpose-built forts, and in larger military bases at Mascara, Auragh, Saint Denis-de-Sug, and their most famous base of all, Sidi-bel-Abbès, ninety kilometres south of Oran. This fort began life as a supply dump for the flying columns, but by 1845 was earmarked as a fortified town to become the official home of the French Foreign Legion.

From its beginnings as a military base with a population of little more than 400, Sidi-bel-Abbès grew ten-fold within the decade, and to a city of 150,000 by the time the Legion was forced to evacuate and give way to independence little over a century later.

The Foreign Legion, growing stronger and more influential, though no less flamboyant, found itself on the front-lines of the Crimean War (1850s), and later the Italian War of Unification (1860s). It added both conflicts to its role of honour. Next came its adventures in Mexico . . . a costly campaign in a war that no one really cared about.

2

1863: CAMERONE, MEXICO

The infantry colonel who saved the lives of the remaining legionnaires took them to his commander, who uttered the famous description: 'Truly, these are not men but devils'.

JIM WORDEN from Bermondsey, south London, was at the 1998 Camerone Day commemoration in London, when representatives of the Legion presented him with an illuminated address for his many years' work as Secretary General of the British Association. He is one of the Legion's accredited historians who provides a graphic description of the moment he discovered the importance the Legion places on its past, especially on its heroes. None more so than those who took part in a small battle in Mexico which became the most famous in Legion history.

Although the Battle of Camerone (1863) had always taken its place high in Legion honours, the reasons for its importance were not crystalized until the 1920s, during a revamp of the war-ravaged army. It was to be used and promoted as the foundation for the new Legion code of *Honneur et Fidélité* to demonstrate to new recruits that the Legion was about courage in the face of extreme adversity, and equally important, that they should remember with respect the heroes of these conflicts.

Worden explained the significance of the one special day on which legionnaires everywhere salute the heroes of Camerone:

I first heard the account of the Battle of Camerone while standing rigidly to attention and presenting arms on the main Legion parade ground at Sidi-bel-Abbès, watching the wooden hand of Captain Danjou, which had been picked up after the carnage, being carried with reverence by a veteran adjutant. I could not help noticing that despite the black patch over an empty socket where an eye had once been, tears were running down his cheeks.

30 April is by order and by desire a very special event at which, every year, the *Récit du Combat de Camerone* is read aloud to all present on the parade ground. After the ceremony the legionnaires will sit down to a banquet, followed by a complete relaxation of formality and discipline, and a legionnaire can celebrate the remainder of the day in any fashion he wishes. It is on this day that the legionnaire will be unlikely to be charged with any minor infraction of rules and regulations, and it would be rare indeed if on this day a legionnaire found himself in the cells for any reason short of murder. Drunkenness has never been an offence in the Legion, unless a legionnaire has been unable to carry out his duty, and on this day, even if a legionnaire has fallen to the ground in a drunken stupor, he will only be considered by his superiors to be 'resting'.

However, such is the ingrained sense of discipline held by most legionnaires, each will realize that like Cinderella, his day of celebration will end on the stroke of midnight. He will have previously discovered also, that Legion NCOs, like elephants, have very long memories. Payment will be obtained later for any infringement of this particular code.

The fact is, Camerone is more than a day of celebration and tradition, it is almost a credo to both legionnaires and ex-legionnaires. It is an absolute requirement to understand why it is that this day above all others is the one most celebrated by the Legion. Why should a tiny battle in Mexico on 30 April 1863, at a place that no one has ever heard of, mean so much to the Legion, especially as this was a battle that had been lost? The fact is, that it was an outstanding example of what the Legion is about – *never surrender* – and what it would stand for in the future. That is why it is still celebrated with such reverence.

This is how it began . . .

Two years before the Battle of Camerone, the new Mexican president, Benito Pablo Juarez, suspended payment of interest on the country's debts. The French King, Napoleon III, having recently purchased some of the Mexican debts from a Swiss bank, demanded military action to secure his investment. He proposed the installation of a puppet monarch, Maximilian of Hapsburg, younger brother of Franz Josef of Austria. The French would send an expeditionary force of 3,000 to support him. They were joined by moderate and less than enthusiastic contingents from Britain and Spain. The French infantry arrived early in 1862, began their march inland and were promptly driven back to the beach where they had landed. The British and the Spanish withdrew their troops after heavy losses, but Napoleon III refused to accept the humiliation of retreat.

By the year's end, the French had ferried 40,000 men across the Atlantic, falling ever deeper into another guerilla war. The Foreign Legion had not been called upon to support this intervention. It had been considered that the international forces of the French, British and Spanish regular armies would have neither need of the Legion, nor of their methods of fighting. The French army were laying siege to Mexico City, and developing large concentrations of forces at Puebla.

The Legion, languishing at Sidi-bel-Abbès, in Algeria, began to get restless. They complained they were being used simply as police troops and construction workers. Junior officers, fearing dissension and stagnation, petitioned Napoleon III, begging that they be allowed to participate in the 'Mexicana Affaire'. On 19 January 1863, approval was received from Paris. A regiment of march, comprising two battalions of infantry, a base company and the band left for Mexico. The Legion's 3rd Battalion would remain in Algeria to hold the garrison and train new Legion recruits for Mexico.

On 9 February, the 2,000-strong Legion contingent sailed from Oran. It consisted of 48 officers, 1,432 Legionnaires along with sundry support forces which included eight canteen managers. They arrived on 28 March at Vera Cruz, 250 kilometres from where the French army had stalled in the face of strong local resistance at Puebla. The legionnaires discovered they were not being thrust into battle. Their task was to secure and safeguard French supply lines which travelled through 120 kilometres of tropical swamplands. The French Commander-in-Chief, General Forey, made no secret of his decision to place the Legion on guard duty. 'I preferred to leave foreigners, rather than French, to guard that most unhealthy area,' he wrote.

As the legionnaires soon discovered, their enemy was not the Mexicans but disease. Malaria, yellow fever, typhus and many infections not yet existing in the textbooks of their medical orderlies were soon attacking the newcomers. Within weeks, sickness had taken a huge toll on the Legion's strength. So much so that when the Legion's commanding officer, Colonel Jeanningros, was summoned to muster two companies to protect a slow-moving convoy, he had difficulty in staffing it.

The convoy was of particular importance. It consisted of sixty horse-drawn wagons filled with heavy guns, ammunition, supplies and three million francs in gold pieces bound for General Foley, bogged down at Puebla. Two days later, on 29 April, Jeanningros received news from a spy that the convoy was to be ambushed, not by guerrillas but by the Mexican army, anxious to avail itself of the new weapons, and the gold. Several battalions of Mexican regular infantry were already moving into position. Jeanningros detailed the 3rd Company of the 1st Battalion of the Legion to go out on patrol and hopefully make contact with the convoy and/or track the movements of the ambush troops. The Company was a sorry sight, decimated by sickness. Only sixty-two of the original 120 were still standing, and not a single officer among them.

A member of the commander's own HQ staff, Captain Jean Danjou, volunteered to lead the Company, and he was joined by two lieutenants promoted from the ranks, Vilain, not yet thirty, and a dour veteran sergeant named Maudet who had also fought at the Crimea and Magenta. Among the NCOs was Corporal Berg, who had given up a career as an officer in the French regular army to join the Legion, and Corporal Maine, who also left the regular army at the rank of sergeant major, having decided that only in the Legion would he find what he believed was his true vocation, as a fighting soldier. With Captain Danjou at their head, and with his newly promoted officers and the Company drummer, Legionnaire Lai, immediately behind, they set off marching in the cooler temperatures of the night towards Palo Verde, stopping only for a coffee break at a post held by the battalion's Grenadier Company.

Danjou pressed on and at dawn they were making their way through the foothills and deep ravines of the Mexican mountains, dotted only with scorched and withering trees. They were already suffering from the morning heat when he called a halt as they reached the humid plains close to Palo Verde around 7 a.m. The men sat down on the parched ground, tired and hot. Out of the dusty packs came the mess tins and soon the smell of coffee rose in the morning air. Danjou, a square, tall man with a small goatee beard walked among them, fiddling occasionally with the leather strap that attached his articulated wooden left hand to his forearm. The men had hardly time to drink their coffee when from the crest behind them, a sentry reported a cloud of dust from approaching horsemen, heading from the direction they had marched.

Danjou called the two lieutenants and ordered the Company to draw their arms and move out. The barren spot they had chosen to rest was no place to meet the oncoming Mexicans and he decided to head back to the tumbledown collection of farm buildings near Camerone which they had passed earlier, about half a mile or so away. They didn't make it. A swarm of Mexican cavalry, guns firing, reached them when they were still some distance from the farm. They took up position in thick, low scrub.

'Form a square,' Danjou ordered. 'Fire only on orders.'

The Mexicans divided into two squadrons, to attack the legionnaires from opposite sides. They approached in a controlled walk, then at fifty metres, the 'Charge' order was given, and with sabres flashing the Mexicans headed in at the gallop.

Simultaneously Captain Danjou screamed, 'Fire!'

The legionnaires opened fire with their first round and then waited for the second command: 'Fire!' Another sixty rounds exploded into the horseflesh and the riders. The Mexicans took some heavy casualties, pulled up and turned away. Danjou barked another order: 'Fire at will!'

The legionnaires, with one foot forward, and heads down fired volley after volley into the mass of men and screaming horses. In the pandemonium, the Mexicans drew back, evidently surprised at the resistance. The legionnaires took the chance to make a dash for cover in a roadside hacienda, leaving their dead where they had fallen and the mules carrying their supplies disappearing into the distance.

Within fifteen minutes of the start of a running fight, Danjou, the two officers and forty-six legionnaires reached farm buildings, surrounded by a stone quadrangle. The large rickety wooden gates were rapidly slammed shut and barred with timber. Danjou deployed his men at strategic points in the buildings, some at windows in the farmhouse, others inside and on top of the stable block, more still lining the walls of the yard. Another Legion veteran, a Polish sergeant named Morzycki, climbed to the highest point of the roof, and came back with the gloomy report that there were 'hundreds of Mexicans all around us'.

Meanwhile, a cavalry rider had reached the encampment of the Mexican infantry, an hour's march away, under the command of Colonel Milan. His reaction erred on the side of overkill. He ordered his three battalions to move out and head for the scene. Under a blazing sun, the Mexican cavalry had reduced the pace of the battle, sending in snipers or rushing the weakest parts of Danjou's defences. They fought for two hours with little change in the situation until, at 9.30, the Mexicans put up a white flag and sent Lieutenant Ramon Laine to the gate of the hacienda, offering to accept an honourable surrender so as to end the slaughter.

'There are 2,000 of us, and more on the way,' said the lieutenant. 'We guarantee you safe conduct as prisoners of war.'

Danjou sent him packing.

By 11.00, he had lost another twelve men. Every quarter of an hour, crawling on his hands and knees, he made a tour of his defences, talking to his men. He asked each one to take an oath to fight unto death. One by one they took it.

At 11.30, Danjou was shot, a bullet in the throat. Lieutenant Vilain took his medals and his sword. He was now the leader of the company's remaining thirty-two men capable of continuing the fight. At 12.00 the legionnaires heard bugles and drums. For a moment they thought that their own regiment had come up to their rescue. Their hopes were quickly dashed as another 1,000 Mexicans, having secured the convoy, appeared on the horizon.

Lieutenant Vilain took a bullet in the forehead and died instantly at 2.00. Maudet took command. The heat was now overpowering and they had no food or water and were running low on ammunition. They had been fighting for nine hours and had eaten nothing since the day before. The surviving legionnaires took Maudet's command and carried on, loading and firing, their faces now black with powder and stumbling over the dead and badly wounded. The deaths mounted as the afternoon wore on and towards 4.00, the Mexicans, whose own casualties now reached 280, set fire to the sheds and straw. The Mexican colonel, Milan, made a speech to his men about national pride, and sent a new attack with his own infantry bearing modern American carbines, firing on the hacienda from all sides.

Morzycki was shot from the stable roof, along with three others. By 5.00, only Lieutenant Maudet, Corporal Maine and three legionnaires, Wenzel, Catteau and Constantin were still standing. They fought on for another fifteen minutes, huddled, choking and retching in the smoking ruins of a shed. When each man had one round of ammunition left, Maudet gave the signal.

Corporal Maine's account of those last minutes remains in the Legion archives:

> We had held the enemy at a distance but we could not hold out any longer as our bullets were almost exhausted. It was six o'clock and we had fought since the early morning. The lieutenant shouted, 'Ready, Fire!' and we discharged our remaining five bullets and, he in front, we jumped forward with fixed bayonets. We were met by a formidable volley. Catteau threw himself in front of his officer to make a rampart with his body and was struck with nineteen bullets. In spite of this devotion, Lieutenant Maudet himself was hit with two bullets. Wenzel also fell wounded in the shoulder but got up immediately. There were now three of us on our feet – Wenzel, Constantin and I.

We were about to jump over the lieutenant's body and charge when the Mexicans encircled us and held their bayonets to our chests. We thought we had breathed our last when a senior officer who was in the front rank of the soldiers ordered them to stop and with a sharp movement of his sabre, raised their bayonets which threatened us. 'Now will you surrender,' he called to us. I replied, 'We will surrender if you will leave us our arms and treat our lieutenant who is wounded.' He agreed and offered me his arm and gave the other to help Wenzel. They brought out a stretcher for the lieutenant.

The Mexican infantry colonel who saved the lives of the three remaining legionnaires was named Cambas. He took Maine and the other two like VIPs to his commander, Colonel Milan, who uttered the famous description: 'Truly, these are not men but devils'.

The Mexicans moved off. There were twenty seriously wounded legionnaires still lying in the hacienda, although several of them were so badly wounded they did not survive long. Meanwhile, scant rumours of the Camerone battle had reached the Legion's Colonel Jeanningros by nightfall and the following morning, he set off with a relief column in search of the missing company. Twenty miles away, he came across the battle scene, which had been cleared up by the Mexicans. Only the bodies of the dead lay naked in a ditch.

It was another two days before Jeanningros could return to bury the dead according to Legion convention, or at least all that remained of the bodies after the vultures and the coyotes had had their fill. One thing that no one noticed and which had remained untouched by the animals was the wooden left hand of Captain Danjou. It was discovered by chance by a local rancher who, realizing its potential value, offered it two years later to the Legion for fifty piastres. After lengthy negotiation by letter, the money was eventually paid and the hand returned to the Legion headquarters at Sidi-bel-Abbès, to take pride of place in the Legion's *Salle d'Honneur*.

There were many other battles which litter the Legion's record of combat during the Mexican adventure, and several with similarly bloody results.

The Legion remained in Mexico until 1870, and tales of battles won were overshadowed by the weakening of its reputation, by the political debacle and the overall losses which France sustained in this disastrous war. The 'Mexicana Affaire' cost 250 million francs and 7,000 French lives. Napoleon III, frantic and depressed, could stomach it no longer. The Americans, having concluded a rather long war among themselves, did not fancy having the French on the doorstep and were already supporting the fugitive Mexican president Juarez by supplying modern weapons.

Napoleon III ordered the withdrawal of his remaining 28,000 men from Mexico forthwith. They were all on their way home within eight weeks, and found no quayside welcome or the customary ceremony with which France normally greeted her soldiers returning from war. The would-be monarch of Mexico, Maximilian of Hapsburg, was not among them. He was captured by the opposition and executed by firing squad. His young bride, Empress Carlotta who had returned to France to plead for more troops to be sent, fell into a state of total breakdown when told and spent the rest of her life locked in a lunatic asylum.

So ended the Legion's tour of Mexico, a disaster in every respect, and the starting point of its own particular version of 'lest we forget . . .'.

3

1870: FRANCE; 1883: INDO-CHINA; 1894: DAHOMEY

'The edict banning the Legion from mainland France was set aside. With the main French armies roundly beaten, two of the Legion's four battalions were brought into the fray.'

THE LEGIONNAIRES returned ragged and for-lorn, but the Legion's reputation was spreading. The early accounts of its exploits began to portray the Legion as a tough but mysterious fighting force, allegedly consisting of vagabonds and criminals. France did not cheer the homecoming of her troops from Mexico, and virtually disregarded the Legion altogether. The costly adventure had ended in ignominy. The Legion itself suffered heavily. Not counting desertions, it lost 2,000 officers and men in the Mexican campaign, 1,500 of them from disease. In spite of the Camerone debacle, Legion casualties in action were the lowest in the whole French army, yet it was to become the scapegoat in military cutbacks. The Legion returned to Algeria to discover a country racked by drought, starvation and typhus. Within months, the Legion was ordered to cut its force from 5,000 to 3,000 men. More than 1,000 foreigners had their contracts terminated and were sent home. The remaining force was dispersed into small units to far flung outposts from the coast to the Sahara, although the tribesmen were in no mood for a fight.

The legionnaires busied themselves building more roads and camps but suffered badly from fatigue and ill-health through poor diet, especially in distant posts which were ill-served by the supply corps. The Legion was further decimated by an outbreak of cholera which began in the summer of their return. By the year's end, military inspectors were reporting a hefty resurgence of drunkenness among legionnaires which, because of their low pay in a high-cost region, was financed by selling their equipment.

Spasmodic battles with the Arabs and the need to police the territory to protect the settlers brought long, unwelcome marches to track the rebel bands, especially those based in neighbouring Morocco. Legionnaires in these faraway places, without adequate supplies, were plagued by disease and simple fatigue. One company marching to Géryville was so badly in need of sustenance that nineteen of its men committed suicide, and an officer who simply wandered off was caught by a marauding band of Arabs and tortured to death.

The onset of the Franco-Prussian war in July 1870 gave them hope of better fare, but initially they were to be disappointed. The edict of 1831 barred the Legion from service in mainland France and, furthermore, a large number of legionnaires and NCOs emanated from the German states. Two Legion battalions were sent to a desolate post to relieve French infantry, at a place the Arabs called El Hasaiba, the Place of the Damned. It was a malaria-infested region that had claimed many lives among the units they were replacing; legionnaires would soon be joining them in the cemetery.

Germany's overwhelming march through French territory brought an instant, if temporary, change in the rules. The edict banning the Legion from mainland France was set aside. With the main French armies under heavy attack, and roundly beaten in several key cities including Sedan and Metz, two of the Legion's four battalions were brought into the fray, arriving in France in mid-September. German-born legionnaires remained in Algeria as garrison troops.

A battalion of 1,350 fresh foreign volunteers was also raised at Tours and went straight away into battle at Orléans under the banner of the 5th Battalion, *Régiment Étranger*. They were met by fierce combat in which they gave a good account of themselves until the command structure collapsed. Unaware of an order to withdraw, many legionnaires fought on in the face of heavy Bavarian opposition until almost two-thirds of its strength was lost, with 580 dead or wounded and 253 captured.

By October 1870, the situation in France was desperate, Napoleon III had fled to England and a revolutionary council in Paris declared the arrival of the Third Republic. It was too late to save France's dire position. The Germanic armies were already encircling Paris, ready for the push south, and soon the new government decamped to Versailles.

The Legion suffered a second round of heavy losses at Orléans, so great that only a single *Bataillon de Marche* was formed out of the remains of what had been three battalions. Scores of them, dog-tired and starving, simply died of exposure after several consecutive nights of sleeping in blizzard conditions with no protection and little food. A month later, France capitulated, humiliated by the superior Prussian armies, and agreed to an armistice.

The Legion had been supporting the French lines in the east. In spite of the peace talks, they had carried on fighting for another month or so, taking further hefty losses, its strength being topped up with young conscripts largely from Brittany, and later with a large number from two French infantry regiments. When they arrived at Versailles at the beginning of April, they were sent immediately to Paris to help put down an insurrection by the Communards who had been holding the city against the German invaders and army of the new French Republic.

It was a controversial episode in the history of Paris, one that the Legion tried to distance itself from, although 100 years later they were still being held partly to blame for the atrocities which occurred as the siege was broken. The Communards, or *fédérés* as they were known, were at the barricades encircling the city with snipers and cannon. They held the advancing French army, which included the Legion, at bay for days on end. Gradually, the government troops pushed through, amid appalling bloodshed, most of which was among the Communards.

The advancing soldiers showed no mercy and well over 20,000 Parisians were killed, many summarily executed in batches, while others were shot as a matter of course as the troops overcame successive barricades. Countless others were wounded. The Legion was held partly to blame, for allegedly importing its less reputable tactics, founded at the time of the battles to quell al-Qadir in Algeria. A century later, in the mid-1970s, the Communist Party of France was still admonishing what it describes as Foreign Legion mercenaries for their role in the suppression of the Commune. Generally, historians seem anxious to record that the majority of assassinations were at the hands of French soldiers, either in the regular army or temporarily bolstering the Legion's ranks.

In the meantime, there was plenty of intermittent action in Algeria to keep the Legion occupied, and by the mid-1870s it had been revamped into five eight-company battalions.

France also began to colonize Indo-China, and by the late-19th century was attempting to match British activity in the Far East. The French focused upon what is today modern Vietnam, which then encompassed the historic areas of Tonkin and Annam. They launched a navy mission in 1858 to bombard Da Nang, supposedly as punishment for the persecution of Roman Catholic missionaries, and marched into Saigon the following year. Anxious to gain absolute control of a region ripe for exploitation, the French Chamber of Deputies voted 5.5 million francs to send a task force of 3,000 men to take the remaining territories of Vietnam.

Colonel François de Négrier was promoted out of the Legion to the rank of brigadier general in the French army to lead the expeditionary force, and he made sure that the Legion came with him ... thus ensuring its presence in the Far East for decades to come. He personally greeted them on the dockside at Haiphong on 27 September 1883 with the reassuring news: 'You legionnaires are soldiers in order to die, and I am sending you where you can die'. It was no exaggeration, and they went straight to it.

They were to meet a formidable enemy in the Black Flags, bands of mercenaries enlisted by the King of Annam, supported by the Chinese army. They, like their successors of the Viet Minh, were not the disorganized rabble that the French had imagined, and what began as a garrison of 3,000 French regulars in the summer of 1883 was extended to a force of almost 40,000 by the autumn of 1885.

The Legion was first in action when it was sent to support French marines clearing out mercenaries from two centres at Son Tay and Bac Ninh. On 16 December the marines were having difficulty penetrating the stockaded fortress of Son Tay in the face of an enemy who outnumbered them several to one. General de Négrier called up the Legion who also found the barrier impenetrable until a large Belgian legionnaire, Corporal Minaert, dashed forward wielding an axe, siezed the black standard of the brigands and, shouting '*Vive la Légion!*' leapt across a moat, followed by his colleagues, who, with him, forced their way through a gap in the wall. The Chinese, so taken by this astonishing sight, crumbled and ran ahead of the legionnaires' bayonet charge. The corporal's commanding officer later awarded him the Military Medal and added: 'If you had shouted *Vive la France!* it would have been the *Légion d'Honneur*'.

Among the Legion party was a young NCO, Edward Husband, who was born in France of an English father and French mother, but who had been brought up in England. He joined the Foreign Legion at the age of 18 and with five years' service completed, had signed again for a further five. In doing so, he was immediately promoted and at 23, found himself to be the youngest sergeant major in the Foreign Legion, achieved largely through the influence of de Négrier.

In the last week of January 1884, after numerous running battles and treacherous hand-to-hand combat against the Black Flags, Sergeant Major Husband was at Tuyen Quang, a small garrison fortress seventy-five miles north-west of Hanoi. It was virtually encircled by jungle, apart from the eastern side, only 100 metres from the bank of the River Claire. He was the senior NCO with a force made up of men from the 3rd and 4th Companies of the Legion, consisting of 399 legionnaires and eight officers under the command of Major Marc Edmond Dominé.

They had arrived to support 210 French regular soldiers engaged on building the fortress, measuring 300 yards square. They had barely installed themselves inside the quadrangle when a mass of Black Flags appeared from the undergrowth and put the fortress under siege. More arrived the following day, and according to Legion archives, the 517 men inside the fort were soon under attack from 20,000 Black Flags.

For three weeks the Legion's few fought off repeated attacks. Sometimes they engaged in hand-to-hand fighting, and at night the legionnaires crept towards the enemy and mined their approaches. The Black Flags responded in kind and sometimes the squads from the two sides on identical missions would meet and fight it out.

On the morning of 13 February, a huge explosion laid by the Black Flags blew away part of the south-west corner of the stockade, killing five legionnaires at their posts on the internal catwalk established at each corner. Sergeant Major Husband along with his section stumbled towards the smouldering crater and fought hand-to-hand against the hordes of Black Flags attempting to burst into the fort.

With rifle, bayonet, knife and boot they fought until the invaders were ejected. With the coming of the dawn, Husband and his legionnaires realized they had held the gap for more than five hours. The battle raged on for another week. The Chinese had reduced its attacking force, being pressed elsewhere, but they still hugely outweighed the declining Legion garrison. On 20 February, Husband was wounded in the thigh. Yet another gap had been blown in the stockade wall, this time causing the deaths of Captain Moulinay and a dozen legionnaires, killed instantly in the blast, leaving a further thirty legionnaires blinded and burnt, lying on the ground, cursing their wounds and the Chinese.

Captain Catelin took Husband and Sergeant Camps and a handful of legionnaires to plug the opening, hurling themselves at the advancing enemy with fury at the sight of their maimed comrades. The sheer violence of their bayonet charge, even against overwhelming numbers of the enemy, again stopped the Chinese breaking through. Each night and day the garrison continued to repulse assaults and apart from the attacks to the walls of the stockade, shells would fall with unfailing monotony in clusters within the compound, creating a desolate scene. The garrison had also run out of food, and on the 26th another disaster – one of the Chinese shells landed among the last barrels of wine.

This barrage was followed by half a dozen explosions at different parts of the stockade and again at the south-west corner. Husband, still limping from his wound, led the remnants of his section into another charge, firing their guns as fast as they could load. In the final few steps

ABOVE …then, legionnaires in 1893.
BELOW …and now, legionnaires in the 1990s.

ABOVE The World War I victory march by the Foreign Legion along the Champs-Elysees in 1919, led by Lieutenant-Colonel Rollet.

RIGHT Lieutenant-Colonel Rollet (centre) 'father' of the modern Legion.

ABOVE The Legion marching in France after the final departure from Algeria in 1971.

FOREIGN LEGION

RIGHT The front cover of an English language publicity brochure published in the early 1960s outlining the history and traditions of the Legion and the life and career of a legionnaire.

THE 5TH FOREIGN LEGION REGIMENT (5ᵉ R.E.)

Located mainly on Mururoa and Tahiti but also on the Tureïa, Totegegie, Tematangi and Reao atolls (outlying garrisons), this regiment is made up mainly of legionnaires but also of sappers.

In Tahiti :
— a transit element and an electrical supply unit.

In Mururoa :
— HQ company,
— one pioneer company,
— one ordnance company,
— one water-energy supply company,
— on transport and maintenance company.

The regiment performs some tasks for the Pacific Experimentation Center : water and power suppply, transport and maintenance, the building of road facilities.

The regiment is also in charge of the Command and supply of the outlying posts.

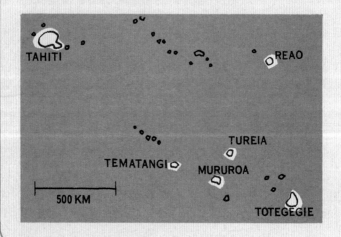

A page from the brochure showing the location of one of the Legion's far flung regiments.

before the hand-to-hand fight began, Husband fell, wounded again. Standing over his body, Husband's legionnaires held off the attack. Husband shook himself and tried to stand up but discovered that his second wound had been a bullet that had entered the same thigh, penetrating the bandage dressing protecting his initial wound.

By the beginning of March, the legionnaires were at their lowest ebb. Their commanding officer had been killed, they had only 180 rifles in working order for the defence of 1,200 yards of stockade, of which large sections had been blown up by Chinese mines. On 1 March, the legionnaires heard gunfire but no attack came that day. They awoke the next morning to discover that the Chinese had simply cleared out. The reason was soon apparent. That afternoon, a relief column of French regulars which left Lang Son on 16 February, finally arrived.

Before them, as they made their way down towards the long approaches to the garrison, they saw a scene of impossible desolation and ruin: six miles of trenches filled with the debris of thousands of troops, a churned and blasted landscape. In the distance, the wrecked fort was surrounded by rotting bodies of both sides which gave off a putrid stench that brought instant sickness to young soldiers as they approached. An eerie silence hung over the fortress itself.

The French company commander issued the order to signal the fort as they reached the approaches to Tuyen Quang. After almost half an hour, so the story goes, the legionnaires had still not appeared. The French CO inquired of his capitain why they were still inside.

The junior replied, 'I have seen this before with these devils. They are cleaning up.' As the French reached the final few hundred yards, the gates of the battered fort swung open and a single bugler and drummer playing *Le Boudin* marched out ahead of the remaining legionnaires in the smartest uniforms they could muster. There were 187 of them still standing, although not one was without a wound of some sort. Sergeant Major Husband, at their head, went on towards a glittering military career in the French army and became the only British member of the Foreign Legion to achieve the rank of general in the French army.

As in Mexico, the Legion's losses in this first encounter with the hazards of Indo-China came not so much from battles won or lost.

From 1887 to 1909 legionnaires who died of diseases such as cholera, malaria and dysentery, totalled 2,700. Their bodies were often buried in the swamps and the jungles where they fell. Many who survived illness were so severely disabled that they were discharged.

In spite of these discomforts, the legionnaires established a rapport with the locals in Indo-China that was unmatched in Algeria. The friendliness of villagers was not out of the goodness of their hearts; everyone benefited from trading with the garrisons. Prostitution became a growth industry, as ever, and most legionnaires had a personal mistress, known as *congaï*, meaning simply young girls in Vietnamese, in nearby villages. Another thriving cottage industry was the supply of opium. Local opium dens did good business among the soldiers. A single pipe would cost a few pennies to smoke, and few obeyed the general command issued to all French soldiers to avoid it. For those who escaped drug addiction, venereal disease or cholera, early experiences in Indo-China were to be looked back upon with nostalgia. 'For me,' wrote Legion marine officer L. Huguet after his serving in 1885:

> ... these moments are unforgettable ... an incomparable landscape ... soft lights of the moon reflecting off the fan-palm trees ... the continuous murmur of insects in a sleepy atmosphere in which a transparent vapour seemed suspended ...

The less poetic among his colleagues may have attributed his words to the fever. Another who saw the delights and also noted the pitfalls was Charles Martyn, a British Sandhurst man and former officer in an Hussar regiment enlisted as a plain legionnaire under the name of Fred Brown. He was sent to Indo-China in 1889, and although the war in Tonkin against the Chinese emperor was virtually over, bloody skirmishes with the Black Flags continued against the backdrop of villages nestling in beautiful countryside.

Martyn's graphic account of bitter fighting in dense but picturesque jungle ought to have been read by the generals of the succession of armies who would follow into these unwinable conflicts in the region in the next century. Legionnaires, he wrote, sweating from sickness and the weight of their flannel uniforms had to hack their way through the flower-filled landscape with machetes:

> ... imagine geranium, fuschias and such like flowers thirty feet high and trunks twice the thickness of a man's body ... imagine, multiplied a hundred thousand times the scent of an old-fashioned flower garden thickly planted with stocks, wallflowers, pinks, carnations and other sweet-smelling flowers that come into your mind. Picture gigantic flower trees ... palms, bananas, magnolias, frangipanis and every other tropical tree you can call to mind ... and a great many other you have never heard of ... covered with ivy and clinging plants of all descriptions until the whole was a glorious tangle of scent and colour ...

It was through these mountains of greenery that the legionnaires had to hack their way to track the elusive bands of Black Flags. Poetic descriptions do not sit easily with the realities of Legion life, especially in Indo-China where it began to pick up a reputation for social unruliness almost from day one, and was still doing so well into the 20th century. After one of the French army's reverses, withdrawal from the town of Lang Son was ordered. Lieutenant Colonel Herbinger instructed the legion to destroy all its artillery, weapons, munitions, food ... everything that could not be carried on the backs of men.

That night, virtually reduced to tears at the prospect of leaving fresh barrels of wine and tafia, cases of meat and biscuits and newly delivered clothes and boots, legionnaires had to go about their mission, leaving an 'unbelievable spectacle of wreckage'. When it came to the wine vats, it was all too much for them. Rather than tip it away, they tried to drink it. Most collapsed in a drunken stupor after their biggest ever free binge. The following morning, a number of them were still totally immobile through drink. Herbinger ordered that they should be stripped of their arms and equipment and left where they lay by the departing forces.

The colonel was so intent on getting rid of unnecessary baggage that even the brigade money chest containing around 600,000 francs was dumped into the river, along with unwanted ammunition.

At his court martial on charges of bringing the French army into disrepute, Herbinger explained that he did not want to distribute the money between the men because they were already laden and, in any event, they would merely have spent it on drink, and so many of them were already drunk.

The continuing Legion presence in Indo-China meant an upsurge in recruitment to the Algeria forts. They were also called into action elsewhere, establishing a pattern that would be repeated through to the beginning of World War I. The huge continent of Africa which was to be the place of so much Legion activity in later years, was also being opened up by the ambitions of both civil and military entrepreneurs.

In 1892, the Legion was in Timbuktu, Senegal, then Dahomey, in West Africa, adjoining Nigeria's western boundary and the French colony of Togoland. Successive governments pursued the dream of having French influence across the African continent, although not without considerable local opposition.

In Dahomey, the legionnaires were confronted by warriors of King Gezo's army – Amazon levies – female conscripts who were considered the king's crack troops. They wore a uniform consisting of full skirt with a cartridge belt slung over one shoulder across their bare breasts and hooked to the waistband. Souvenirs of their active service were also hung from their waist, such as human bones and skulls.

The French regular army first encountered them as early as 1851, when around 2,000 women came screaming towards them as they marched into the country. Forty years later, in September 1894, they were preparing for another confrontation with the French. Two battalions of legionnaires found themselves on this front-line and among them was the Englishman Charles Martyn, now recovered from his Black Water fever which he contracted in Indo-China, and enveloped in lush countryside and thick bush, interspersed with mangrove swamps in Dahomey. They lived off the land, slaughtered wild animals as they trudged up country from Porto Novo on the Gulf of Guinea.

They carried nothing but their arms and 150 rounds of ammunition for each man, but in the sweltering heat, the column travelled at less than two miles an hour, alternately hacking through dense bush or wading through insect infested swamp. At dawn on the morning of

19 September they had their first encounter with the Dahomans, attacked by a force of almost 5,000 men, double the Legion's strength. The Legion encampment was just stirring as the attack came. Men were running around still in their shirts and undershorts, grabbing their rifles from the stacks outside their tents. Charles Martyn described the scene:

> We could barely make out what we were firing at ... as fast as we could ram the cartridges in and loose off we fired into moving black shadows and saw them topple over like corn falling under the sickle ... then we launched the first charges ... ramming our bayonets into their bodies until the hilt came up against flesh with a sickening thud, and then pushing them off to make room for another, like a farm labourer forking hay, until we had to clamber over dead and dying men piled two or three high to get at the living ... but they could not run away because a great mass behind them were pushing them onto our bayonets. It was a terrible slaughter.

The ground was covered with black bodies and the carnage was not yet over. Among the corpses of the Dahoman warriors were dozens of wounded. The Legion neither had the means nor the men to either treat them or keep them as prisoners and, as was customary, they were finished off where they lay.

The column continued on its trek north, and battled through regular encounters with smaller groups of warriors. The legionnaires' first meeting with the Amazons came on 4 October when they joined a battle already in progress between the Dahomans and other French army units. The attack waves were often led by the Amazons, whose prelude to the charge was their erotic dance of death. Martyn wrote of them:

> Their uniform was a sort of kilted divided skirt of blue cotton ... the garment barely reached to the knees. It was supported at the waist by a leather belt which carried the cartridge

pouches. The upper part of their bodies were quite nude but the head was covered with a coquettish red fez into which was stuck an eagle's feather ... [they] were far and away the best men in the Dahomeyan army ... they fought like unchained demons.

In this battle, at Dogba, the force of the Legion once again outgunned and outcharged the Dahoman army. Among the dead and wounded were many of the Amazons, often just young girls. The rest of the women took flight, and by the end of 1894, Dahomey had succumbed to its new colonial rulers.

The Legion was once again severely hit by disease and the terrible fatigue suffered on the four-month march through the bush. Almost a third of its men fell by the wayside.

4

MISTY-EYED RECRUITS

'That training was sadistic and brutal, there was no doubt.
And, like so many other aspects of Legion life, once adopted
it became an accepted part of the organization's tradition.'

THE MYTH and the mystique began to take hold as word of the Legion's exploits spread. As the years passed, writers and journalists began to seek out the truth about this strange and blood-stained army. There were also a confusing mixture of views about it, depending where in the world the reader happened to be.

The Germans had some particularly unpleasant memories of the Legion during the invasion of France and never really warmed to the idea that so many legionnaires were of German origin. They continued to show real animosity toward it, preferring the version promoted by its military chiefs and peddled by many of its writers, that it was manned by a bunch of desperados, drunks and madmen – people hiding from trouble. France itself was shunting criminals and vagrants of foreign extract into the Legion, rather than spending money keeping them in jail. Several stories emerged of recruits of various nationalities, mostly German, who had been arrested for some misdemeanour or other in France and, however slight the offence, had been given the option of hard labour in prison or 'volunteering' for the legion – a situation that continued well into the 20th century.

Another popular theme was at the other extreme – the romanticism which was attached to the Legion on the grounds that it had become a haven for the adventurer, the lovelorn, poets and other gentle beings or outcasts from society, who had suffered a downturn in their lives. But who were these volunteers? Where had they come from? Why did they join? The world wanted to know. Major PC Wren, author of *Beau Geste*, provided the most definitive answers – as they applied to his time with the Legion from 1895 to the early part of the 20th century. His story famously centred on three orphaned Geste brothers, Beau, John and Digby, who were adopted and raised by their aunt, Lady Patricia Brandon. In order to raise money, she sells the family jewel, a sapphire called the 'Blue Water', secretly replacing it with a fake. Knowing of the deception, Beau remains silent rather than disgrace his aunt. Years later, the grown Beau again protects her, with a gallant gesture to spare her any humiliation. When the stone is brought out to be sold to pay her husband's debts, it is stolen by Beau who runs away to join the Foreign Legion. He is joined by his brothers, the three of whom end up commanded by the sadistic Sergeant Lejeune who knows of the jewel and also wants to possess it. Lejeune commands a company at Fort Zinderneuf, where Beau and John are stationed: 'I may kill half of you in training . . . but the half that lives will be soldiers. You will all get the chance to die with your boots on . . . I promise you!'

In an interview at the time of publication, Wren expanded on his view of the Legion—in which he never served, incidentally, and whose commanders described the book as a libel:

The Legion takes every sort of man who may have any sort of reason for joining. The reason affecting by far the greater majority is bitter necessity, so the recruits are chiefly poor men out of work, labourers in times of unemployment, ex-soldiers who have no trade but soldiering. A smaller class is drawn from the romantics, the born adventurers, the type of men who form the subject of a poem we learnt in our childhood, the soldier of the Legion who sang . . .

> But I was aye a truant bird
> And thought my home a cage

Drawn from such varied sources, Wren went on, a legionnaire's comrades will not only be men of literally every nation of the world, including Negroes and Arabs, but also from every social stratum. And he added:

I have known princes as well as noblemen, generals and even priests at one end of the scale and at the other . . . Paris apaches, unskilled labourers, crooks and criminals while some are so devoid of both education and intelligence that they have to make their mark instead of signing. Yet, when they come together as legionnaires, they accept the necessity of honour, a marked manifestation of which is his honesty. The legionnaire may and does do terrible things but he does not steal from his comrades that which is his comrade's own property. He may steal property of *Madame la République* temporarily in the charge or possession of his comrade. He may therefore steal articles of uniform and equipment, but nothing else. At least, not twice. The barrack-room thieves receive far more terrible punishment than the authorities or civil law can ever inflict. It is undoubtedly true, as I can vouch (although it has been denied) that men caught stealing from their own trusting comrades have been nailed to the barrack-room table with bayonets through their hands.

Punishment by the authorities, meanwhile, is also frequent and free and consists of various forms of imprisonment, varying from confinement in the barrack-room to solitary confinement. What makes punishment so easily earned is that NCOs can themselves inflict it. Should a legionnaire be so foolish as to err repeatedly or be so unfortunate as to look to the sergeant like one who may, he may well find himself the subject of a court martial. The sentence of penal servitude may last six months or more and, if he survives it, the period equal to the sentence will be added to his term of Legion service.

Yet, the Foreign Legion does France infinite credit from a military point of view . . . She gets the highest form of heroism. The question whether France is a great asset to the Foreign Legion cannot be answered so clearly . . .

The truths that Wren revealed did nothing to dissuade writers, who promoted the aura of romanticism which had begun to surround the Legion. A London writer informed his readers in 1895:

> To be a French Legionnaire, strange as it may appear, requires no qualifications either as regards birth or character. The German deserter, the Italian anarchist or the Englishman fleeing from justice are all equally welcome. The Legion is a corps of bold spirits, many of whom are driven to its fold through coming under the ban of society. Foreign recruits would, if laid bare, make exciting and often lurid reading. The life, if eventful, is undoubtedly a hard one, and it is certainly more than mere love of adventure which attracts the vast majority of those who join.

The web of fact merging with fiction was already being spun. Novels and accounts began appearing to bolster myth and legend, but a series of contemporary sketches published in France provided a more truthful view of legionnaires as lean, fit, saturnine men who were typically poor, hard and brave, and who could be distinguished only by courage and endurance in some distant colonial war for a nation for whom they bore no particular liking.

At the time, details were only just beginning to emerge on the training regime which itself was in its formation as the Legion moved to firmer ground in the political arena. It was conducted almost entirely on location in Algeria, out of sight of the French public and military hierarchy. That training was sadistic and brutal, there was no doubt. It had to be, said its instructors then as now, given the scope of its recruitment policy and the language barrier. And, like so many other aspects of Legion life, once adopted it became an accepted part of the organization's tradition.

The four-month ritual of tough physical training began then, and continues today with only modernizing modifications. It comprised long days of hard slog, beginning at 4 a.m. and lasting to well after dark, of forced marches of fifty miles with a full 80lb pack, in temperatures that varied between day and night from below freezing to 80°F, of imprisonment for the most minor of offences, and of the kick of an NCO's boot for even lesser ones.

The routine of Legion life described by recruits at the end of the 19th century has also altered little. A contract was signed which was more of a disclaimer that neither the volunteer nor his relatives would have call on the French government should he be injured, disabled, killed or stricken with disease whilst in their service. Nor, then, would he have a claim on a pension until he had completed fifteen years' service.

The recruits were brought by rail to the southern ports, usually Marseille, from all over France. At Marseille they were met by a corporal who led them into Fort Saint Jean, one of two medieval stone compounds at the entrance to the town port. Once inside, contact with the outside world was at an end for many months. A guidebook of the day, dated 1880, made Sidi-bel-Abbès, to which they were bound, sound quite presentable:

> The town is cut in two parts by a wide street . . . on the west lies the military quarters which can house 6,000 men, on the other side is the town where the Hôtel de France is very good and reasonable. Madame Perrot, the proprietor speaks excellent English . . . '

When enough recruits were gathered at Fort Saint Jean, a process which might take several days, they were put aboard a ferry to take them across the sea to Oran. It was the last many of them saw of France, for the country had no particular desire to have them back. One of the earliest British accounts of this journey into the unknown came from a gentlemanly figure, PR Gallichan, who, according to his own unpublished memoirs, could be classed as an Englishman attracted to the Legion purely through a sheer love of adventure and the burning desire to be a soldier at all costs. What is surprising in reading his account is the similarity to those volunteers who joined the Legion almost a century later. He wrote:

I had tried in vain to join the English army. I was refused owing to my being rather short-sighted but as I was determined to be a soldier at all costs I prevailed upon my friend, Charles O'Rourke, to enlist with me in the French Foreign Legion. After a somewhat cursory medical examination, I was accepted, as was Charles.

Gallichan's arrival in Algeria, barely a month after leaving England, came as a shock. There were recruits around him who spoke neither French nor English. Most, he said, were dishevelled and had been given false names and imaginary pasts which usually bore no resemblance to their confessed origins. This was the rule rather than the exception.

Gallichan soon learned that it was not the done thing to question a man's reasons for volunteering. Whatever the reasons, they were now all in the same boat – and once they were cleaned up, heads shaved and uniforms donned, they would all look the same. In Algeria, the new recruits had a choice of destinations, to which they would be carried by a narrow-gauge railway, either to Sidi-bel-Abbès which became the official home of the Legion and its 1st Regiment in 1875, or the smaller post of Saïda, home of the 2nd Regiment.

Around both posts a diverse, scavenging local civilization had built up which relied heavily upon the spending power of the Legion garrison. It provided all the amenities for the serving soldier, ranging from brothels, money-changers, purchasers of second-hand goods (including Legion kit), and bars. The official welcome at both was the same. The Legion band would strike up one of its favourite songs on the arrival of the new recruits and marched cheerfully ahead of them from the railway station into the parade ground of the base, watched eagerly by the prostitutes, pimps and sundry purveyors and bar keepers who lined the route.

Gallichan and O'Rourke joined the 2nd Regiment at Saïda. The daily routine was the same here as at Sidi-bel-Abbès: up around 4 a.m. for breakfast of bread and thick black coffee; then a variety of tasks for the day, from route marches, lectures, general duties, rifle practice, battalion drill or practical field fortification. The day was packed, and seemingly endless.

The two adventure-seeking Englishmen were horrified, first at the harshness of the routine and, second, at the pervasive air of violence which persisted both on the parade ground and in the barrack-room. They were scared by NCOs, kicking or punching those slow to pick up their commands in language they did not understand. They were shocked by the easy manner in which legionnaires brawled violently among themselves, with fights in the barrack-yard.

Gallichan and O'Rourke were there for only three days before deciding to desert, along with another Englishman named Hides, a fisherman from Hull. Gallichan's attempts to escape go down in the annals of Legion history as one of the most persistent, which might be seen as something of a blueprint of do's and don'ts for the thousands who in succeeding years would attempt to desert by the same route (see Chapter Five).

Desertion was, and is, as much a part of the Legion story as any other, though veteran legionnaires – the ones who stayed – are likely to disagree. Desertion has always been present, and although annoying, never a real problem in terms of manpower because there were always plenty of volunteers. It was, however, an expensive business putting them through the training routine, only to have a quarter of them run off at the earliest opportunity. From quite an early stage, the Legion had anti-desertion pickets on permanent duty wherever there was leave or a stopover.

On overseas excursions, such as to Mexico, Indo-China or Africa, deserters risked their lives in more ways than one. Some went over the side to swim for it in shark-infested waters, or dodged pickets' bullets by swimming ashore during docking manoeuvres. At Suez, a popular spot for desertion attempts, five prospective runaways were shot and killed before they reached the bottom of the landing stairs. The shots were fired by the sentries, made up of French marines, not legionnaires. The latter were never likely to shoot their runaway comrades; they might beat them to within an inch of their lives if and when they were caught – but shoot them? They'd open fire but would be affected by a sudden attack of blindness.

In Algeria itself, the possibilities of a successful desertion from the Legion were even more hazardous, which is why most bided their time, to make a run for it during an overseas posting. The rule was that a man who ran away could not be classed as a deserter until he had been missing for six days. The chances of surviving in the Algerian country-side for that length of time without being picked up by Legion trackers or Arab bounty hunters, or alternatively shot by either, were not good. Stories of the harsh treatment meted out to deserting legionnaires were common in the late 1800s, especially in Germany where a campaign was launched in Munich under the banner of The German Protection League Against the Foreign Legion. This group sought to warn its nationals against joining the Legion which, it claimed, was a murder-ous organization whose men were treated like animals, subjected to appalling violence, even death. There is enough published testimony from the era to confirm that in some of the more remote outposts of Legion life, unsuccessful deserters were lucky if they escaped with their lives. Dr Alcide Casset, a former officer in the French military, later published a pamphlet on his experiences in 1911 in which he claimed that the Arabs who went in search of runaway legionnaires would be paid whether they brought them back dead or alive. The doctor dis-covered that since the reward would be paid in full either way, the trackers found it infinitely less troublesome to simply kill the deserter and bring back only his head as proof of capture. The doctor himself said he was called upon many times to verify a legionnaire's death, simply by looking at his head, to which would be attached his papers.

Another story of beheaded deserters came later from Morocco, where one of the Legion commanders was said to have offered the locals twenty-five francs for the return of a deserter, dead or alive, and 100 francs if they brought back only his head. To those who challenged the necessity for killing deserters, there was a ready excuse that many of them were armed and, more to the point, armed with weapons they had taken from the Legion. In the struggle, the legionnaire may well lose his life. This extreme solution was generally confined to the wilder regions of Legion service. In the main, the treatment of deserters was less harsh than the stories. Many were quickly captured and spent no more than a few weeks in jail, although the punishment was gradually increased for persistent offenders . . . of whom PR Gallichan was one.

5

A DESERTER'S STORY

'Many tried, and kept on trying, to get out, and while accepted as a part of the Legion's make-up, it did become a real problem – and a threat – that desertion encouraged by an enemy could hamper its performance.'

LEGIONNAIRE PR GALLICHAN'S story is not so much about the Legion, but a derivative of it and one which would be repeated often, in different forms down the decades. It demonstrated not only the desperation of men who realized they had made a mistake in joining the Foreign Legion but, once in, how difficult it was to get out. This is Gallichan's account of his escape, with his comrades O'Rourke and Hides:

Taking food with us, we left camp after Last Post had been sounded and struck into the mountains steering our way north by the Pole Star. After rough climbing and many falls in the dark amongst the hills, we eventually found our way barred by a dense forest. We therefore halted, made up a fire, using branches as fuel and all three went to sleep within the circle of the genial warmth for the nights are often very cold in Algeria, in striking contrast to the burning heat of the day.

In starting on that eventful journey we had each supplied our-selves with a thick cudgel to use in our tramp. Our idea was to travel only by night, as we feared being seen by the Arabs who usually put French deserters to death with horrible torture. Our aim was to reach Oran, annex a fisherman's boat and then to sail out into the Mediterranean on the off-chance of being picked up by a passing steamer. It was a desperate scheme, but the only one we could devise.

We were awakened by the cold, the fire having gone out. Our teeth chattered uncomfortably, and we thereupon decided to walk on till daybreak when, after surveying our position we took another nap. We remained in this second encampment until dusk had again fallen, and then resumed our march, always following the direction of the North Star. Before daybreak our passage was barred by a river, so we called a halt, lighted a fire, and once more sought oblivion in slumber.

I awoke before my comrades and speedily woke them whereupon I seriously warned them of the dangers we incurred by loitering in so exposed a spot. Hardly had I uttered the words when, on looking up the river, we were startled to see two Arabs approaching us rapidly. They were yelling wildly and were soon joined by others. I promptly sprang into the river and dashed towards the other side, followed by my companions.

Despite our obvious danger I could not help laughing, because all the other two seemed to trouble about was the fear of wetting our small stock of bread which O'Rourke carried in a haversack. Finally we succeeded in clambering up the slippery bank but, being completely worn out with fatigue, could go no further, our wet clothes being an additional impediment.

Always of a practical turn of mind, I suggested that as we were likely to be caught and murdered and were, furthermore, very hungry, we had better eat our bread. This we accordingly did as fast as we could. During this time the Arabs remained on their side of the river, being evidently under the impression that we had some trap laid for them, for when I pulled out my sodden handkerchief and waved it as a flag of truce they thought it was a revolver, and they scattered right and left.

Eventually we managed to make friendly signs and, plucking up

44

courage, they came across the river in Indian file. Having seized us, they took us to their encampment. There the women and children turned out to see us. The prospects of coming to an untimely end did not make me forget the pangs of hunger only whetted by the saturated bread and I quickly made them understand that we were both hungry and thirsty. After a time they gave us some buckwheat cakes and sour goat's milk which was welcome but very unpalatable. The palaver was ended, we were told to get up, and a few of the Arabs, armed with pistols and knives, escorted us about two miles from the encampment. Now, thought I, we are going to be dispatched. But the natives disagreed among themselves, and appeared to be hestitating before shooting us there and then or taking us to Mascara, the nearest military station, where they would have received twenty-five francs for each of us from the military authorities. Eventually one came up to me and, pointing towards the north, told me to go.

I could scarcely believe my ears, but quickly stepped out a couple of yards, although expecting to be shot down instantly. My comrades speedily followed my example and finally set off at a good pace. Having escaped what we fully expected to be certain death, we resumed our wanderings. Eventually we sighted a small town, Ain-Fekan by name, lying in a hollow, and upon approaching nearer we found a deep stream, from which we drank deeply. We proposed entering the village to purchase a stock of drink and eatables and then to strike north again. Entering a café we ordered absinthe and bread and cheese. We were thoroughly enjoying the fare, seated at a table, when someone touched me on the shoulder. I sprang to my feet in dismay, to find myself face to face with a *gardechampetre* [rural policeman]. My first impulse was to run but the policeman pointed to a group of soldiers outside and tersely informed us that the game was up. We all rose but our captor politely told us to finish our meal, after which he conducted us to the *gendarmerie* where we were put in the same cell and on the whole treated very well. Our description was promptly wired up to the depot and the military authorities claimed us as deserters.

Next morning the three deserters, chained together, were marched out of the village, escorted by two mounted *gendarmes* armed to the teeth. On arrival at Saïda, they were taken to the guardroom where, after a short interrogation, they were placed in cells. Three weeks of what Gallichan described as 'durance vile' followed. They were chained two by two and marched to the railway station en route to Oran. On the way, they stopped at Perregaux, there confined in a large prison and made to sleep on a wooden bed lying at an angle, and having a long wooden plank for a pillow. They were each shackled to an iron bar running along the bottom of the bed. One of the prisoners refused to let himself be shackled whereupon, Gallichan wrote, a comrade knocked him down for his own protection as one of the *gendarmes* threatened to shoot him if he resisted. Gallichan went on:

> The following day we were forwarded by train to Oran and marched to the military prison at Santa Cruz, built on a small mountain of the same name which overlooks the town and harbour. We now knew that we were waiting to be tried by court-martial, the specific offence not being desertion, as we might have imagined but of having made away with our military effects. The minimum punishment is two years' hard labour and the maximum five years.
>
> After a week's detention O'Rourke and I were taken before a lieutenant of *Chasseurs d'Afrique* for a preliminary examination and upon his ascertaining that we had been such a short time in the Legion and that we had no knowledge of French military law an 'ordonnance de non lieu' was filed against us which meant that the crime we had committed was considered not to have occurred. We were conducted to the Fort Ste Thérèse in Oran to await our transfer back to Saïda.
>
> As the fort overlooks the port and the walls are not very high I suggested to my comrade that we might, by tying a couple of blankets together, easily let ourselves down one night, take a boat and provisions and chance being picked up by some passing vessel. O'Rourke, however was not enthusiastic over the scheme, and it

was lucky we did not make the venture, for it blew a hurricane the night I had selected for the attempt.

After a few days' detention at Fort Ste Thérèse we were sent back to the depot at Saïda, where Hides again joined us, having been tried by court-martial and acquitted. After leaving the military prison I made acquaintance of an American named Howard and we two planned a second escape. Howard by the way, had also previously deserted but, like myself, had failed in the attempt. My chum, O'Rourke, this time refused to join us but we enlisted another recruit in an Englishman named Quilter who suggested what we considered was the best plan of campaign. There is a large export of alfalfa grass from Algeria, principally to England, this grass being taken to the different railway stations and forwarded on to the coast towns. We learnt that a large consignment was about to be sent to Arzew, a small town between Oran and Algiers and was there to be shipped on an English steamer lying in the offing.

Our idea was to climb into one of the alfalfa wagons and to hide between the grass and the tarpaulin covering the load. We anticipated arriving in Arzew during the night and we intended slipping out in the darkness and swimming to a vessel – a somewhat risky undertaking as sharks abound around the coast.

One evening found Howard, Quilter and myself waiting in a cornfield near the railway station but just before the bugle sounded Last Post, Quilter's courage failed him and he returned to barracks. Howard and I lay low among the corn. I went to sleep while Howard kept watch, and at two in the morning he woke me up and we climbed over the wooden fence and made for the wagons. Once inside, we shook hands and imagined that all our troubles were over.

We went to sleep under the tarpaulin covers, to be awakened at six by the noise of the railway workers who were shouting to each other preparatory to shunting our wagon. Soon the train began to move, and, after various stoppages, we arrived at Perregaux, which was barely half-way on our journey to Arzew. After remaining stationary for half an hour, we found to our consternation that the wagons were not likely to go farther. Our plight was now becoming serious, for we were gradually getting stifled by the hot midday African sun, which beat down pitilessly upon the tarpaulin which covered us.

Finally, I could endure it no longer, for the flesh was scorched off my left hand. Bidding Howard goodbye, I let myself down from the wagon and crawled on my hands and knees into a shed, feeling very sick and dizzy, for I was suffering from sunstroke. A railway employee was in the shed, sitting at a desk. He stared hard at me but said nothing. I asked him for water and he handed me a quart bottle of the precious liquid which was dashed with absinthe. This revived me wonderfully and I then returned to the wagon without, as I thought, being perceived.

My object was to fetch my kepi which I had left there; and having recovered it I crossed the station and hid in an empty second-class carriage where I remained until seven o'clock in the evening. The train with the alfalfa wagons attached left for Arzew about this time and my first intention was to remain in hiding until darkness came on and then follow the railway lines to Arzew. On second thoughts, however, I realized that the English vessel would in all probability have left before I could get there and the possibility of having my throat cut by the Arabs en route convinced me to abandon my intended tramp. Unarmed as I was and worried by thirst, there was nothing to be gained by needlessly exposing myself to unknown dangers. I accordingly left my hiding-place and walked towards the town, quenching my thirst on the journey from a stream.

Meeting a Spanish teamster, I asked him the way to the *gendarmerie*. He recognized me as a deserter and informed me that the *gendarmes* were scouring the country around Perregaux in search of me. Realizing the hopelessness of my position now that I could not reach the coast, I decided to give up the struggle, and accordingly went straight to the *gendarmerie*.

Upon the prison door being opened, to my utter astonishment, I beheld my friend Howard, with his head wrapped up in a blue military handkerchief and looking very ill. It appears that after I left the wagon the railway worker who supplied me with water gave information to the police. They came to the shed, and while looking for me they noticed the tarpaulin on one of the wagons move. A ladder was promptly placed against the wagon and Howard was hauled out, in a dreadful condition. He was in a fit from the heat and the hair on his head was almost all singed off. He was at once taken to the *gendarmerie* and medically attended.

That night we lay on our wooden plank, each with a foot shackled to the iron bar running along the bottom. Chained together, we were next day sent up by train to Saïda, where we each received a punishment of twenty-eight days' solitary confinement in the cells. The food rations consisted of about half a pint of soup a day and a pound-and-a-half of bread. Given a healthy appetite, this means torture. We duly completed our term of imprisonment, and upon rejoining my detachment I was not so eager to plan or attempt escapes, realizing fully the almost insurmountable difficulties unless a very favourable opportunity presented itself.

After I had been some considerable time in the regiment we were asked if any of us were willing to volunteer for Tonkin, the French possession of Indo-China. Quickly realizing the possibility of escaping on the journey, I promptly volunteered but my friend O'Rourke, now being in the band, would not do so. We were formed up and the names of volunteers were called out, mine being among them. I passed the doctor as fit for foreign service. I well remember how the major, after making us form a circle around him, told us that he was confiding the flag of France to us; that he knew it could not be in better hands and that he felt sure we would spill our life's blood in its defence. During this stirring speech I confess I felt very mean, for I fully intended to desert, given a favourable opportunity. Life in this corps of modern mercenaries was not at all to my taste.

We soon commenced our journey, travelling by train from Liaret to Oran. Arriving at Oran we marched to where our tents were pitched, headed by the band. Our reception by the populace was wonderful; in fact, we made quite a triumphal entry. Cries of '*Vive*

49

l'Armée!' and *'Vive la Légion!'* were heard on all sides, and we marched to camp amid salvos of applause and a pyrotechnic display of Bengal lights.

On the following day I made the acquaintance of an Englishman named Heaton Shillaker who belonged to the 1st Regiment. Needless to say, we speedily became friends. That same day we volunteers left for Marseille on board the *Russie* packet. At Marseille we were to re-embark on the hospital ship *Cholon*, which, before steaming for the East, was to call at Toulon to pick up marines.

Arriving at Marseille after a rough passage we found no welcome extended to us as at Oran. In fact, the attitude of the populace was one of utter indifference. We marched up to the Fort des Incurables and the first night the whole detachment had permission to leave barracks. Sixteen men promptly attempted to desert, but were captured and brought back next day by the *gendarmes*.

The second day we were confined to barracks, but on the third night our captain who was, by the way, an Italian, prevailed on the colonel to let us out, remarking that it was probable that very few of us would see France again since we were likely to be killed or die of some foreign plague. The colonel yielded and, once clear of barracks, I said to my new friend and fellow Englishman, 'Tonight we bolt,' a remark to which he readily assented.

We were supposed to re-enter barracks at nine o'clock, but we two were still roaming round aimlessly at half-past, though this slight infraction of duty would not have entailed punishment, the circumstances being exceptional. We kept a sharp eye open for the pickets who would speedily have gathered us in, but though still at large we appeared as remote as ever from evolving a successful plan of escape. At last we came across a café over which was written the legend in English, 'The Irish Consul'.

This struck me as being so funny that we entered. At a small table sat four men, whom I saw at a glance were English sailors. They were listening to the more-or-less musical strains of a melodeon played by a woman. Saluting these men, I said, 'You are Englishmen, I believe?'

'Yes,' came the reply.

They next asked us if we were British, and upon receiving a reply in the affirmative remarked that we did not look it, which was not surprising, for we were dressed in long blue coats and duck trousers, and wore white helmets and long blue cholera sashes around our waists. We sat down with these British Tars, and, without any beating about the bush, informed them that we were anxious to rid the Legion of our presence. The men then informed us that they were sailors from the steamship *Goolistan* trading from London to the Persian Gulf, and that they were homeward bound, having touched at Marseille en route.

They volunteered to stow us away on board if we could manage to get so far undetected. After several near misses, we finally made our secret boarding of the *Goolistan* and I felt that we were, so to speak, on British soil, and heaved a mighty sigh of relief ... we were stowed away for the night and at eleven o'clock the next morning, we heard the bugles and drums of the legion, who were marching down to the transport, en route for China, and we thanked our lucky stars we were not with them. At two o'clock the same afternoon, to our great joy, we heard the propeller of our vessel begin to revolve and knew that now we were quite safe.

When thirty miles out our kind friends (as per agreement) 'found' us and marched us before the captain as stowaways. When everything was explained he was very kind, and though we offered to pay for our passage he would not hear of it, but told us that as he was rather short-handed, we would have to work our way back to England as deck-hands. In ten days we were in London, and here I took leave of my good friends the sailors and my comrade Shillaker. After an absence of nearly three years I felt inexpressibly pleased at being once more under the protection of the Union Jack.

Gallichan's story was unique in its persistence. Many tried, and kept on trying, to get out, and while accepted as a part of the Legion's make-up, it did become a real problem – and a threat – that desertion encouraged by an enemy could hamper its performance. This method of weakening the opposition had been tried elsewhere.

Legionnaires and regulars alike had been tempted to the other side in many conflicts, but soon after the turn of the century, it became apparent that manpower was haemorrhaging from Legion positions in Morocco and that the runaways were largely of Germanic nationals. The discovery of the underlying cause almost brought an early start to World War I.

6

1914–1918:
THE 'MAGIC OF BARAKA'

The story was told around the fires at night in Legion encampments, when the
'Magic of Baraka' invariably came up. It was an old Legion description applied to
legionnaires blessed with an ability to dodge enemy bullets time and again.

BY THE EARLY 1900s most of Africa had been
carved up and earmarked by the colonialists of Europe's leading
nations. France had control or influence over a large portion of north
and west Africa through the states of Algeria, Tunisia, Mauritania,
Senegal, Guinea, Berkina, Cameroon, Gabon, and the Congo. Its
possessions in Central Africa included Chad and the Central African
Republic, while in the east it had French Somaliland and Djibouti (at
the southern mouth of the Red Sea) to balance the British presence in
Aden.

Britain largely concentrated her interests in the south, while
Germany became increasingly agitated over its meagre share of the
spoils. Morocco was a particularly thorny issue and one which eventually led to heavily populated graveyards of legionnaires. Britain,
France, Germany and Russia all had designs on the place, but the
French had already darted across the Sahara and laid claim to the lion's
share. A force of 2,000 men of the French army, equipped with 4,500
camels 'commandeered' from locals, picked up a large chunk of the
borderlands. The Legion was instructed to send a representative force

of 409 officers and men of the 2nd Regiment, who made an epic 1,200-mile trek across the Sahara in sweltering temperatures well in excess of 100°F in just 72 days. Their bodyweight decreased at a dramatic rate and their boots and feet were ripped to shreds.

Countless skirmishes followed as the Saharans and other local tribesmen recovered from the speed of the French invasion and hit back. The Moroccans were a hard and fanatical enemy, with large bands of well trained warriors at the disposal of regional rulers and desert warlords across the country. The story was as before: the Legion in the forefront of activity. From those early beginnings France eventually won effective control of Morocco after agreeing a trade pact with Britain.

Germany was left to pick up the crumbs. In accepting that it would provide for Morocco's internal security, France had once again bitten off more than she could chew. Originally, it had been agreed that France would send a small force of 3,000 men to police Morocco and keep the tribesmen under control. Within six months, that total had risen to 14,000, including a large contingent of legionnaires.

It was at this point that the Legion realized that there was suddenly a high rate of desertions among its forces in Morocco and closer investigation revealed that the runaways were mostly Germans. In 1908, 217 legionnaires deserted through Casablanca alone; 114 were German and 80 were Austrian. The reason was only discovered when six of the deserters (worse for drink) were recaptured – that German residents in Casablanca, still smarting over the French incursions into Morocco, were running a highly organized escape line. German legionnaires, it seemed, were not only being helped but encouraged to desert, so weakening the strength of France's most feared fighting force.

The captives were hauled off to a military prison where they confessed that the German consulate had provided them with clothes and passports, and there were effective lines of communication to two very active groups in Germany, the German Protection League and the Association to Combat the Enslavement of Germans in the Foreign Legion. Very soon the German government itself stepped into the fray with a demand that France release German nationals among those deserters recently caught.

France refused, and the issue was promoted to the level of a diplomatic crisis when Britain and Russia sent formal word that they would stand firm behind France. Next, the German Chancellor von Bülow, followed by Crown Prince Wilhelm, heir-assumptive, and finally Kaiser Wilhelm himself, all rattled their sabres. For some months, the issue of Foreign Legion deserters came exceedingly close to becoming an excuse for a resumption of hostilities between France and Germany which would ultimately draw in Britain.

The Crown Prince, primed by his government, said it was high time 'this insolent group in Paris experienced anew what the Pomeranian Grenadier can do ... the Casablanca incident is a test of force'. The German Chancellor weighed in with the comment that there would be no war with France without a war against England, while the Kaiser declared that Germany only wanted peace – a sure sign of trouble ahead.

The Moroccans were becoming more restless. The Sultan of Morocco, Abd-el-Aziz, was ousted by his brother, Moulay-Hafid, who in turn was besieged by his own people at Fez. He was rescued by a French relief column, consisting largely of legionnaires. The new monarch formally placed the country under the protection of France, who thus achieved colonization through the back door.

Legion losses, meanwhile, were heavy, including a company of the 6th Battalion, weakened by desertion, cut to pieces by tribesmen close to the border with Algeria. Amid the internal strife of Morocco, for which France had now become the self-appointed policeman, there were other more dangerous political manoeuvres.

Germany continued its harassing tactics to demonstrate displeasure at France's sneakiness, and the refusal to honour trade agreements with Morocco. The Kaiser resorted to gunboat diplomacy when the German vessel *Panther* appeared off the coast of the Morrocan port of Agadir, supposedly to protect German nationals from the French. As Winston Churchill described it, the Moroccan farce in which the Legion had been used as something of a pawn, was simply 'a milestone on the road to Armageddon'.

The dispute with the Germans was settled in 1912 when everyone agreed to adhere to international arbitration, accepting a formula which gave Germany a larger slice of Central Africa. Germany had backed down, though the world had already received the message of clear and present danger: Germany was shaping up for a scrap and next time she would not turn away, nor would she bother with a trumped up excuse like the desertion of a party of drunk legionnaires. Instead, it was the assassination of the heir to the Austro-Hungarian throne, Archduke Franz Ferdinand, on the streets of Sarajevo on 28 June 1914 that lit the fuse.

Within a month, Europe was at war, a situation which was cheered on the streets of London, Paris and Berlin. There was also popular support from around the world from men who displayed their allegiance to the anti-German cause by immediately flocking in their thousands to France to join the only regiments designed for foreign volunteers.

The French Foreign Legion in World War I is today the subject of a deserving tribute at their museum at Aubagne. The rapidly assembled force of men equipped itself in a manner that was ranked among the best under French colours. A detailed account of the Legion's campaigns in the four-year war is beyond the scope of this work, because so often its campaigns were part of a larger panoply involving other units of the French and Allied forces. However, a glance through the statistics, the personalities and some of the offbeat individual accounts of that war will provide an alternative insight.

Frederic Sauter Hall, a young writer of mixed Swiss–Scots ancestry, better known by his pen-name of Blaise Cendrars, and less well known as a corporal in the Foreign Legion during World War I, was among the first of many intellectuals across Europe to call for international support for France, even before mobilization formally began on 1 August. He wrote:

> Every man worthy of this name must act today, must forbid himself to remain inactive ... in the midst of the most formidable conflagration that history has ever experienced.

Within the month, Cendrars had volunteered for the Foreign Legion, along with thousands of others from more than fifty nations. Other personalities in the first batch included the American Harvard graduate and poet Alan Seeger, and songwriter Cole Porter.

Cendrars reported for duty on 3 September, at the Hotel des Invalides, on the Left Bank. It was a scene of chaotic enthusiasm, not helped by the insistence of a Canadian volunteer who was desperately trying to find a home for 300 near-wild horses he had shipped across the Atlantic at his own expense to aid the war effort. For the record, more than 42,000 foreigners enlisted in the French military during the course of the war, whereas at the outbreak, the Legion had four battalions in Algeria, five in Morocco and three in Tonkin, the largest number it had deployed in its history, with 10,521 men in December 1913. Battalions were needed in all those places to maintain and secure French interests, and to keep its colonialists safe.

Within the year, the Legion's strength doubled to 21,887, after which it declined once again through numbers killed or wounded in action, or through foreign nationals moving to their own armies as more countries were drawn into the war. The marriage of veteran legionnaires and raw recruits was not a happy one, and Cendrars was one of the loudest complainants about the treatment meted out by the old hands to himself and the other artists, writers, intellectuals and professional men. They were all thrown together with what Alan Seeger described as 'dregs of society'.

There were exceptions. An unlikely friendship developed between Arthur Griffiths, a scrawny, ill-educated Londoner, and Cendrars, who was intrigued by the Englishman. The story of Griffiths was told around the fires at night in Legion encampments, when the 'Magic of Baraka' invariably came up. It was an old Legion description applied to legionnaires blessed with an ability to dodge enemy bullets time and again.

Among those said to have the magic was Arthur Griffiths, a man with a mysterious past. He won no medals, nor had he aspired to the rank of sergeant, but he did possess this bullet-dodging ability, *baraka*. Jim Worden, legion archivist, reckons he has established the truth, as near as it's possible to get. This is his account:

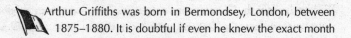

Arthur Griffiths was born in Bermondsey, London, between 1875–1880. It is doubtful if even he knew the exact month or day. He left school at 13, hoping to become an apprentice lighterman, but being a puny waif, failed to find employment on the docks. In 1905, he enlisted in the Foreign Legion at Marseilles, with a declared age of 30. What had he done in the years of his early adult life? In the Legion, no one would ever ask. The information had to be volunteered, and that did not happen in Arthur's case.

Griffiths was not an ideal recruit by any means. His face was pinched and his body thin to the point of emaciation. He was soon on his way to Sidi-bel-Abbès, finding little difficulty adjusting to his new life. It suited him, and compared with his natural habitat of the grimy, smoke-filled, fog-bound slums of London, North Africa was a paradise in spite of the wars: wide open spaces, clear desert sky with its thousands of stars and the smell of tamarisk plants used for the fires to prepare morning coffee.

He also struck up a close friendship with a long-serving German, Weidermann, who spoke broken English, and who improved it through Griffiths' tuition, albeit with a Cockney accent. Both renewed their contracts after five years' service and their company commander suggested they should go on a corporals' course. Weidermann agreed, but Griffiths had no desire to put himself through the rigours and discipline involved in the training. During the 1911 riots in Fez, Captain Paul Rollet, his company commander, complimented him on his tenacity and called him Johnny Englishman, a name which was subsequently applied to all English members of the Legion. As France called for general mobilization of its troops at the end of July 1914, Griffiths and Weidermann were among the first contingent of legionnaires moved to the French mainland, with other members of the Legion's 1st Regiment of Infantry. They were to act as instructors to the thousands of volunteers clamouring at Legion recruiting offices throughout France. Among them was Blaise Cendrars, who had trained with Weidermann and Griffiths in the Rhône Valley.

Weidermann and Griffiths were in a battalion which included fifty or so American volunteers, but when they joined the war in the trenches of the Somme, they were no longer in the same section. Weidermann was sent off in one direction with a group of

Americans, among whom was Alan Seeger. On New Year's Eve, Legionnaire Griffiths stumbled into the trench occupied by a section commanded by Blaise Cendrars, now a corporal, and reported his arrival as a replacement for duty. Cendrars was shocked by the man's physical appearance. He was obviously a sick man and appeared to be years older than the first time they had met. Griffiths had developed a hacking cough and lost all evidence of his years under the African sun. The trenches were no place for a man in his condition. Griffiths kept going, attaching himself like a second shadow to Cendrars in their dashes through enemy fire. Both men, it was assumed by others present in the company, were blessed with the 'Magic of Baraka', time and again demonstrating it by surviving a hail of bullets.

During the latter part of June, while resting among beech trees, Griffiths told Cendrars why he had joined the Legion. He explained how at the age of 20, he had found a job in the City of London as a sewerman. Day after day, he climbed down into the stench and muddy waters, clad in hip-length canvas and pitch-coated waders that weighed almost as much as himself. Armed with an iron bar to ward off rats, his carbide lamp held above his head, he adjusted to his underground life by making each routine descent into an expedition.

One day, he heard voices through one of the grills built into the high walls and roofs of the sewer. He began to investigate what lay beyond those grills and made a remarkable discovery, that they led directly into the underground chambers of the Bank of England. Furthermore the final chamber gave him access to a room filled with gold. Griffiths decided that he must report his discovery at once to the Governor of the Bank. The appearance of this shabby little man in black cap and red-coloured knotted handkerchief around his neck brought only laughter from the beagles at the main entrance to the Bank. He was told to clear off before they called a policeman. For more than a month, Griffiths repeated his attempts to get a personal interview with the governor, and each time met with the same response. Finally, he handed in an envelope addressed to the Governor, containing two gold coins he had taken from the vault and a message asking to see him immediately. Hardly believing what he was hearing, the Governor agreed to go down to the vaults at an appointed time. Griffiths left the Bank and at the appointed time, the Governor discovered him sitting on a pile of gold smoking his pipe! He was asked to sign a pledge that he would never reveal this story, in exchange for £1000, and to leave England immediately. It was then that he went to France, travelled to Marseilles and joined the Legion.

That was Griffiths' story, and one believed by Cendrars to whom it was recounted. He had no reason to doubt it because it was virtually a deathbed confession by Griffiths – he died from consumption eight days after their conversation.

The Legion brought together many comrades with unknown pasts who would never normally meet. Another unlikely pairing came together towards the end of October 1914 when John Ford Elkington entered the gates of Chateau Vincennes, the Legion's headquarters in Paris and applied to join. The Legion had no hesitation in accepting him for service. Although he was 49 years old, Elkington had completed previous military service with the British army. His section, made up largely of American civilians, was under the control of Arthur Griffiths' pal, Corporal Weidermann, who had already completed sixteen years service. Elkington found himself teamed up with one of the Americans, David Wheeler, who, like himself was twenty years or so older than the average recruit.

Neither of them was aware of the other's past, nor was it ever raised. Elkington was mentioned in dispatches for his acts of bravery at the Battle of Artois, when he had led a section forward to recover the wounded. He survived the slaughter at the infamous Hill 140, where more than fifty officers and 1,900 legionnaires were killed. The battle was acclaimed as one of the Legion's most significant of the war, in which legionnaires displayed great courage in spite of the inexperience of many of the volunteers who made up the regiment's strength. The Hill was won, at great cost among the first line of attack, made up of veteran legionnaires who were acting as cadres. The regiment was awarded the *Croix de Guerre* for their part in the action.

Elkington and Wheeler were also praised for their courage at the Battle of Givenchy, where twenty-one officers and 624 legionnaires fell, and at Souchez cemetery where the two comrades wiped out a German machine-gun post. Elkington was promoted in the field to sergeant. His colleagues were beginning to say that Elkington and Wheeler were also blessed with the 'Magic of Baraka'.

However, in September 1915, Elkington's company joined with the rest of the regiment at Souain. His battalion had been earmarked for the attack on Horseshoe Wood and Navarin Farm. Few legionnaires had any illusions about surviving the battle. German defences were known to be almost impenetrable, and everything pointed to another episode of death, despair and misery. Their commander, Captain Junod, fully kitted out in the dress uniform of a Legion officer, even down to the ceremonial epaulettes, stood erect on the parapet and waved his cane, calling his men to fall in behind. To the sound of a bugle, Elkington and Wheeler, along with their company, climbed out of the trenches and advanced in columns of four behind Junod, hardly noticing the gaps appearing in their own lines as the dead and wounded fell to German machine-guns.

They had passed two lines of the German defence wire and had already over-run the first line of the German defence trenches. Legion casualties were enormous, yet only one more line of German trenches had to be overcome before reaching the final objective, Navarin Farm. Elkington and Wheeler were ahead of their section, hurling grenades as they ran towards the final defensive trench. The Germans pulled back and then halted to make a counter attack. Elkington turned to wave his men on, but he fell back into a trench wounded in the legs by a burst of machine-gun fire.

Wheeler rushed to his aid but he too was shot, and fell wounded into the same trench. Only now did Elkington discover that David Wheeler was a surgeon of some repute. Wheeler examined his injured comrade and found several bullets had smashed Elkington's right leg. He cleaned and dressed the wounds with bandages that he always carried, saving Elkington from gangrene. It was only after giving treatment to Elkington that Wheeler attended his own wound, a bullet that had slashed across his calf. Then, he promptly fainted. They lay together in the trench for ten hours, until found by the stretcher bearers and corpse collectors.

At the field hospital, the medics concluded that only Wheeler's prompt action had prevented Elkington losing his leg. The wound was serious enough for him to be hospitalized in Paris. Legion casualties at Navarin Farm were so great that the company was disbanded. David Wheeler continued serving with the Legion until the entry of the United States into the war in 1917, at which time he was allowed to leave the Legion. He became an officer in the American army to be killed in action in the final throes of the war, in August 1918.

Lying in hospital in Paris, John Elkington reluctantly became something of celebrity, although if the truth was known he regretted that he had not given a false name when he joined the Legion. French newspapers picked up his story when he was awarded the Military Medal and the *Croix de Guerre*, the highest awards that could then be conferred on an enlisted man. The past life of John Ford Elkington was now revealed. Before enlistment in the Legion he had been a professional soldier for most of his life. At age 20 he joined the Royal Warwickshire Regiment and served with distinction, first in India and later in the Boer War. During the latter, he was awarded the Queen's Medal with four clasps for conspicuous service.

At the beginning of World War I he had been a Lieutenant Colonel in the same Regiment, in which he had enlisted almost thirty years before, commanding the 1st Battalion which formed part of the British retreat from Mons, with the war only a few weeks old. Elkington's battalion had suffered heavy losses when his battle-weary men arrived at Saint Quentin.

Devoid of rations and supplies, Elkington requested the mayor of the town for permission to rest his troops there. The mayor refused, fearing the imminent arrival of the advancing enemy soldiers. He told Elkington that he did not want his town destroyed simply because it was full of English soldiers.

Elkington pleaded with the mayor again. They could not move on. They had been on the march for days without proper food. The men were exhausted, many wounded. The mayor finally agreed but only on the condition that if the Germans arrived, Elkington would surrender his troops immediately and without a fight. The issue was academic, because Elkington's unit had virtually no ammunition left; many of his men did not even have guns. The battalion had lost nearly all its officers, the command staff had gone away by train and they had no artillery whatsoever. His concern was only feeding his men and treatment for the walking wounded.

The mayor of Saint Quentin, not content with the officer's undertaking, produced a document for him to sign, confirming his agreement to surrender. Elkington, with little thought of the possible consequence, scrawled his signature. The Germans did not turn up and Saint Quentin was spared the bombardment the mayor had feared. The mayor had already sent the British officer's surrender note to the Germans, just in case, and they made use of it for propaganda. In September, having rejoined the rest of the corps, Lt Col Elkington was relieved of his command, and ordered back to England. The document he had signed for the mayor brought to an end his military career with the British army.

He was court-martialled on 14 October 1914, and details of his dismissal were published in the *London Gazette*. He became the first British officer in war to be cashiered, with the implied disgrace of cowardice in the face of the enemy. He immediately left for Paris, to enlist in the Foreign Legion, hoping to put this unfortunate incident behind him.

In 1916, King George V, having read of the honours awarded to John Elkington for his outstanding bravery, recorded in the French Official Gazette, personally prompted an inquiry. In September, the *London Gazette* announced: 'His Majesty King George V has been pleased to approve the reinstatement of John Ford Elkington, with the rank of Lieutenant Colonel, and all previous seniority, and the immediate award of the Distinguished Service Order in consequence of his gallant conduct whilst serving in the ranks of the Foreign Legion of the French Army.'

In September 1916, with the blessing of the Foreign Legion and with the aid of a stick, John Ford Elkington went home to England and his wife and two children. He returned to his British regiment, although he would never wear the medals he had won for gallantry.

7

THE WAR THAT NEARLY
ENDED THE LEGION

'The Legion downplayed the view of some
historians that they became the sacrificial unit
of the French army.'

THE ROMANTICISM and mystique of the Foreign Legion received a boost through the number of literary figures, intellectuals and bohemian characters who enlisted in 1914. The Legion of old was diluted by eager but inexperienced volunteers, and often the two groups were at loggerheads.

The American newcomers had a hard time, as the poet Alan Seeger recorded in his diary and letters home. The 'true' legionnaires did not hold out the hand of friendship towards these men. Nor did they temper either their treatment of raw recruits, or their own general behaviour towards them. The Legion was the Legion, take it or leave it. Most veterans simply did not want these high-flown amateurs.

Alan Seeger was among the first of his group to enlist, even before Blaise Cendrars. Born in New York in 1888, he was educated in Italian studies at Harvard. He edited the *Harvard Monthly* in 1906, and graduated in 1910, when he moved back to New York to become a struggling writer in the American heartland of bohemia, Greenwich Village. He decamped to the original home of that fashionable lifestyle, Paris, in 1912 and settled in the Latin Quarter which he found to be his spiritual home.

Seeger was so in love with Paris that he felt honour-bound to help defend the city when the war came. On 25 August 1914, Seeger carried the American flag at the head of around four or five dozen US volunteers marching along the Avenue de l'Opéra and onwards through Rue Auber to the rail terminal Gare Saint-Lazare, to board a train for Toulouse and their training camp. They were a fairly mixed bunch, men of true French extract mingling with idealists, adventurers, romantics, the pseudo-serious and two black Americans. They, like many other Afro-Americans, felt strongly enough about France's plight to enlist, long before their country's entry into the war.

Eugene Jacques Bullard was the grandson of slaves from Columbus, Georgia. His father, Octave Bullard, came from Martinique, an Overseas Department of France in the West Indies. He had often told his son stories about France. Years later Bullard wrote in his diary: 'My father had told me that in France there are not different white churches and black churches, or white schools and black schools, or white graveyards and black graveyards. People, coloured and white, just lived together and treat each other the same and that was where I wanted to go.'

Gene Bullard was forced to leave home at the age of seven, after his family was attacked by a lynch mob. He roamed around until, at the age of 10, he stowed away on a ship bound for Germany, hoping to reach France. He ended up in Britain, where he eventually put his physique and temper to good effect by working as a boxer. He finally reached Paris in 1913, just after his 19th birthday: 'When I got off the boat train in Paris I was as excited as a kid on Christmas morning. Here I was in the place I had wanted to be in and to see all my life. And it was wonderful.'

Bullard joined a travelling dance troupe, Freedman's Pickaninnies, and remained in Paris after the troupe left as war threatened. He teamed up with Bob Scanlon, another African American boxer he had known in London, and in August 1914, they joined the Foreign Legion. Reasons for joining remained varied. Seeger confessed in his diary that 'it is for the glory alone that I engaged'. On their march through Paris, they were cheered by crowds, watching what was for the Parisians a gladdening sight of foreigners once again coming to the aid of France. At the time, groups of volunteers from individual countries tended to gather together – Russians, Poles, Greeks, Swiss and a large contingent of Jews. This melting pot of nationalities was no challenge to the Legion. The intellectuals, curiously enough, were largely assigned to the regiments of march which housed the tough old soldiers of the Legion. There was a distinct difference between the old and the new, as Blaise Cendrars noticed:

> There was not a single peasant among us . . . tailors, furriers, upholsterers, leather-guilders, sign-writers, coach painters, goldsmiths . . . a few sons of noblemen . . . plus a few intellectuals from Montparnasse who like me were enchanted by the obscene language of these exhilerating companions and their enchanting exuberance.

The legionnaires spat hatred, or at least appeared to. Most had just sailed in from various extreme situations in other parts of the world, sun-scorched and already bloodstained, having left behind Legion dead in Algeria, Morocco, Indo-China and elsewhere. They were not at all caught up in the romance of fighting for France in the way that had captured the imagination of the volunteers. They snarled and drank a lot, and the only clues to their pasts, as Cendrars noted, were the medals on their chests.

The Americans in Alan Seeger's group found it incredible that the legionnaires should regard them with such indifference and lack of understanding. Europeans were less shocked, although they were naturally put out that they who had volunteered were treated with such awfulness, being kicked, punched, beaten up, hit with bottles, sworn at, derided, scorned, stolen from and generally treated with great hostility. Relatives of one British volunteer wrote to the Legion's commander to complain that their son should never have been placed in such a regiment with such animals and could he please be released immediately? The request was refused.

The legionnaires proper, on the other hand, could not believe or understand that all these men had come to fight gratuitously. Neither did they feel bound by their honour-bound code that thou shalt not steal from your comrades: the newcomers, often wealthy, well attired and equipped, were natural targets. Seeger blamed the rising tension on the fact that the Legion was not engaged immediately, and thus during a period of relative inactivity when legionnaires of old filled their time taking a bottle of wine or four, animosity between the two groups grew into an almost stand-off situation. Seeger commented rather sniffily:

> ... discontent has more than usual to feed upon, where a majority of men who engaged voluntarily were thrown in a regiment made up almost entirely of the dregs of society, refugees from justice and roughs, commanded by *sous-officiers* who treated us all without distinction in the same manner that they treated their unruly brood in Africa.

Then, they all went to war and began loosing off some of their frustrations against the Germans. In the heat of battle they were all just men, fighting in the most horrendous conditions. Inexperience of everything that lay before them was indeed a common bond. In January 1915, Seeger and a group of other Americans were on duty at a forward observation post in the wreckage of a chateau. They included Paul and Kiffin Rockwell, two US college kids from Atlanta. Kiffin heard a muffled crash and saw something roll spluttering to his feet.

'What's that?' he asked, reaching down to pick it up.

Seeger yelled, 'Good God, it's a hand-grenade!'

They looked at each other, mystified, and then Kiffin tossed it away as hard as he could and it exploded in mid-air. It was only then that the significance of a hand-grenade dawned upon them. If someone had thrown it, they must be close by. The Germans were very close indeed.

Seeger decided he'd better get the corporal. His name was Weidermann, Arthur Griffiths' friend. As the two men came running back, another grendade landed at Rockwell's feet. Weidermann called out a warning. Rockwell threw himself to the other side of the room just as the bomb exploded. They all survived and bolted, knowing full well that the Germans would come in very quickly now. They had barely reached the cover of trees when gunfire was heard behind them. Corporal Weidermann fell wounded, and shouted for the others to go on. They looked back as the Germans reached the veteran legionnaire whom they quickly identified as one of their own nationality, a German fighting against Germany. His time was up. They stood over him and crushed his skull and face with their rifle butts. And that night, the young American legionnaires heard the howling, taunting cries of the Germans high on a hillside.

The Americans continued on with their fight, but were diminishing in their numbers daily: through the first year, and half way to the next, battle after battle, sometimes going around in circles. In September it was their turn to try to eject the German reserve from Navarin Farm which the Legion had unsuccessfully attacked in the early summer. They put 2,000 officers and men into the battle, the legionnaires thrusting forward time and again in the face of murderous fire from German machine-gun nests. After seventy-two hours of constant fighting, the forward ground towards the farm lay cluttered with Legion dead and wounded, 603 having fallen before the commanders ordered a retreat.

Once again, they had failed to dislodge the German reserve, but the angry protests of Legion commanders to the French high command made it plain that they considered they had done everything in their power to take the farm; it was simply too well fortified and manned – which they already knew, but their advice had been disregarded for the sake of an over-ambitious strategy.

Another major confrontation was on its way and the Legion, having recovered its composure, was heading for what would prove to be one of its costliest operations of the war, in the ferocious Battle of the Somme. They were part of the Allied force committed to drawing the German fire in the Somme to relieve the pressure on the French army in that other great slaughter house called Verdun.

The Somme campaign began in the third week of June, with the Legion fielding 2,850 men and sixty-two officers, as part of the overall Allied force including a substantial British contingent which had been holding the line for ten months. Legionnaires were not among the first wave of 100,000 men who went over the top on the first day of July when 57,000 were killed or wounded.

The legionnaires were held in reserve, for a particular attack that, in the event, was something of a suicide mission. Battalion commander Major James Waddell, a New Zealander, had many of the surviving Americans under his wing. He was a popular man, a courageous leader and one of the most respected of all the Legion's officers. Waddell had quit university in England in 1895 to join the British army and saw service in India and Afghanistan.

In 1900, at the age of 27, he joined the Legion and went off to Tonkin. At the outset of the war, he commanded the nucleus of the Algerian legionnaires who included Weidermann and Arthur Griffiths, before transferring with a Legion battalion to the Dardenelles where he was wounded in 1915. By 1916, he had already been awarded the *Légion d'Honneur* and the *Croix de Guerre* with seven palms. Among his soldiers at the Somme were two who were to become famous in Legion history, Alan Seeger and the renowned Sergeant Major Max-Emmanuel Mader, a former soldier in the German army who had joined the Legion in 1904, married a French woman, had one son, became a nationalized Frenchman and the most decorated legionnaire of all time. Seeger had just written a card to his mother in New York: 'We have changed sectors at last . . . the country here is very beautiful.'

And so, on 5 July 1916, these personalities of Legion history, old veterans and young Americans, were together for the assault on their designated target, the heavily fortified village of Belloy-en-Santerre which was a rabbit-warren of German gunports and defensive systems that was judged to be almost impossible to attack with any real hope of success.

The legionnaires, with the burden of 60lbs of gear slung on their backs, were to make their attack in two waves, each to provide covering fire for the other. The first went dashing across open countryside and seemed to be having a charmed advance until they were about a couple of hundred yards away. Then, the German machine-gun fire cut them down. Seeger was in the second wave, led by Mader, charging on and shouting the men forward. Half way across, Seeger fell screaming in pain into a bomb crater. He was heard crying for water and his mother, and then silence. He was one of 844 legionnaires and twenty-five officers killed that day. The survivors who reached the other side faced fierce house-to-house combat, and then finally hand-to-hand scraps until the Germans retreated to regroup for the first of many counter-offensives. They too suffered heavy losses, and the Legion also took 750 prisoners. It was a spectacular victory for the legionnaires and a few nights later, they were asked for a repeat performance at Chancelier where they took another 400 casualties in a battle that cost the three armies almost 1,300,000 men.

Seeger's personal effects included a number of poems, his diaries and other writings which were gathered up and returned home. None had been published in his lifetime, but made their appearance in a book a year after his death.

Alan Seeger's *Rendezvous* echoes a letter he wrote in 1915, in which he said: 'If it must be, let it come in the heat of action. Why flinch? It is by far the noblest form in which death can come. It is in a sense almost a privilege.'

And so the poem that reflected his feelings at the height of World War I, written in the trenches, demonstrated an eerie and prophetic notion that he was about to die:

Rendezvous
I have a rendezvous with Death
At some disputed barricade,
I have a rendezvous with Death
At some disputed barricade,
When Spring comes back with rustling shade
And apple-blossoms fill the air—
I have a rendezvous with Death.
When Spring brings back blue days and fair.

Legionnaire 19522 Seeger was posthumously awarded the *Croix de Guerre* and the *Médaille Militaire* and took his place in the history of the French Foreign Legion which, in the end, he would have wanted.

The two black Americans who joined at the same time had no complaints either. Eugene Bullard, in particular, moved to greater glory from his early days with the Legion. He was seriously wounded by shrapnel in May 1916 and was awarded the *Croix de Guerre* for his bravery. After his recovery he trained as a flyer, transferring to the French Air Service in October 1916. He became an ace pilot with the Lafayette Flying Corps, a group of American pilots who fought for France until the US came into the war, and he earned the title of the 'Black Swallow of Death' for his daring in battle.

Blaise Cendrars' view of the Legion also changed quite dramatically in a comparatively short time and he wrote gushingly of his comrades after the war. The change began on his first leave after months in the mud and afterwards, he wrote a passage which now stands as one of the most incisive and superbly expressed explanations ever written as to why men who join the Legion, and having done so decided to tough it out, are totally taken by its comradeship and will defend it to the death:

> I was prepared to follow the consequences of my action [in enlisting] . . . but I did not realize that the Legion would make me drink this chalice to the dregs and that these dregs would make me drunk and that by taking a cynical pleasure in debasing and discrediting myself I would end up by breaking free of everything to conquer my liberty as a man. To be. To be a man. And discover solitude. That is what I owe to the Legion and to the old lascars of Africa, soldiers, NCOs, officers who came to lead us and mix with us as comrades, these desperados, these survivors of God knows what colonial epics but who were all men, all. And that made it well worth the risk of death to meet these damned souls who smelled of the galleys and were covered with tattoos. None of them ever let us down and each one was willing to sacrifice himself, for nothing, for kudos, because he was drunk, for a challenge, for a laugh, to stick it to someone, By God . . . these were professionals, and the profession of a man of war is an abominable thing and leaves scars, like poetry. You have it, you don't.

Another young Briton who came to form a quite incredible love-hate relationship with the Legion was Adolphe Richard Cooper. He was also unique in that he was under 16 when he joined, left on four occasions and re-enlisted each time. He first described the Legion as a desolate, soulless army of thugs and ended up virtually recommending it to every young man with no purpose in life.

In between leaving the first time, in 1916, and the final time in the early 1930s, Cooper wrote two books, the first of which was published while he was briefly out, entitled *The Man Who Liked Hell.* It had a vitriolic tone, intended as he said to 'expose' the Legion, its practices and the terrible habits of its men. It was devoid of the romance and heavily punctuated with the Legion horror stories – that homosexuality was rife, that there were almost daily fist-fights among the men and the 'death marches' in which legionnaires were expected to trek an impossible 1,000 miles in eight days and those who didn't make it were buried by the wayside.

Jim Worden points out that Cooper's second book, *Twelve Years in The Foreign Legion,* seemed to have been written as an apology for the first and that his conclusions were more honest. Cooper's life in the Legion began in October 1914. He was cabin boy on a British merchant ship. He walked off at Algiers, and at the age of 15 years four months enlisted in the Legion. When signing his first contract, he accepted the alias 'Jean le Bruin' and for a young lad did very well. In fact, in the annals of Legion personal histories, his own service dossier at Legion headquarters was remarkable. It reads as follows:

ADOLPHE RICHARD COOPER – SERVICE HISTORY

1 Enlisted 8 October 1914 at Algiers. Alias Jean le Bruin.

2 Discharged at request of the British Consul 1916, following appeals by his relatives; subsequently served in the British army for the duration of the war.

3 Re-enlisted September 1919 under own name: Adolphe Cooper.

4 Completed his five-year contract and was discharged September 1924 as second class Legionnaire.

---

5 Re-enlisted December 1924.

6 Completed corporal training, promoted 16 April 1925.

7 Reduced in rank May 1926 after thrashing a subordinate.

8 Transferred to 4th Regiment 28 March 1928.

9 Discharged December 1929 (still a second class Legionnaire) on completion of his second five-year term.

10 Re-enlisted January 1930 for a further five year contract; promoted again to corporal and later to sergeant.

Back in 1914, Cooper had managed to talk himself into the Legion at two-and-a-half years under the minimum age which was, in Legion terms, something of a miracle. Cooper spent six months at Sidi-bel-Abbès with a training cadre preparing soldiers for war. He was disappointed to find that as a fully trained legionnaire he would not be fighting in France. He was among a single battalion of the Legion sent into combat at a little known place, Gallipoli, at the entrance to the Black Sea. The Legion battalion was to be part of the series of ultimately disastrous naval and shore battles launched by joint Anglo–French forces with the object of easing the pressure on the Russians on the eastern front. Cooper arrived there on 26 April 1915. Gallipoli is most famously remembered as the battleground of the Australians. The Legion was part of a combined French force which went under the name of the *Armée d'Orient*.

All units faced well dug-in Turkish troops commanded by German officers. Curiously enough, virtually all the Legion NCOs were also German. The multi-national Legion troops showed spectacular courage storming ashore in cutters towed by steam pinnaces. At some beaches, the opposition was minimal. At others, they were mown down by machine-gunners lodged in the surrounding hills.

Adolphe Cooper, having secretly celebrated his sixteenth birthday soon after his arrival at the Dardenelles, took part in several battles, including hand-to-hand fighting, lunging with his bayonette, surrounded by legionnaires bawling instructions in languages he could not understand. In the fierce action, Cooper's company commander and his officers were all killed and Sergeant Major de Leon took over command.

It was specifically for his courage in that particular battle that Cooper was among the first legionnaires, and certainly the youngest, to be awarded the *Croix de Guerre* for gallantry in action. Of the 1,000 men of Cooper's battalion, less than 400 survived by the time the force was evacuated in January 1916. Cooper himself was wounded by shell fire, and returned on a hospital ship to Sidi-bel-Abbès.

While recovering from his wounds his family finally learned of his whereabouts and with the assistance of the British Consul secured his release from the Legion. Adolphe Cooper went on to stake many claims to fame in the Foreign Legion, after re-enlisting in 1919. He became one of the highest decorated legionnaires at Sidi-bel-Abbès. During his first full five years between 1919 and 1924, he also held the record for his service in both the legion prison and the company discipline cells at Columb Bechar. He made it to corporal, and was then busted – a not uncommon occurrence for tough young men. He had been promoted to sergeant when he left in 1935, joining the ranks as one of the longest serving legionnaires of all time.

The sheer fact of staying alive in the Foreign Legion, with or without the so-called 'Magic of Baraka', was a feat in itself. Historians generally accept that the Legion was consistently put up for difficult tasks by the war managers and this could be seen especially in many of the final campaigns when the Legion faced a crisis of diminishing manpower. Volunteers had virtually dried up because of the call on manpower by other nations. By the end of 1917, there were fewer than 100 volunteers a month, a totally inadequate number to keep pace with the killed and wounded. The high casualty rate and the fire engine tactics of the French military, using legionnaires to fill gaps left by major desertions in other French line units, continued right up to the end. By then, some Legion companies were already reduced to fewer than four dozen men, and yet in the last weeks of the war, legionnaires were thrown into a succession of hotspots.

In April 1918 at Hanguard Wood, soaked still in German mustard gas, legionnaires backed by British artillery and tanks thrust themselves against the German 19th Division and were cut down by machine-gunners at an alarming rate. With one battalion reduced to 187 and only one officer, two other Legion battalions moved in to exact their revenge in fierce hand-to-hand combat. The total cost to the Legion was 833 men and eight officers killed or wounded, while Allied casualties reached 160,000 in the overall offensive.

In July, with the Legion still below strength, it was in action again in a desperate struggle close to Paris, at Soissons, where they were designated to storm a number of fortified German positions. The operation was a total success, but the Legion took another 1,400 casualties. They included Max Mader, the German born stalwart who in more than ten years of dodging bayonets, bullets and bombs had become a living legend. Max had half his right arm blown off and his shoulder riddled with bullet holes. The ambulance corps picked up his motionless body and took it to the field hospital, expecting Mader to be one more candidate for the mass graves.

The legionnaires made a particular fuss of Mader's seemingly inevitable demise and arranged for the padre to read the last rites. As he did so, Mader's huge form shuddered into life. Treatment for his wounds was hastily resumed and Max Mader went on to live a long life on his meagre Legion pension.

By the end of the war the Legion's strength had slipped to its lowest level. During the war the Legion had accepted 42,883 volunteers from 51 nations of whom almost 31,840 were killed or wounded. This figure included those who were at some stage later transferred out of the Legion into French army units or to armies of their own nationality. The casualty figures, judged from another standpoint, provided an even more illuminating picture from the Legion's point of view. The number of 'true' legionnaires at the start of the war has been put at around 13,000, and historian Hugh McLeave estimated that of the original 8,000 legionnaires who went from Sidi-bel-Abbès, a mere fifty survived.

Set against the one million lost souls of the French army and the appalling overall cost of human life, the Legion downplayed the view of some historians that they became the sacrificial unit of the French army. But the heart had been cut from the French Foreign Legion.

8

POST-WAR REFORMATION

'Concerns were swept aside, and as the Legion's new regiments began to take shape, a large percentage of its men were drawn from nations who were but a matter of months earlier bitter enemies of France.'

For A WHILE in post-war France, racked by the guilt, recriminations and bitterness shared by all nations who participated in the carnage, a question mark hung over the Foreign Legion. Its performance had been regarded as generally exemplary and the Legion took place of honour at the head of the 1919 Victory Parade on Bastille Day down the Champs Élysées, with its band playing *Le Boudin* and other popular songs of the day. Such was the greater glory of the French Foreign Legion that its band left soon afterwards for a triumphant tour of the United States, drumming up quite a large number of aspirant legionnaires in the process.

Behind the cheering, the future of the Legion was uncertain. More than 30 per cent of all French males aged between 18 and 27 had succumbed to battle wounds and tens of thousands more were so badly injured as to be incapable of work for the rest of their lives. After the devastation of human life the immediate future of the Foreign Legion was hardly rated on the scale of priorities, but the determination of some of its top brass, and especially one of its new regimental commanders, Colonel Paul Rollet, had other plans.

Rollet, revered today as the Father of the modern Foreign Legion, was instrumental in bringing it back to becoming a powerful force in the military strategy of France. The Legion had taken a grievous knock in World War I. Some said it was beyond repair; but Rollet believed differently. He was a die-hard, if somewhat eccentric, legionnaire. The product of a military family and Saint-Cyr officer training where he was unimpressively placed 311 out of 587, his physical appearance was untypical of the Legion. He was small, slender and seemingly of nervous disposition. The latter was not true in reality. Behind his sharp blue, darting eyes, set above a long pointed nose and a tufty point-shaped beard, was a forceful character. Apparently destined to an unin-spiring career in a line regiment, Rollet volunteered for transfer to the officer corps of the Legion in December 1898. He was soon involved in the Legion's colonial battles, with service in Algeria, Morocco and Madagascar. He was injured two or three times. Although a strong dis-ciplinarian, Rollet endeared himself to his men for his indifference to his superiors, with whom he argued strongly on any strategy with which he did not agree. Though he himself would challenge and ques-tion, he had no compunction about enforcing the code of blind obedi-ence upon his men.

He never wore a shirt under his tunic and invariably wore light-weight safari clothes. He usually carried an umbrella, like Louis-Philippe, creator of the Legion, even on to the battlefield and where possible was accompanied by his dog! He never wore anything other than a kepi on his head, regardless of shellfire around him, and was only once known to divert from this rule when he was forced to con-form and wear a metal helmet for the 1919 victory parade. He was out front, leading the parade and carrying the regimental colour, swathed in honours.

Rollet left the Legion briefly, at the outset of the war, when he was promoted and given a line command. In 1917, however, the Legion, which because of losses had been rolled up into the *Régiment de Marche de la Légion Étrangère* (RMLE), welcomed him back as its chief when the incumbent commander, Lieutenant Colonel Duiriez, was killed at Aubérive.

The injection of his personal charisma and established methods in handling the Legion brought the weakened RMLE to peak condition at a particular time. It was selected to attempt to form a bridgehead movement near Verdun. Three Legion battalions marched then ran into pitched battle, grabbing the desired stretch of territory, and almost 700 German prisoners, well ahead of schedule.

Paul Rollet used this and other examples as testimony when, towards the end of the war, he began to submit his case to save the Legion from being disbanded:

> . . . and so would disappear this excellent school of energy, of will, of courage which formed the heart and character of ardent young officers full of fire who would go afterwards into the regiments of settled garrisons, animated with sacred fire . . . it would not be a simple unit which would disappear with the Legion, but a notable part of the world of the French army.

Rollet had a strong supporter in the post-war political arena in General Jean Mordacq who had served in the Legion before the war and had since risen to a position of influence within the French government. Mordacq believed the time had come to expand the army of foreigners into divisions, each with their own particular identity and specialities in infantry, cavalry and artillery.

This was also the view of General Hubert Lyautey, French military supremo in Morocco, who had led the initial incursion by French troops there in 1908 and had held the fort in the colonial outpost throughout the war years. Lyautey had run his defence of France's colonial interests in North Africa with single-minded devotion. He ran his own war and took all the men he could get, regardless of background, although he complained that many seemed to be there only because they might get arrested on the outside.

All that now changed. There were men aplenty queueing up to volunteer again and Lyautey – like Mordacq – suggested a minimum Legion strength of 30,000. The Legion, he wrote, should introduce an immediate recruitment drive carried out with tenacity which would provide not only a good number of recruits but also the 'right type', a task which would prove rather more difficult than he appeared to have imagined.

To his strong campaign for the revitalization of the Legion was added the weight of Paul Rollet who returned to Sidi-bel-Abbès with the exhausted, disillusioned, battle-weary remnants of a once great fighting force after the clearing up had been done at the end of 1919. In the spring of the following year, the reformation of the Legion was formally approved by government decrees. These gave it power to vastly increase its numbers and create cavalry and artillery regiments, marking the end of the Legion as solely an infantry unit.

Recruitment began immediately, but a question mark, unforeseen at the time, hung over the suitability of the men who were volunteering. For a while, they would change the face of the Legion entirely. Vast numbers of former soldiers were idling across Europe, including a large number of Russians who had simply walked away from the war in 1917 when the Czar was murdered by the Bolsheviks. There were many Britons volunteering and, as ever, a large number of Germans, despite their pre-war propaganda against the Legion. Successive French ministers of war had always been wary of the number of German nationals, particularly NCOs, in the Legion and that fear was heightened as more and more were accepted. One of the great heroes of the French military, Marshal Ferdinand Foch, a prominent figure in the peace negotiations, warned against packing the Legion with German volunteers. It was only a matter of time, he repeatedly predicted, before Germany would invade France again and so the Legion was only storing up trouble.

The concerns were swept aside, and as the Legion's new regiments began to take shape, a large percentage of its men were drawn from nations who were but a matter of months earlier bitter enemies of France. The 1st Infantry Regiment, for example, consisted of 72 per cent of former 'enemy' nationals. The 4th Regiment included the largest number of Germans, 42 per cent by 1922. Within a decade, 44 per cent of all legionnaires were Germans.

Germans and Eastern Europeans also tended to crush the romanticism of the Legion, although it was not completely overwhelmed. Post-war writings of ex-legionnaires (like Blaise Cendrars and the poems and letters of Alan Seeger) helped. So did the entry into the service of men later regarded as 'characters'. There was the immaculately attired and suave young man who stood before a recruiting officer in Paris:

'Name?'

'Prince Aage of Denmark', replied the man.

'Occupation?'

'Banker . . . or should I say bankrupt!'

The Prince, a member of the Danish royal family, was also a distant relative of Louis-Philippe who founded the Legion in the first place. Aage thus became an officer with immediate effect and very soon became a battalion commander in Morocco. And then there was the middle-aged man of some bearing who attracted the attention of Colonel Rollet:

'And what did you do in civilian life?' inquired Rollet.

'I was a general, Colonel.'

There was a colourful post-war mix of volunteers: Hungarian lotharios, Russian counts, hot-tempered Cossack horsemen, German sergeant majors, ill-educated Turks. But overwhelming numbers came not from adventurers, but from men who simply could not find anything else to do with their lives. Prince Aage, who rose to a place in the Legion hall of fame, reckoned that in the immediate post-war period the Legion was different for two reasons.

First, the core of the old Legion had had such a shocking wartime experience that they were physically and emotionally drained, and they simply did not want to get involved with newcomers. Second, one of the vital elements missing in the new Legion, initially at least, was the lack of adventurers and 'men with troubled pasts' who needed and would accept strict discipline. There were simply too many Central European mercenaries. Douglas Porch produced similar evidence, unearthing the regimental diaries of the 2nd Regiment which noted in 1921 that the legionnaires seemed not to have come to the Legion in search of new adventures. They were simply men waiting for better times. The legionnaires of this epoch were 'therefore different from before the war. They seemed more malleable, less drunken but also thin-skinned'.

Another significant difference was seen in the 'rather large number of letters that they write and receive . . . [which] show that they have not broken with their old countries. That is why we receive frequent requests to end enlistments coming from parents of young legionnaires less than twenty years old.' As Porch noted, new officers coming to the Legion in the immediate post-war period expected to rub shoulders with the bronzed lascars, but instead found a collection of 'adolescents with hardly any fuzz on their chin'. A quarter admitted to being less than twenty years old and 64 per cent were under twenty-five.

The Legion had changed beyond recognition, according to Adolphe Cooper on his re-enlistment for a second term in 1919. At the time of his first enlistment in 1914, he was thrust into the midst of tough battle-scarred legionnaires. Now it was different. He blamed the influx of Russians, although being British, he wasn't that keen on the Germans either. 'I realized I had made a terrible mistake in coming back,' he would write later. Mistake or not, the Legion gripped him once again and as we have seen from his service record in the previous chapter, he remained for another fifteen years.

The evident post-war change in the character of the Legion was uppermost in the mind of Paul Rollet. The re-organization of it was going to take far longer than they had imagined. Rollet's answer to the youthfulness and inexperience of the force was to revive the traditions and the fighting reputation of the pre-1914 Legion. Many of the informal rituals, the symbols and even the myths of the past had simply emerged out of the ether to become part of Legion life and history. Rollet became determined to gather up those traditions, even invent new ones, and hand them back to the new breed of legionnaires. He designed a whole new platform of conduct on which the post-war Legion would be built, all linked to past achievements.

He worried that the newcomers did not show enough respect for either Legion history, such as Camerone, or to the veterans and the more recent heroes of the Western Front. Those men, physically tired and who had themselves slumped in their self-esteem and habits, were taking a less active role and drinking heavily. They complained bitterly that the newcomers had no regard for the unwritten rules of the Legion that demanded respect for seniority, a community spirit of sharing and mutual aid and that the young recruits should accept the teaching of the *anciens* through their recollections and, admittedly, appalling jokes.

Rollet's first step was to make sure the newly enlisted men showed deference to the old-timers and learned from their experiences. Those who did not could expect a kicking. Discipline was to be a prime factor in the rebuilding; physical punishment came instantly and excessively for wrongdoers and 'wrong' might just be a sideways glance at a bellowing German NCO. The memories of the survivors and the symbols and practices of the pre-1914 Legion alone were insufficient in themselves to bridge the gulf left by the war. Rollet and his fellow commanders agreed that they had to resurrect past glories and the old ways to form what would become the central plank in the Legion's re-creation.

Camerone Day was revived. It became a sacrosanct celebration and the symbol of a Legion committed to making the supreme sacrifice. Rollet personally designed and supervized the installation of the *Monument aux Morts* at Sidi-bel-Abbès (moved in its entirety in 1962 to the new headquarters in Aubagne) and an updated *Salle d'Honneur* provided a visible connection with the past, so that the history of major Legion battles was to be told and retold.

The names of heroes were engraved in marble, and ingrained into the memories of new recruits. The Legion's favourite songs were to be learned and sung by all and the family spirit which Rollet believed to be so important was to prevail. Family traditions, such as Christmas, became an important time of leisurely celebration, regardless of the legionnaires' religion. On that day, they could relax and they would each receive a gift from their company commander. Men who had cut themselves off from their families and the world were to be encouraged to view the Legion as their home. The whole concept of *Legio Patria Nostra – The Legion is Our Fatherland –* was to be established. Even the Legion's motto would be changed from *Valeur et Discipline* to *Honneur et Fidélité*.

That was the Legion according to Paul Rollet. Throughout the 1920s the new Legion was being restructured and expanded. Nor was it merely a question of getting the psychology right. Recruits themselves had to be physically honed, and standards were set down that remain in place today. Most of the volunteers had come through harsh times. Food had been short and many were skeletal shadows, hardly equipped for the tough regime of Legion life. To them, the Legion offered a life of relative luxury compared with what they might expect in their home towns. They were given three meals a day and wages at the end of each week, plain food and meagre rewards but as American Charles Jackson, a volunteer of that era, wrote in his diaries:

> To some of my colleagues in this odd amalgam, the Foreign Legion provides the stuff of their wildest dreams, noticeably when they receive cash in hand which is apparently a novel experience to some. They clutch their few coins as if it were a fortune; I have seen men reduced to tears. Yet, it will not remain with them for long. The town of Sidi-bel-Abbès is well equipped to divest them of their riches and should any of it remain, the old soldiers of their company will beg and borrow from the innocents so that they, having already spent theirs, may buy more drink. The town resembles in many ways our imaginings of an old wild west town, dusty and dirty with a main street along which you walk through lines of local populace waiting to relieve you of your cash. The first hurdles are most attractive diversions which are to be found virtually at the gates of the camp. They are of course the brothels. There are three *Le Moulin Rouge, Au Palmier* and *Le Chat Noir*. The hostesses as they are so politely described are of mixed origin, some Arabians, a couple of Europeans and even a South American. They can be quite intimidating, especially in *The Cat*, where they line the bars in waiting, and are virtually naked. Thus, those in the Legion to whom spending money has not been plentiful cannot wait to get to these places which, I have to admit, have a certain attraction to those of us desiring the warmth and pleasure of female company, so lacking of late.

The Legion began to revert to its well tried and tested training regime enforced by the heavy-hands of NCOs who were often beyond the control of young and inexperienced officers. They liked to see the days of new recruits filled from dawn to dusk with press-ups, running up and down hills and sand dunes laden with backpacks, doubling up by carrying a heavier man, and the forced marches under the daytime swelter of the Algerian sun or the cold nights.

These aspects of Legion life would barely change down the decades and nor could they, according to Legion historian Jean Planchais:

> Under the terms of the 1908 Hague Convention, a legionnaire could not be forced to fight against his own country. That condition apart, the Legion exacted total obedience from its volunteers and expected nothing less than total adherence to the contract every one of them signed which included the stipulation that a non-commissioned officer was free to marry only after six years service, and the private soldier twelve years, if he remained in service that long. As an admirable instrument of war, the Legion was forged by absolute obedience and an entire devotion to rigorous traditions. It could never be described as a troop of mercenaries, because the pay is too small to justify that description. Even so, men are never wanting at the Legion.

Recruitment went on at a pace, and by the mid-1920s more and more men were needed to bolster the Legion's presence across North Africa. Continuing uprisings among the Moroccans, who General Lyautey fought to keep under control during World War I, ensured the need for the presence of the Legion. Lyautey was always a supporter of Legion tactics and as Commander-in-Chief of all French troops in the region, he asked for large numbers of legionnaires to cover the roughest terrain deep into the desert and high in the hills, death-trap country for all but the most experienced of regimental commanders. The era was a great test for the inexperience of a youthful Legion.

Never-ending battles with the anti-colonialists in Algeria continued, and the upsurge in nationalism in Morocco engulfed the Legion in dramatic skirmishes with Berber tribesmen who were becoming increasingly agitated by the empire builders stealing their lands and resources.

The Berbers had inhabited the coast of North Africa, from Egypt to the Atlantic Ocean for centuries, although they had been pushed back into areas in and near the Sahara. After World War I the Berber and Arab populations began actively to seek independence. In the summer of 1920, the Berbers opened their campaign of attacks in Spanish Morocco. The emir of the Rif regions of Spanish Morocco, Abd-el-Krim, a well-travelled intellectual, mustered vast armies of horsemen and foot soldiers and repeatedly defeated Spanish troops. The most emphatic victory by any African leader against a European force was recorded the following year. El-Krim's spectacular gathering of 30,000 warriors annihilated General Sylvestre's Spanish regiments at Anual in July. More than 12,000 Spanish soldiers were killed.

The Legion had already begun to expand its forces in Morocco with its companies of relatively inexperienced men. The 2nd Regiment, which had been in training at Saïda, was posted to a new garrison at Meknes. The old RMLE became the 3rd Regiment under the command of Colonel Rollet who moved his headquarters to Fez. The 4th Regiment formed up at Meknes and was posted to Marrakesh. In 1926, its resources were severely tested as el-Krim launched his long-expected attack on French Morocco.

For this, he had secured some valuable inside information. He was already well known to have captured deserters from the Legion in the past and far from torturing them, or cutting off their heads or other unpleasant acts, el-Krim offered them money, food and women if they would join him and help eject the French from his homelands. At least a couple of dozen were known to have accepted his offer.

By mid-April 1925 el-Krim led the Berber army of 30,000 into French Morocco and stormed across the countryside. With such vast numbers travelling in the Berber columns, tactics were simple and effective. They arrived at remote Legion forts and offered the commanding officer the chance to surrender. None are known to have given in voluntarily. They would then be surrounded and left to the mercy of a large force, while the rest of el-Krim's army moved off in search of another conquest. Tales of courage among the legionnaires began to sound like re-runs of Camerone or the heroics in Tonkin.

One far away fort withstood attack after attack for almost eight weeks until they were virtually out of ammunition and supplies. As the Berbers began to prepare for the final onslaught, the fort's commanding officer, Lieutenant Paul Lapeyre, ordered all available explosives to be placed in a strategic position. Then, as the rebel tribesmen crashed through the gates, he gave the order and blew the fort up, killing himself and thirty of his soldiers along with a large number of the enemy.

By the end of April, more than half the entire line of French forts and outposts on the border had been put out of action, two dozen were evacuated and nine had been captured. General Lyautey who had appealed for reinforcements feared that French Morocco was heading towards disaster as more tribes who had previously been 'pacified' by French forces rebelled and joined el-Krim's army.

They marched on towards Fez and by the end of the month were gathering outside the capital, ready for the attack which they might well have won. But el-Krim suddenly pulled back. His reasons for doing so were the subject of much conjecture later. Some suggested that he believed that the Legion and other French army units, headquartered in Fez, were lying in wait. The delay in attacking Fez, which was in fact quite unready for such an event, allowed the French the breathing space they required. Marshal Pétain was already heading towards Morocco with an incredible fifty battalions of French troops drawn from the Rhineland army of occupation. Lyautey was relieved of his post as military governor and sent home to Paris. Pétain, in negotiation with the Spanish, masterminded a joint attack from both armies. The massive movement of manpower brought equally huge artillery support with reconnaisance planes overhead.

El-Krim made his last stand before the largest army ever assembled by a European nation in North Africa. He surrendered in 1927, realizing his 30,000 warriors had been totally outgunned by Pétain's armies numbering, in all, 250,000. They were made up of 120,000 French troops, 40,000 native soldiers and 90,000 men contributed by the Spanish. El-Krim was exiled to Reunion in the Indian Ocean, having signed a surrender document calling on all tribes to accept French and Spanish rule.

It was another seven years before the last of the rebel strongholds was quelled, which meant a continued strong presence from the Foreign Legion.

The Legion became an integral part of France's permanent occupation for and during more settled times, legionnaires were put to work, joining French engineers building new roads and barracks. In one place, on the road from Marrakech to Ouarzazate, an Atlas mountain stood in their path. Legionnaires, largely using hand tools and explosive, cut a tunnel four yards high and seventy yards long and set up a plaque inscribed with the legend: 'The mountain barred the road. The order came, all the same, to go through it. The Legion executed that order.'

The Legion forged ahead. New regiments were formed to take its strength to 33,500 men by the end of 1933, made up of eighteen battalions of infantry, six cavalry squadrons, five mounted companies and four companies of sappers based in North Africa. It had also had three battalions in Indo-China. Of its total force, approximately 40 per cent were of Germanic origin, a fact which had not been overlooked by the Nazi regime and by German military intelligence in particular.

9

ALL-AMERICAN HERO

'Talk to your son and his comrades, and you may judge for
yourself whether he will welcome your interference in the
life which he himself has chosen.'

AMONG THE young men rushed into combat
in Morocco during the last uprisings of the Berbers in 1932 was Peter
Ortiz, the son of a New York art dealer. His father, Philip, was
wealthy enough, even in those years of depression, to send his son to
Europe for two years to complete his education. In 1931, he was
attending Grenoble University where he should have remained until
the end of 1932. In January of that year, his parents received a letter
from their son, brief and to the point: 'By the time you receive this
letter, I shall be on my way to Sidi-bel-Abbès to join the French
Foreign Legion for five years. I know what I am doing and I am not
afraid.'

Ortiz senior, whose business interests involved frequent travel
between New York and Paris, caught the next ship across the Atlantic,
and on the way made himself aware of the life his son might expect in
the Foreign Legion by reading books on the subject, including *Beau
Geste*, and other less reputable tomes, often written by deserters. As he
journeyed on towards Paris, Philip Ortiz became determined that he
would free his son from the brutal and vice-ridden life that he was
convinced Peter had entered.

As soon as he arrived in Paris, Philip Ortiz sought the help of a business acquaintance to secure an interview with Marshal Franchet d'Esperey, one of the most powerful military figures in France. Ortiz informed d'Esperey that his son was a minor and had been under the age of 18 when he enlisted in the Legion. The marshal agreed that this was sufficient to get the boy's enlistment annulled but suggested that before this step was taken, Philip Ortiz should travel to Sidi-bel-Abbès. 'Talk to your son and his comrades,' said the Marshal, 'and you may judge for yourself whether he will welcome your interference in the life which he himself has chosen.'

Ortiz travelled to the Legion headquarters in Algeria, where he was met by his son who first took him to the Legion museum, explained the significance of Camerone, showed him the *Monument aux Morts,* introduced him to some of his comrades in the regiment and at the end of the guided tour, insisted he wanted to stay put.

Philip Ortiz met senior Legion officers who went to some lengths to prove to him that the army of foreigners was not stacked with vicious psychopaths, sexual deviants or fugitives from justice. There were some of these characters, it could not be denied. The majority, they submitted, were men of courage who preferred a hard and dangerous life, freed from the abject misery of the depression and unemployment in their homelands. Philip Ortiz concluded that the portrait of the Legion painted by the literature he had read was at best an exaggeration and at worst, make-believe. To be certain, he decided to go on a tour of all Legion bases within striking distance of its headquarters. It was a grand tour, lasting several weeks. When he returned to Sidi-bel-Abbès, Ortiz agreed that there was nothing better he would like than for his son to remain in the Legion.

Back in Paris, he had further talks with the military establishment, this time with three marshals to whom he floated an idea for what amounted to a public relations effort to improve the image and reputation of the Foreign Legion. He persuaded several business friends in Paris and New York to join him and with the backing of the three marshals of France formed a committee under the name of *Les Amis de la Légion Étrangère*. Housed at 18 Rue Louis-Le-Grande, it was formed for the specific purpose of counteracting what were considered 'slanderous attacks' on the Foreign Legion. Branches of the association soon began to spread throughout the world. The news came as a particular pleasure to Colonel Rollet who was on the verge of becoming Inspector General of the Legion. He hated PC Wren's book, *Beau Geste*. He claimed that the sadistic Sergeant Lejeune in his book was 'untypical' of Legion NCOs. They were generally harsh martinets but not 'villainous'. The reading and filmgoing public were not convinced. Since *Beau Geste*, a large industry had built up around the Foreign Legion both in the published word and, annoyingly to the French military, in popular film and radio.

Philip Ortiz began his own campaign to get the French government to subsidize a film promoting the virtues of the Foreign Legion. They always refused on the basis that it was more prudent to remain silent. They were prepared to allow the word of true Legion life to be spread by true legionnaires, those who completed their contracts with satisfaction and pride and who resumed their place in society without regret. This, in many cases, was quite true. In 1937, the War Ministry did commission a film, *Legions d'Honneurs*, but this was not so much in answer to Ortiz's pleas as to counteract the resurgence of an exceedingly hostile campaign against the Legion opening up in Germany. In the mid-1930s, as the rule of the Nazis became ever more severe, there was actually a decline in German volunteers to the Legion, and indeed the numbers of German personnel fell for the first time in more than a decade.

By 1937, only 20 per cent of legionnaires were of German nationality. This was in part due to an overall reduction in Legion manpower after the French government ordered it to be cut by a quarter in the wake of the depression. By natural wastage and by curbing enlistment, the Legion strength was reduced by almost one third to barely 21,000 by 1936. The decline continued in 1937, when fewer than 11 per cent of all volunteers were German, and many of those were, upon investigation, found to be opponents of the Nazi regime, or Jews seeking escape from it.

This dramatic reversal of German recruits was inspired by the Nazi's chief propagandist Dr Joseph Goebbels, who had prodded the German press into launching a vitriolic campaign, violently attacking the

Legion and demanding that the government took steps to halt the flow of German youth into this despotic regime. Books about the Legion were publicly burned in Germany after Goebbel's department claimed that their innocent young men were being hypnotized into joining. In 1938, a professional hypnotist, Albert Zagula, was arrested in Karlsruhe and charged with such a crime.

There was clearly some suspicion of a smokescreen behind the propaganda, especially when a sudden upsurge in Germans applying to the Legion occurred in the early months of 1938 when the French Government took the brakes off recruitment with the threat of war ahead. The Legion's intelligence unit was charged with conducting a close vetting of Germans who might in reality be foreign agents. It was instructed to seek out possible secret agents from the incoming volunteers and to place under surveillance any 'doubtful elements' already in service. There was real concern that the influx of German volunteers had to some extent been orchestrated by German intelligence, the *Abwehr,* with two specific objectives: to place spies in key positions, especially in the area of radio operations, and to destroy the Legion from within by undermining its morale. Forthcoming developments would only heighten those fears.

Elsewhere, the concerns of Philip Ortiz and the Legion hierarchy over the bout of what they saw as bad publicity for the Legion, were somewhat misplaced. Far from putting the Legion in a bad light, they had increased its visibility as a fighting force with an heroic past around the world, even in Germany, where it was feared as much as it was loathed by the military. A decade of unremitting press, publishing and film interest had substantially raised the Legion's profile and renewed to another generation an awareness of its traditions and its past, along with the mystique and even the romance.

Even so, Philip Ortiz and his friends persevered in their aims while his son, Peter, was playing his own supporting role, turning in an exemplary true-life performance as Rollet's perfect legionnaire. He attained the rank of sergeant when his five year contract was completed in 1937 and, in spite of his family's wealth, he decided to re-enlist for a further five. A brief summary provides the highlights of a military career of this Legion-trained American that, in the end, resulted in a shower of medals for bravery.

Peter Ortiz was transferred to the Legion's 11th Regiment of Infantry formed in October 1939, and one of the first to see action in France. Out of his own unit of 1,630 legionnaires, only 300 survived. Peter was wounded and taken prisoner by the Germans, only to escape in October 1941. Over the next three weeks, he made his way out of Germany and into France on foot, still dressed in the tattered remnants of his French uniform.

He arrived at Marseille and called at the Legion base at Fort Saint Jean to obtain his official discharge from the Legion and the passport he had deposited with Legion authorities on his enlistment. As an American citizen, he made his way to Lisbon with funds provided by the Legion. He was given priority air passage from Lisbon to the United States, arriving home to discover that America had now entered the war.

He enlisted in the US Marines and returned immediately to the fray, organizing scouting groups behind enemy lines. He was wounded a second time and found himself back in Algiers, in a US military hospital. On his recovery, he was sent to England to join the Office of Strategic Studies (OSS) and spent the rest of the war engaged in many daring missions, parachuting into enemy territory. In the summer of 1944 his team, once again engaged on a mission behind German lines, was engaged in heavy fire in which one of his sergeants was killed. Peter Ortiz again became a prisoner-of-war and at the end of hostilities was among Allied troops freed from a prison camp at Marlag-Milag, north-east of Bremen. He ended his military career with the rank of Colonel and collected an array of medals for bravery beyond the call of duty, including the *Légion d'Honneur* and the *Croix de Guerre* with palm. From the British he received the Order of the British Empire and from his own country, he was awarded two Navy Crosses, two purple hearts and the Legion of Merit. Thereafter, the man who had lied about his age to join the Foreign Legion and whose father became one of its greatest supporters, led a peaceful life, until his death in 1988.

10

FROM SELFRIDGES TO ALGERIA

'They began their training with marches. There was one every Thursday and every one was tougher and longer than the last. Many recruits were marked down as possible failures, and John Yeowell suspected he was among them.'

THE LAST years of the 1930s briefly saw the Legion in calmer waters, although there was a veritable hurricane blowing up just ahead of them. Only those who were in it can provide us with a true glimpse of that era. Crystal-clear recollections of the Foreign Legion in the run-up to World War II came from John Yeowell.

Yeowell had a military background of sorts. His father was killed in World War I, at Cambrai. He was born four months after his death, in April 1918, and his mother became a lady companion to the wife of a brigadier-general in the British army. The general had a large house near Brading on the Isle of Wight and a town house in Clapham Gate, London, which was later bombed. The boy Yeowell was treated like one of the family and the general paid for his education:

I suppose I rather let him down. In my late teens, I was a bit of a drifter. Film extra, a bit of tramping, soldier of conscience in Spain, even a spell as a pavement artist outside the National Portrait Gallery. In short, I hated the idea of being tied down. One morning at the end of August 1938, I found myself with a girlfriend in Selfridges. They had a travel agency on the third floor and while she was attending to her own business, I was studying a free-standing map of the world and my eyes lit upon North Africa and all those romantically sounding places north of the Sahara. I thought 'Well, I could be out there tomorrow if I joined the Foreign Legion'.

I knew absolutely bugger-all about the Legion. I'd never read *Beau Geste*, or any other books on it for that matter, but it just kept swirling around in my mind: 'Well, why not?' I was the sort of chap at the time who, once having set my mind towards something, I had to do it. So I decided to go to France and join up. I had no idea how to go about it but I was sure that when I arrived in France I'd see notices all over the place saying 'Join the Foreign Legion and See the World'. I went down to Brighton and set off on a day trip, costing fifteen shillings to Boulogne.

When I reached Boulogne there was nothing to indicate where I should report for the Foreign Legion so I bought a rail ticket to Paris and booked into the Hotel Russie on the Boulevard Rocheschouart. I had no luggage and the remains of about £10 left in my pocket and I assumed there was no point taking money into the Legion, so I might as well spend it. I had a marvellous time on those few pounds. It was just after a state visit by King George VI and Queen Elizabeth and the English were regarded with some favour, or at least tolerated. And we were comparatively well off in terms of the exchange rate.

I was able to indulge myself in some quite expensive places, and a few less savoury but more interesting places, too. I had about £2 left and decided it was time to move on. On the morning of 7 September 1938, I hailed a taxi and ordered the driver to take me to Rue Saint Dominic. After a few minutes, he turned to me and asked why I was going to that address. In English, he said: 'You are going to join the Strangers' Army?' It sounded like an accusation. 'Well, don't do it. Don't do it. You must not go,' he said quickly. 'Brutal. Terrible. A friend of mine has just come out. He said it was awful.'

'Don't worry,' I said reassuringly. 'I'll survive.'

The driver didn't seem so sure and persisted. He told me he was

Russian and many Russians had joined the Legion. He clearly wasn't going to give up. He offered to take me to the British Embassy, free of charge.

'No, no,' I said. 'Rue Saint Dominic.'

He dropped me in the courtyard to an elegant nineteenth century building, which was the War Ministry. He refused to take any fare and wished me *Bon Chance*, and I must say that did make me a little nervous. Whoever heard of a taxi driver refusing his fare, for God's sake! I went into the building and came into a long room with a counter along one side and notices beside each *functionaire*, scribbling away. One man was in uniform with a notice which said *Légion Étrangère*. He was an elegant looking sergeant, sucking on an empty cigarette holder, a black and red kepi set at an angle over his eyes. I said to him in English, 'I want to join the Foreign Legion'. How stupid that sounds now!

He looked at me, didn't say a word and simply pushed a pile of leaflets towards me. I found the English version of the Legion's terms of service. But it didn't matter much, my mind was made up and I'd have gone ahead whatever the terms.

The Sergeant gave Yeowell a form and for no particular reason, he signed his name as John Jerningham. Others, he concluded, gave false names and so he decided he should too, although later he discovered that not everyone did. He left his profession blank; he could hardly put down pavement artist. The sergeant said he must fill in profession, and asked a few questions. Could he drive? No, he couldn't drive. Could he ride horses? He stammered, remembering that he had handled a horse in the transport section of the London and Scottish Territorials for a short while. He took that to be a yes, and immediately put down in the space for profession: Jockey.

Yeowell was sent into a neighbouring room which was virtually empty. Bare floorboards, creaky chairs and over a shabby fireplace was a print of Patrice McMahon, Duke of Magenta and Marshal of France, who had been president under the Third Republic and had been an officer in the Foreign Legion in its early days. There were three other men already in the room and they looked a sad bunch. One of them called himself Tommy Black and insisted he had born at 'Plymoot'. Another man, a wide-boy type named Bontemps, more or less took charge and said he knew the system and how to beat it.

The medical officer turned up as Bontemps was explaining the secrets of the Legion. The MO was a small man, a civilian wearing a dirty white coat, steel-rimmed glasses, wizened features and stubble on his chin. He examined them, one by one, and passed them all. Yeowell heard afterwards that it was unlikely they would be failed:

> The French had a vast colonial empire that was policed by mainly legionnaires. Why should young Frenchmen go out and die on the frontiers of the empire when all these stupid bloody foreigners were more than happy to do so?

They were all given rail warrants and a baguette, sardines and wine and travelled overnight to Marseille, reporting to the Legion fort where a sentry in pale blue uniform did not trouble to challenge them as they passed by. Further interviews took place, first with the Deuxième Bureau, the military intelligence department. The officer had his forms in front of him, and to his surprise addressed him in perfect English. He also called Yeowell by his real name and:

> ... there was a glint of satisfaction in his eyes when he noticed that for a while, in 1937, I had joined an outfit called the Irish Brigade which went to Spain. He said, 'Ah ... you have good taste'. I could only guess what he meant. The interesting thing was that the Legion intelligence officer knew all about this, including my real name. All who came with me from Paris were interviewed. We had our photographs and fingerprints taken, whereupon my new friends, with the exception of Bontemps, were ejected and we never saw them again. Apparently they were taken to the front entrance and as soon as they stepped outside were arrested by the police. So you see, this rumour that the Legion was full of wanted men was, by then, 1938, not entirely

true. If you had committed a serious crime, the last place to go was the Legion.

The next day Yeowell was among sixty or so new legionnaires who boarded the *Ville d'Oran* ferry and were allotted accommodation in the bowels of the ship, deep down in the hold. There was a pile of stinking mattresses which had clearly been used a thousand times by other recruits. The atmosphere was dreadful, the food was appalling and the rough wine, which he did not attempt to drink, was by all accounts awful. There were one or two fist fights over cards on the journey and a rumour that war had broken out in Europe. It was around the time that Prime Minister Chamberlain was to meet Hitler at Munich.

After a two-day journey, they reached Algeria and were marched to a miniature barracks in Oran, where they were assigned their first task:

The Legion, as I soon discovered, never allowed you time to sit around plotting mischief. You had to be kept busy. Our first experience of this was here at this tiny barracks, unoccupied but for ourselves and there we were lined up by a corporal who showed us a tiny stone. Now, he said, we had to advance over the ground and pick up every stone larger than the one he was holding, which meant pretty well every piece of bloody gravel around the entire building, and put them into a heap. This, by the way, was to be done by hand, stone by stone and not with brush and shovel. I suppose the next batch of recruits who came through would be ordered to spread them out, one by one. I conjectured that the same stones must have been handled by successive generations of legionnaires for the past 100 years.

It was here that the dreadful thick uniforms we had been given in Marseilles were replaced. In the stores, there was an old legionnaire, wearing a thick grey beard in charge, standing in front of shelves packed with rows and rows of neatly folded uniforms. On the wall was a framed motto, in French: 'Everything in its place and a place for everything'. The Legion was very fond of wall texts.

After one day in Oran we went by rail to the Legion headquarters at Sidi-bel-Abbès. The Legion was to Bel-Abbès what the University is to Oxford. We were given our numbers, taken to our barracks and began our introduction to the ways of the Legion which are like nothing you have ever experienced before. We each had an iron bedstead which, when not in use, folded to half size. Above the bed was a shelf containing a box, about eighteen inches square, to hold private possessions. On top were placed greatcoat, uniform, boots, every item of clothing and leather equipment. The boots, by the way, were wonderful, strong leather all made by legionnaires at Bel-Abbès. I remember sometime later looking into a room where there were row upon row of men sitting on the floor making them. Another workshop contained stonemasons. When I first saw it, they were making a memorial to a group of legionnaires who had been killed in a railway accident near Fez about three years earlier. It showed you that time was of no importance in the Legion.

Yeowell now had the opportunity to talk to some of the men in his room. Some were less reticent than others and had interesting tales to tell but regardless of their willingness to converse, they represented a fair cross-section of the population of the Foreign Legion. There was a Hungarian, Ziegler, who'd been an officer in the Hungarian army and was in his country's fencing team in the 1936 Olympics. He spoke very good English, and was an Arsenal fan. José Gomez, a huge Texan of Mexican descent became a good friend. Constantine Netchaeff whose father had been a member of the last Russian parliament before the Revolution had himself been a taxi-driver in Paris. Hans Goeppel, a smallish German, had also been in Spain. He'd been a lieutenant in the Germany navy. He was half Jewish but in spite of that his father was a medical officer in the German army in Hanover. When Hitler came to power Hans had jumped ship when it called at New York and got a job at Brooklyn Ladies' College, but got the sack because he drove a car into the swimming pool when it was full of ladies. He then got a job in a New York restaurant as a waiter but fell in love with his boss's girlfriend and was sacked. So he then shot himself but it was dark and he only shot an eyebrow off. The scar was still evident. He was eventually reported by his former boss as an illegal alien and was arrested. It was at this point he became something of a public figure. A group of anti-Nazis in New York heard about his escapades and a chap called Dave Glendenning bailed him and caused an outcry by dressing him up in German naval uniform and carting him around to anti-fascist meetings.

The German embassy protested and called for this masquerade to stop. It was at that time he volunteered for Spain and sailed with the Washington-Lincoln battalion of the International Brigade. They were subsequently interned having fled to France and given the option of joining the Legion or stayed indefinitely where they were. Hans, like a lot of others from the Spanish Civil War, ended up in Sidi-bel-Abbès. John Yeowell continued:

> We now began our period of indoctrination, not a word they used in those days, but true nonetheless. It was to fill our heads with the traditions of the Legion. Much the same happens even today, I gather. One of the first things they do is to take you around the museum of the Legion, the *Salle d'Honneur* where the great battles of the past were described to us, along with the exploits of the heroes. We saw the captured battle colours, ancient swords, rifles and other relics. They gave us each a little book with our names inscribed inside, a rather cheap little book in French, which highlighted the Legion of the past. It really did work. Every day on the parade ground there was some kind of traditional activity going on with the Legion band playing all the trumpet calls which we had to memorize and which always ended with a performance of *Le Boudin*. It was all very moving. And the traditions of the spirit of the Legion began to sink in.
>
> The *caserne* dated from about 1840 and sometimes I'd be lying on my bed staring at the darkened walls that had remained unchanged in 100 years and imagine what it was like then. The thought occurs that one of those heroes they had been talking about probably slept in this room, probably in this very same bed. It does get to you and in a curious way you feel proud of that past, which, incidentally, gradually becomes your own past.

Also at Sidi-bel-Abbès was a fine concert hall which was built by legionnaires. It was one of many such buildings. The legion used to receive grants from the government for building projects but the skills of the manpower available to the Legion were so diverse that they did virtually everything themselves, from small building work to major civil engineering projects. They had their own architects, surveyors, builders, electricians, plumbers, labourers and so on. It was a very self-contained organization.

The concert hall was the venue for films and concerts. Apart from its fine military bands, the Legion had its own symphony orchestra that broadcast weekly on Radio Algérie. They had also built an Olympic-sized swimming pool, the first and only one in North Africa. Yeowell did not have time for swimming. After a week or so, he was sent to one of the training depots at Saïda, some miles south of Bel-Abbès. The *caserne* there was two storeys, the upper floor reached by a rickety old staircase, with twenty men in each room. He was the only Englishman in the room at the time and his French was virtually non-existent. He teamed up with Helmut who spoke German, English and French. He had been a member of the Hitler Youth but seemed more interested in western dance-band music than politics, and in any event, political discussion or activity in the Legion was banned. It was strictly non-political although songs which were borderline cases could be heard in the barrack room.

They began their training with marches. There was one every Thursday and every one was tougher and longer than the last. The NCOs kept a scorecard for the duration of training. Many recruits were marked down as possible failures, and John Yeowell suspected he was among them. Pay-day in the Legion was fortnightly, the amount was too small for it to be paid weekly – about a halfpenny a day. Money, in the Legion, was seen as a common commodity, to be shared. There was no planning, it just evolved. Two francs would buy a litre of wine. Cigarettes were also very cheap.

The canteen was a scruffy smoke-filled room which could hold about forty people standing. Outside there were tables by the side of the parade ground, for the evening. The canteen was the gathering place of every Legion post. In the larger *casernes* the canteen, called the

Foyer du Légionnaire, was sometimes an elegant club-like place where the barmen wore white tunics. Food at Sidi-bel-Abbès was very good. At Saïda it was good but not so very well presented: breakfast of coffee, bread and sardines or black chocolate, then two meals a day, starting with soup thick with peas or lentils, meat which was eaten by itself, vegetables and local fruit.

When they went out on a march they had to take everything with them:

> ... and I mean everything we possessed, absolutely everything, including the food, water and utensils for cooking. The idea was to march out under moonless skies and it took some getting used to, because invariably someone would fall over rocks or unseen objects. It was easier to march in single file. We rested for ten minutes every hour and I learned to take a nap each time we stopped. The officers had horses but on the outward march, they usually walked ahead of us and their batmen led the animals. They would ride them on the return, and on re-entry to the outskirts of town the band would be waiting for us. Each *caserne*, incidentally, had its own *musique*, and even in small detachments stationed in isolated places, they had their *clique* of drums and trumpets.
>
> As the *caserne* came into view, we would be marching to attention, the officers would mount their charges and the band would strike up *Le Boudin* and lead us back to base. It was all very inspiring. My section commander, de Vienne, was a great guy, an aristocrat and I heard after the war that when he retired from the army, he became a Roman Catholic priest. Legion officers were mostly French. They tended to be rather distant. There was very little contact between them and the men. It was all made through the *sous officiers*, rather like God using priests as his intermediaries with the Christian rank and file.
>
> At the time, and certainly in the units in which I served, there was no physical abuse from the *sous officiers*, none whatever. But there were plenty of ways to punish men, usually by a spell in the regimental prison for minor offences or for more serious crimes, such as

desertion, the disciplinary company at Columb-Bechar on the edge of the Sahara between Morocco and Algeria; a terrible place by all accounts.

The prison at Saïda was a small single-storey building surrounded by a high wall and with a courtyard running parallel to it. As you went into the compound, you were confronted by a painted text high up on a white-washed wall: 'You come in like a lion and go out like a lamb'. And believe me, they did. I went in as a relief guard. My job was to stand at one end of the courtyard with slung rifle, another sentry was at the other end. Between us there was a group of prisoners who were walking round and round, nothing else, just walking. Over the years, the cobblestone courtyard had been worn into a groove where they walked. The sergeant in charge was a German named Schwarz, a very unpleasant man. Everyone in the Legion knew of him. He bellowed at me and said. 'Keep these men walking, otherwise you will be here'. *Blutiger Schweindhund*. These poor devils who were all deserters started this march half an hour after reveille. Twice during the day they were allowed to stop to eat their food, standing up facing the wall. Schwarz would be standing behind them shouting obscenities in several languages. It was said that at least one man had died during Schwarz's reign of terror. I wasn't surprised to hear that. They marched all day, until 6.30 p.m. There was never much sympathy for deserters but there were always men in the Legion who'd had enough, for one reason or another and wanted to go home. It wasn't easy to get out, being in North Africa. There were no tourists to hitch a ride with, and then there were the *Moghazni*, a kind of irregular police force wearing blue burnouses and mounted on fine Arab horses who were paid handsomely if they captured and returned a deserter.

One afternoon when we came back after training and in front of the guardhouse there were three men who had been picked up by Arab bounty hunters and brought back. Their heads were bare under the hot sun and their legs were manacled and chained to a flagpole. Christ, they did look miserable. This is how they spent their first day back, without food or water.

One of them was still wearing his Arab disguise. It was pathetic. He was easily recognizable as a legionnaire. As we marched past them, some of our men spat at them. There was no sympathy whatosever for them and such scenes provided an easily assimilated lesson for the rest of us. They would later be placed in the prison, and join those men walking around and around which they would do every day until the travelling *tribunal de guerre* arrived to deal with courts martial.

The gap between visits of the tribunal could be weeks and many of the poor devils in the prison would finish up in the infirmary. If they happened to be in the infirmary when the tribunal came around, they would miss it, and have to wait in prison until the next time. The usual sentence for first time deserters was eleven months served at Columb-Bechar. When they finished their sentence, they resumed the five years again with the latest bunch of recruits. If a man did escape, the Legion would never forget him. So, if he was spotted anywhere on French soil at any time in the future, he was liable to be arrested and brought back to complete his contract. I met a legionnaire in Morocco, an Austrian who was a dentist before he first joined the Legion. He had deserted and managed to get back to Vienna where he resumed his profession and established a successful practice, married and had a family. Then, confident that the Legion had forgotten all about him, he took his family to the south of France for a holiday. He was by chance recognized and arrested, brought back to Sidi-bel-Abbès and after completing a prison sentence for desertion, he was made to begin his five-year contract all over again.

Desertion, however, may well have been in the minds of some as Hitler's Nazis began their march across Europe. Germans in hiding, Jews from across Europe who had sought refuge and others of questionable status suddenly became nervous for a variety of reasons.

11

1940: ARCTIC BOUND

'We were quickly out in open countryside which was covered
in snow. It was so deep in places you would sink right up to
your thigh. Then we had our first meeting with the enemy.'

THE LEGION was spread across North Africa,
Indo-China, French Guyana and other less vital colonial interests
when the war in Europe was declared. In a curious way, said John
Yeowell, it didn't seem anything to do with legionnaires in North
Africa. It was a long way away, and although regular French military
had been mobilized on all fronts, the Legion was still manning its
distant forts, and the only concession to the outbreak of hostilities for
the time being were patrols organized simply to see if there were any
Germans about whose presence might be detrimental to French
interests. An odd situation also developed – German legionnaires
looking for enemy agents of German nationality. One morning, the
inevitable happened. German-born legionnaires in sensitive barracks
were paraded on the square. They knew that this was the end for
them, and that night there was a muted farewell party. The following
day, they were disarmed and taken to an internment camp in southern
Morocco.

It was, however, John Yeowell's Moroccan regiment that provided
the manpower for the Legion's first mobilization of the war. They
became part of a rapidly formed 13th Demi-Brigade, organized for a

particular mission in the early weeks of 1940. For this, men who had been fighting the Rif wars in the deserts and the hills of Morocco were prepared for a journey to the Arctic, for which they would require snowshoes. They were put under the command of Lieutenant Colonel Magrin-Verneret, another of the Legion's eccentrics who, like Rollet, came out of Saint-Cyr and was also a veteran of World War I. By the law of averages, he ought long ago to have retired from the military. He limped as a result of a shot-up leg and had an awful temper after a head injury, the scars of which were still visible.

The call to the Legion came as France was confronted with a British request to contribute to an Allied force to support Finland against the threat of a Soviet invasion. Even before the Legion left France, the Finns bowed and accepted Soviet terms. Another fight was promptly arranged. The French force was already on its way when Hitler pre-empted the situation by invading Norway to protect ore shipments and to set up a naval base. Soon fierce sea battles raged between the Royal Navy and the Kriegsmarine.

At sea, the British had the upper-hand, but by April 1940, the Germans had occupied all of the main Norwegian west coast ports, from Narvik in the north to Kristiansand in the south, and around the tip of the peninsula to Oslo. Although they had to pull out of southern Norway, the Allies attempted to wrest the northern port of Narvik from the Germans, to prevent ore shipments.

An amphibious assault was planned under the overall command of British Lieutenant General Claude Auchinleck, with the protective guns of the Royal Navy and using Allied troops which included the 13th Demi-Brigade of the Legion, units of the French 27th Chasseurs Alpins, the Polish 1st Capathian Demi-Brigade, and a mountain corps made up of refugees from conquered Poland, with local assistance from Norwegian units.

Opposing them was the Nazi invasion force under General Edouard Dietl, reinforced by the 137th Gebirgsjager regiment, a tough mountain unit who had been parachuted into the snow-covered hills. John Yeowell was still serving in Morocco in February 1940 when the call came:

Our movement into action began when the Legion asked for volunteers to go to Finland. Everyone at Meknes volunteered. Those who were selected moved to Fez, where they formed into the 13th Demi-Brigade which consisted of two battalions under the overall command of Magrin-Verneret. I was in the 1st battalion. We were kitted out with a wonderful uniform for the cold weather that we would apparently be encountering. We had baggy plus-four trousers, very good mountain boots, long stockings, jersey and fur lined jacket and a khaki cape with hood. Beau Geste would have been surprised! There followed several weeks' training in the French Alps with the Chasseurs Alpin before we went to the port of Brest to await embarkation, although not for Finland.

We left Brest on two cargo ships, one of which put in at Liverpool. Collins, another of the few Englishmen on the voyage, went ashore and never came back. The *Providence*, which carried my battalion, made for Glasgow where we spent a couple of days. The Lord Provost invited everyone ashore for a slap-up meal at the university and a tour of the city. They all came back with fifty fags each and a large framed photograph of the Lord Provost. The three remaining English legionnaires, myself, Calthorpe and Mike Horgan, were confined to ship. The miserable bastards had probably heard about Collins's disappearance. We embarked on the Canadian Pacific liner called the *Monarch of Bermuda*, the first troops to sail in this magnificent ship. The staff were still in their white starched jackets as if they had never left the West Indies.

We knew now that we were going to Norway where the Germans had occupied the country from north to south. Our ship travelled alone and unescorted in an area infested with U-boats. When we reached the fjords north of the Arctic Circle, my section under Lieutenant Vardot was transferred to a Royal Navy minesweeper. It was an exhilerating experience to sail silently up these great inland seas at one o'clock in the morning. It was twenty-four hours' daylight and we were able to see in the distance these wonderful vistas of white mountains and tiny nestling villages with their timber houses and pastel coloured roofs and walls. It looked idyllic.

We were billeted on Norwegian families in the village of Balla-gen for the first week. Then, on a Sunday afternoon, there suddenly appeared off the coast the Allied fleet. It was an inspiring sight. My battalion boarded HMS *Effingham* and we were soon on route to another unknown destination. As usual they didn't tell us a bloody thing. We could have been going back to Glasgow as far as we knew. I was able to chat with the crew and tried to establish what we would be doing. One old salt thought we'd be on board for quite a few hours and if I wished I could take a hot bath, which I did, soaking in an old-fashioned tin bath-tub.

The same chap gave me a tin of pineapple and some tomato juice which I stuffed in my rucksack. Later, as I stood at the rails gazing idly at the passing scenery, one of the crew said, 'Look over there . . . that's Narvik. And they've got the bloody Swastika flag flying . . . the cheeky bastards.'

I had never heard of Narvik and couldn't see any flag, but I said 'Yes, the cheeky bastards . . .'

Several miles later we reached the end of the fjord, a kind of cul-de-sac. The small town ahead of us, only 100 yards or so away, was Bjervik. We formed up on deck, still without being told anything, although it was obvious we were going ashore.

Before the 13th Demi-Brigade could attack Narvik itself, the village of Bjerkvik had to be cleared and secured. The high ground behind it overlooked the strategic port. At midnight on 13 May the massive guns of the British battleship *Resolution*, the cruisers *Effingham* and *Vindictive* and five destroyers opened fire on the picturesque village and its surroundings to send the Germans scuttling. Soon afterwards, the troops hit the beaches in infantry and tank landing craft. It was the first time in the war that such combined operations took place in the face of enemy fire:

As we stood on deck, we heard the slight metallic sound of the battle flags, the Union Jack and the Tricolour, as they went up the mast at great speed. It was like the opening of a huge military tattoo for this was the signal for the bombardment of Bjervik to commence. The town's inhabitants had already gathered on a hill at the side of the fjord so that they could be seen, and there they stood watching their homes being shelled and burned to the ground. It must have been desperate for them. A little armoured car, German, was going down the front by the shore firing a stupid little machine-gun at the fleet until it was blasted into kingdom come.

The bombardment of Bjervik went on for a quarter of an hour, then we went ashore in what I suppose were ship's boats. Some had motors, others simply had to be rowed by men of the Royal Marines. One man in my company and one in the company to our right were detailed as scouts. I was one and the other was Calthorpe. Funny really, two out of three English legionnaires in Norway being chosen for this honour! That's what I thought then; in practical terms, however, it meant we had to walk out in front. If we were shot, then it would be unsafe for those behind us to go on. Still, what the hell. You can only die once.

We crossed the narrow beach and went over the road and headed through the blazing town. The place had been shot to pieces. Every garden gate and every fallen telegraph pole I suspected of being booby-trapped, and by God was it hot! We were quickly out in open countryside which was covered in snow. It was so deep in places you would sink right up to your thigh. Then we had our first meeting with the enemy. I had reached a slight rise in the ground and as I lay there looking around, I heard voices and they were very close indeed. Less than three yards in front of me was a man walking right across my field of vision. He was carrying something, but not a weapon. All the enemy were scattered about like this in isolated pockets. It was probably the only method of defence in such a complicated landscape. They did not appear to know we had landed and seemed to be taking it easy for a bit. My grenade killed all three of them, poor buggers.

We never again found a group so unprepared. Not long afterwards, we were actually held up for quite a long time by a single machine-gun emplacement. When one of our own gunners had silenced it, I was sent forward with a corporal to check that indeed it had been put out of action. We found an officer and a sergeant lying dead beside their broken Hotchkiss machine-gun. We went through their ruc-sacs. From the officer's pack came a silver cigarette case which became the propery of the corporal, a packet of tea and a Penguin edition of the *Good Soldier Schweik* was my booty. It was a surprising find, considering it was a World War I novel which made mockery of German militarism. In the sergeant's pack was a huge Nazi flag which we surmised must have been used for airdrops.

A week later, we attacked and captured Narvik. We then advanced northwards through the mountains to within ten kilometres of the Swedish frontier and there we remained in what was a fairly static situation for both ourselves and the enemy. We were to remain stuck there for the rest of our stay in Norway, which would not be for very long.

We were sitting around one day, waiting for the next barrage of German mortar shells when a corporal from another company came along asking for volunteers for an execution. This sounded interesting, but there were no volunteers from my section. We heard later that two men, said to be brothers and supposedly Dutch but now thought to be German, had been seen walking towards the German lines with their rifles under cover of thick mountain mist that descended quite suddenly, sometimes for hours and then rose just as quickly. It rose too quickly for them. They were brought back and sentenced to death. Sometime later, a *sous-officier* shouted: 'Look down there . . . *Regardez!*'

Way down the mountainside, perhaps a quarter of a mile or more, we could see the two men digging their own graves. This was in full view of several Legion companies spread over the mountainside. We saw the firing squad line up and being so far away we saw them fall in their graves before we heard the shots. It was meant to be a warning, although I don't suppose we were much affected by it.

It was the second time we had been asked for volunteers for a firing squad. The first time was also at Narvik, a day or so after landing. My company was supposed to be resting and were scattered around the beach trying to get some sleep when two Germans came picking their way through the recumbent legionnaires. One was carrying a briefcase and the other a spade. It turned out they were naval officers who had trained a mortar on our landing place and very effectively too. My mate from Morocco days, Mick Horgan, was one of their victims. Unfortunately for the two Germans, they were dressed partly in civilian clothes and were condemned to death. I hope they were both awarded a posthumous Iron Cross, First Class.

During their advance into the mountains, the Allied force had at one point to cross the single-track railway line between two tunnels. Inside one was a carriage and several of the soldiers, Yeowell included, climbed inside. It was quite comfortably furnished, an unmade bed and items of clothing scattered about. It had been the sleeping quarters of General Deitl, commander of the German forces in Norway. He had obviously left in a hurry. At another point they came across a small enclave that had been used as an open-air resting place for the enemy. It was even furnished with a couple of easy chairs that had been salvaged from one of the British ships that still lay half sunk in the harbour. On a flat rock was a portable gramophone with a pile of records beside it. The record on the gramophone was *I Saw You Last Night And Got That Old Feeling*.

The most dangerous manoeuvres during the Allied advance came near the highest point of the mountain, when they were suddenly met by sustained machine-gun fire. John Yeowell was lying flat on the ground with an open space of about twenty yards or so in front of him and then there was nothing but thick undergrowth. Next to him, shoulder to shoulder, were two Spaniards, Mihjian with his machine-gun and his side-kick, De Villonga. The soil in front of them spurted up as enemy bullets hit the ground. If the gunner had raised his sights a fraction he could have killed all three of them. Both Mihjian and De Villonga died a couple of days later from mortar fire:

> They were a couple of brave idiots. When you meet a situation like that you're not frightened; you don't have time to be. It's also due to Legion training too, dammit all, what did we use on our training but live ammo anyway? We lost several men on

these heights before Vadot ordered us back, thirty metres and no more, he said, and repeated it. And this being the Legion, we as good as measured it with a tape. As we wound our way back along the tracks something caught my eye in some rocks as I turned. Under some rocks in front of me was a small space, like a tiny cave. I saw a pair of jackboots and I wondered how the hell a corpse managed to get into such a small space. While I was pondering this, the boots moved and I shouted. A young German came up shaking uncontrollably.

'*Nichts schiessen! Nichts schiessen!* Don't Shoot,' he said. He unbuckled his belt and handed me his pistol. I marched him off to Vadot who spoke to him in German and then told me to take him down the hillside to a compound where they were collecting prisoners. As we descended, we passed several groups of legionnaires who were advancing in the second wave behind us. I came across a man I knew, Maurice Chevalier, not his real name. We called him that because he was a great imitator of the French singer at concert parties. Chevalier shouted to me to get out of the way. He was going to shoot this *sal Bosche*. He raised his rifle to take aim but luckily for the prisoner I was in the way. I shouted back that I was under orders from Vadot . . . this man had special information. We got clear of the fighting but could still hear the whistling of the shells as they passed over us and exploded in the distance. I got him through until we reached a place where there was a stream and we took a drink.

As we paused, I tried to question him in my very elementary German. He was 19 years old, a sailor. His ship had been sunk during the recent battles with the British navy. He must have been through hell. I asked him when he last ate anything and he said three days ago. I had sixteen biscuits in my pack and I gave him half.

We were soon exchanging friendly gossip until suddenly it crossed my mind, 'Hey, I'm in the Foreign Legion – what about the spoils of war? I have to live up to Legion traditions!' I noticed on his wrist a very fine watch.

'I'll have that,' I said.

'No, please, don't take that,' he said. 'It was a gift from my mother.' I didn't believe a word of it, but dropped his arm, anyhow.

He told me about his family and gave me a photograph of himself in naval uniform and wrote his name and address, in Bremen, on the back. He even gave me his home address and suggested we got in touch after the war. What an optimist!

A Legion sergeant on his way to the dressing station hobbled past, one leg soaked in fresh blood, and offered the prisoner a cigarette. He told me to get this man down the hillside as soon as possible before someone shot him.

We moved off and I got the German to the compound. There were only two or three other prisoners. I handed him over and was about to go when the *sous-officier* in charge called out '*Attendez*'. He picked up the German's arm and looked at his wrist and saw that he had his watch still in place. He seemed surprised. He asked the German if anything had been stolen from him, and he said that nothing had. So at least I had escaped a *tribunal de guerre*. If the truth be known, he probably thought I lacked initiative. You just can't win with some people.

I began to weave my way back when I came across a strange sight. There was a man in what I took to be a Norwegian uniform sitting with his back resting against the trunk of a tree. I said a few words to him but he did not reply. I thought he must be sleeping. Then, bending down I saw under his peaked ski cap that his face was almost entirely swathed in bandages. I'd had a one-sided conversation with a corpse. God knows how long he had been there.

During our so-called rest period, I was one of the six volunteers to attend a memorial service in Narvik church. I had volunteered because I wanted to see something of the town. We got there just as the brass hats were arriving, but we legionnaires remained outside. We could see three representative coffins in front of the altar draped in French, Norwegian and British flags but, no, we weren't going inside. We had another job to do . . . at the local cemetery. In one corner of it was a large trench, thirty feet long and six feet deep. On one side were a number of empty coffins. All this had been prepared by the Germans for their own dead but we used them for ours instead. Several rows of bodies covered in groundsheets were already lying beside the trench. Among them was my old friend Mick Horgan. A small group of officers' coffins with their names scribbled on the lids in pencil were already prepared for burial. One of them was de Guiteau, my own company commander.

Our duty was one that haunts me to this day – to put the bodies of the legionnaires into coffins ready for burial. The state of the bodies was such that we were able to put two, sometimes three into a single coffin. It was a horrible job, but it had to be done. It was almost dawn by the time we had finished, with brief services by the local Lutheran minister and a legionnaire who now wore the stole of a Catholic priest. None of us had known he was a priest. There were no chaplains in the Legion in those days and the only time we ever saw a priest was when we had to bury someone. De Gaulle, who hated the Legion, changed all that.

After this white night, there was still not much rest. We then had to go over the whole area where there had been recent fighting to collect the enemy dead. We spread out and wandered everywhere, the stretcher bearers ready to cart away the corpses which were gathered some distance away.

While the legionnaires of the 13th Demi-Brigade had been fighting in the Norwegian mountains, dramatic developments had been occurring across Europe. The Germans had overrun the low countries, Denmark and part of France. The Allies were in retreat, the British expeditionary force was heading for evacuation at Dunkirk and the Germans were continuing their march across France. Norway had to be evacuated and all French troops, including the Legion, were being mustered to the defence of France. John Yeowell's section was the very last Allied infantry unit to leave Norway. It was a hazardous operation for it was essential that the enemy should not know they were getting out. They even created dummy legionnaires dressed in parts of old uniforms with a few broken rifles or machine-guns – shades of Fort Zinderneuf in *Beau Geste*. All this was meant to fool enemy scouts who might venture near enough. In this way, they managed to get clean away without being noticed. They were taken off by a British destroyer, halting briefly in mid-fjord only for the funeral of a dead sailor and a dead legionnaire. Then, they transferred to the liner *Duchess of York* and formed part of the last convoy to leave Norway. One ship carried the entire Norwegian government and the Norwegian Royal Family. Another carried German prisoners of war, including the one Yeowell had captured. It wasn't long before the convoy came under attack from the Luftwaffe and several pocket battleships. Several ships, one of them the aircraft carrier *Glorious,* were sunk and so, ironically, was the one carrying the German prisoners, which meant Yeowell would never get to have tea with his friendly captive after the war.

They made it back to Glasgow but never went into port, obviously fearing that some would prefer to depart ship. They took the South Wales Borderers ashore by riverboat. Calthorpe was among them. He'd spun the squaddies a line and they rustled up a spare uniform. As they sailed off to shore, Yeowell saw his ugly face grinning up at him.

The rest of us remained on the *Duchess of York* and sailed on to Brest. We were given our back pay, lashings of wine and cigarettes and a free night out in Brest before we journeyed on to God knows where. No one seemed to know. It was a perfectly orderly night, even though the legionnaires were all as pissed as newts and the *bordels* were full to overflowing. Next morning, we gathered at the naval *caserne*. There was no direction from the military hierarchy and to all intents and purposes at that moment the Legion was on its own. Our commander, Colonel Magrin-Verneret, discovered that the Germans were about to occupy Paris, and decided we ought to do something about it. So, we formed up in the centre of Brest and began marching toward the capital, there being no trains available to take us there. It seemed a ridiculous notion, trudging across country, 700 kilometres as the crow flies but we had to do something, I suppose. Thinking about it at the time, I did have a strong feeling that we were all going to die in the good old Legion tradition, *Bravo mes enfants!* Another page added to the glorious history of the Legion with a special niche for us in the *Salle d'Honneur* at Sidi-bel-Abbès. Personally, I didn't really want to be part of the Legion's history, not yet anyway.

We formed up and marched away towards Paris, sleeping by the roadside and getting supplies from local villages. When we reached Dinan, which was about forty kilometres inland from St Malo, we halted for a rest and dispersed for coffee in the cafes. As we sat sipping our coffee, someone called for silence. A wireless was turned up and we heard an announcer saying *Attention! Attention! Ici Radio Toulouse.* He introduced Marshal Pétain who announced the Vichy Armistice Agreement with the Germans and called upon the patriotism of the French people.

Vive la France!

I didn't have time to finish my coffee in that wonderful little place. We were called outside to be addressed by a captain of the Legion: 'You have just heard someone claiming to be Marshal Pétain saying that France's war with Germany is over. I know Marshal Pétain personally. He is an old friend of my family and I can assure you on my word of honour that was not Marshal Pétain.'

He said, not quite accurately, that this was how the Germans got Warsaw, but they would not get France so easily. But, of course, it was Pétain and the Germans who had got France virtually in their pocket. There was no point now in trying to get to Paris and we did the only thing possible, to march back to Brest. We found an empty goods train at Dinan and a willing driver. As we moved off, the word was passed through the wagons: If anyone had German souvenirs from Narvik, they should get rid of them immediately. Any man who might be taken prisoner by the Germans found with such souvenirs would be shot out of hand. A whole cascade of things, even jackboots, were being tipped over the side onto the rail track.

The sky above Brest was filled with thick black smoke with explosions going off all over the place. We guessed workers must be blowing up their factories. The train pulled into an area signposted Royal Engineers Docks, and hey presto!, a ship bound for England was just about to pull out. We all managed to get aboard the last sailing of the *Twickenham Ferry*, a Southern Railways ship. It was absolutely packed, so many men on board – police, soldiers, even Boy Scouts with long beards – that it was impossible to sit down.

Even as we were leaving, a German plane came over, probably on a recce. The ship's captain stopped, but the aircraft obviously could not see us because of the thick black smoke which now enveloped the whole area. We arrived the next morning at Plymouth. All kinds of tales were circulating at the time about German spies disguised in strange clothes and the term Fifth Column being bandied about. I suppose the local command at Plymouth could not be blamed for viewing our lot with suspicion but after a couple of days we were transferred to river steamers which took us down past a line of massive warships moored in Plymouth, including several of the French navy, and we came ashore to be welcomed by the Royal Marine Band playing *Marche Lorraine*.

The 13th Demi-Brigade had its headquarters in a tented compound at Trentham Park, near 'Stoke-sur-Trent' as it soon became known. After a few days, the legionnaires were visited by an officer from the War Office. There were only a handful of Britishers and they were told to report to the NAAFI. About fifty turned up, Turks, Greeks, Yugoslavs, Russians and Morrison, a black American. Most of them didn't speak a word of English, so God knows what they made of the major's speech. He sounded a bit like Peter Ustinov, imitating a British officer: 'Well chaps, now you're on home soil, and very welcome too. Being British you will not be able to stay in a foreign army and you will be transferred to units of British army units. In view of your disciplined training, it is likely you will go to the Guards.'

Meanwhile, local townsfolk of Stoke and Newcastle-under-Lyme were being kind and welcoming to the foreign soldiers whom they treated like heroes. Once, they organized a tea party in a local church hall . . . and as John Yeowell recalls:

Only a few went, thank God, for it turned out to be a trifle embarrassing with a gaggle of gnarled Foreign Legion chaps not smelling too sweetly after recent experiences and whose social graces were not on top form, being entertained by the ladies' committee of the Congregational Church. The ladies had baked us cakes and made jellies and blancmange and sandwiches using the last of their ration coupons. They had a gramophone and played a record I shall never forget. It was the latest craze of *Hands Knees and Boomps-a-Daisy*, with dance movements to match the words. It's not difficult to picture it, is it? Our lot being invited to perform what looked to some of them like a kind of tribunal dance that had somehow survived from ancient times!

There was one difficult situation while we were in Britain. The Spaniards decided to opt out. As a group, they were fearless fighters, but lousy legionnaires. They didn't mix, kept themselves to themselves and I am sure had their own commissars. They had volunteered for the Legion to escape internment in France, and this was not their war. Magrin-Verneret called us all out on parade: 'You are still members of the Foreign Legion – not some kind of new International Brigade.' It reached such a pitch that the CO had us all on parade. He then ordered all the Spaniards to remove their berets, thus ensuring they would be spotted if they tried to break out of Trentham Park. Later on that same day, three coaches arrived to transport them to Stafford prison. Many, I believe, remained in Britain and served with the British army.

Yeowell was eventually sent to London to help with the organization of the British end of the Free French. A then relatively unknown French colonel, Charles de Gaulle, had fled France and with Churchill's backing had established his headquarters at Carlton House, while the Free French rank-and-file were themselves billeted at Olympia.

The remnants of the 13th Demi-Brigade remained at Trentham Park to await the arrival of de Gaulle. John Yeowell assisted with the establishment of the Central Depot of the Free French near Euston Station and was there when the place was bombed. He left the Legion at the end of 1941 to join the British army. After training at Tidworth with the Royal Armoured Corps, he was sent to the Far

East and spent the rest of the war in India with the 26th Hussars, and then the Special Force (Chindits). He was in Wingate's 2nd Expedition into Burma in 1944. Yeowell remained in the army until 1949, with GHQ 2nd Echelon in Germany, and then followed a position at the Ministry of Agriculture from where he continued to keep one eye on the nation's security.

12

1941–1942:
LEGION AGAINST LEGION

'They made their choice by marching through a tent; the
direction they turned at the end of it signified the side they
elected to support.'

AS WITH World War I, France was deluged
with foreigners seeking to enlist into its armies at the outbreak of
World War II. By the end of 1939, more than 80,000 had registered
their willingness to fight for France. Many would never see a French
uniform before the Nazis went around the Maginot Line and forced
capitulation. Tens of thousands did reach French army regiments, and
the War Ministry took the decision to form special corps of foreign
volunteers, training in France with cadres from the Legion.

The Legion itself was also to be heavily re-inforced and in its
wisdom the French shunted more than 3,500 Spanish refugees from
the Civil War straight into Legion ranks in North Africa. They were
not a particularly willing bunch, although many proved themselves as
good fighters. The Legion, to most of those Spanish soldiers, offered a
more satisfying existence than the internment camps to which they
had been sent when they fled across the border. One of those purpose-
built camps near Perpignan was immediately turned into a training
camp for Legion recruits before their onwards transmission to Algeria,
where they were instantly referred to as 'the communists'.

Another unhappy group who were given virtually no choice but a Legion posting were volunteers and conscripts from the Jewish communities of France and other European nations, including a large contingent of Poles. More than 3,000 were sent to Legion regiments in the first months of the war. Many were of middle-class backgrounds and included academics, doctors and lawyers, some of whom, like the Spaniards, had left-wing sympathies. They were known collectively in North Africa, and sometimes unfairly, as *volontaires forcés* (forced volunteers).

This influx of almost 7,000 somewhat reluctant legionnaires spread across regiments in North Africa did nothing for Legion morale. But the Foreign Legion expanded rapidly so that by the early spring of 1940 in addition to the three new volunteer regiments, it possessed eight full regiments of infantry and artillery (REI), two regiments of cavalry (REC), one reconnaissance division (GRD97) and the 13th Demi-Brigade.

In the early months of the war, when it was called 'phoney', volunteers from far and near were being trained in France by Legion cadres. Three new Régiments de Marche, 21st, 22nd and 23rd, which came into existence on 24 October 1939, comprised 3,860 volunteers from 47 nationalities, although almost a quarter of them were Spanish, and other large groups consisted of Polish and Jewish contingents. Their training had been hasty and unsatisfactory. Full equipment checks on their arrival revealed a complete unpreparedness for combat. Few of the legionnaires had chin straps for their steel helmets, dozens of them had no rifle slings. Some did not even possess haversacks and had to wrap their kit in a groundsheet, secured with string and slung over their shoulders.

The German attack on the frontiers of France began in the second week of May, two days after the arrival of this new volunteer force at its first forward position. They were to be fully engaged by the Nazis for the next two-and-a-half weeks and took heavy casualties. The 22nd was moved to form a defensive line north of Peronne, and even as they took up position, the volunteers came under fire from Stuka bombers and tank shell-fire. The Germans pursued their advance with relentless precision, and on 5 June, in spite of a spirited counter offensive, the legionnaires of the 22nd faced overwhelming odds. Without artillery or armoured vehicle support, they took further heavy losses, more than half the original number killed or wounded in three days. Battalions collapsed one after the other but, refusing to surrender, they took to fierce hand-to-hand fighting, soldier against soldier, bayonette against bayonette.

The short life of the 22nd RMVE ended in the quickly-learned traditions of the Legion. One of its officers who had broken out to try to get a delivery of ammunition was captured by the Germans within yards of leaving his own unit. He was sent back to suggest that they surrendered. They refused point blank. The unit still contained many whom Germany would throw instantly into concentration camps. There were 730 still standing when they were finally surrounded and virtually out of ammunition. They could offer no real resistance and were captured and taken by rail to PoW camps in Moosbourg, Bavaria. More than half eventually escaped. Some joined the French Resistance while others managed to get back to Sidi-bel-Abbès.

On 21 June, the 21st Regiment of volunteers was also overwhelmed and its few surviving soldiers dispersed into the Ardennes forest. Only the 23rd remained in action until the Armistice. Meanwhile, the Legion's own 11th and 12th were in continuous firefights from the declaration of war until the Armistice. The 11th was packed with tough legionnaires from North Africa and recent foreign volunteers enlisted in Europe, reinforced by a battalion of reluctant French conscripts. As the terrorizing sounds of the German tanks and Junkers Ju-87 Stuka dive-bombers approached, many surrounding French units retreated.

The Legion's 11th stood its ground for two weeks until, completely outgunned and outmanned, they were forced to fall back. Colonel Jean-Baptiste Robert burned the regimental standard and buried its tassel which was later dug up and returned to the Legion. Only 380 men out of a force of 3,000 survived to return to North Africa after the Armistice. The 97th Foreign Legion Divisional Reconnaisance Group (GRD 97) was totally wiped out. Manned entirely by veteran legionnaires from the 1st Foreign Legion Cavalry Regiment, poorly equipped and travelling in out-dated and lightly armed recce vehicles, they came up against a line of German Mark III tanks. The legionnaires fought a strong rearguard action to cover other French units as they moved out.

They survived until 9 June when they were blown apart as they made a final stand against the panzers. There were no known survivors. Only the 12th remained at the front when the Armistice came, with just 300 men standing when the fighting ceased. Of all the French units engaged in those first battles with the Germans, the Legion took the heaviest casualties in percentage terms.

When the Armistice between France and Germany was signed on 25 June 1940, all Legion units were withdrawn to Algeria where, for a time, the future of the Legion was once more in jeopardy. One of the first demands of the Nazis was the total disbandment of the Foreign Legion. This was renegotiated so that the Legion's presence in the colonial outposts could be maintained. It was regarded as an 'essential instrument in maintaining order in those regions'. The Germans did however insist upon a drastic reduction of Legion numbers. The first regiments to be dissolved were those comprising the 'hostilities only regiments' and what remained of the newly-formed volunteer units. These were followed with both the 11th and the 12th Legion regiments of infantry, although by then an effective fighting force of 6,000 was left with no more than 1,000 survivors to return to North Africa.

At the same time, the Reich agencies demanded that all remaining German and Italian nationals in the Legion and internment camps should be returned immediately to their homeland. This, of course, included many volunteers who had fled Germany and joined the Legion to fight the Nazis. The number of German nationals repatriated was far fewer than the German authorities had expected. Even in these times, the Legion looked after its own and the true identities and nationalities of many who had given false names was never revealed. Dozens were spirited away into far-flung outposts, although it was inevitable that many were returned. Non-Jewish German legionnaires sent back were offered imprisonment or enlistment in the German army for assignment to a special desert unit attached to the 90th Division of the Afrika Corps.

Still further reductions in Legion manpower were demanded. The Vichy-loyal Legion in North Africa came under constant scrutiny from the Armistice Commission and was kept short of weapons, gasoline and sometimes even food and tobacco. Morale among the ranks was at rock bottom and the rate of desertions and suicides was rising. The 1st and 2nd Regiments of the Legion remained in Algeria along with the 4th Regiment of Infantry and the 2nd Regiment of Cavalry. Both of the latter were later casualties of the cutbacks and by the end of that year Legion commanders could prove to French and German bureaucracy that eight units of the Legion had been axed. The 5th Regiment which was based in Indo-China remained loyal to Vichy France and with other loyal French military units based in the region, allowed the Japanese to effectively occupy Vietnam without opposition in the early months of 1940. The 6th Regiment of the Legion, which was in Syria, remained unaffected, since it too was unreservedly obedient to the Vichy government, on the orders of General Henri Dentz, Commander of the Army of the Levant. In those early months of Vichy rule, the Legion lost two-thirds of its force, down from 50,000 at its peak in 1940 to around 16,000 in 1942, of whom two-thirds were in the French colonies.

Back in England, the 13th Demi-Brigade, in their tents at Trentham Park, faced a momentous decision. By mid-1940, the camp housed more than 4,500 French soldiers, most of whom had fled with the British expeditionary forces from the beaches of Dunkirk in May. Among them were 1,619 legionnaires, survivors of the Narvik invasion and the exodus from France. They were an uncomfortable mix of Legion veterans and middle-class or politically motivated volunteers. There was on each side a core of idealists, soldiers looking for a scrap and those wanting to fight for a particular cause. As had been found in the past, they had little common ground. On 30 June, a further cause for anguish was injected by the arrival at Trentham of Charles de Gaulle.

De Gaulle came to offer the 13th Demi-Brigade a choice. The legionnaires, officers and ranks, could either join him in the formation of a Free French unit or return to Algeria. The implications were laid bare and emotions ran high, especially among the very vocal group of intellectual volunteers who could not imagine any other course than fighting the Nazis. The officers also argued among themselves and one of the Legion's Narvik commanders, General Bethouart, refused point blank to back de Gaulle; 31 of the Legion's 59 officers at Trentham voted to return to Sidi-bel-Abbès, all of them French.

The rest were given twenty-four hours to make up their minds, and in the late afternoon of the following day, the split was made: 938 opted to join de Gaulle. A swift parting of the two groups saved a more public demonstration of allegiance. Their animosity towards each other was evident and the group who remained simply ignored their departing colleagues, bound for North Africa. In Algiers, the 13th Demi-Brigade was formally disbanded. The name lived on however, adopted by the British-based contingent. As part of the Free French Army commanded by General de Gaulle, the 13th Demi-Brigade themselves left Britain on 28 June bound for Africa, where eventually they would join the British Eighth Army in the Western Desert. First, de Gaulle embarked upon a mission to win the support of the French colonies of Africa. His tiny army of 4,300 joined a large convoy escorted by Allied warships, and stopped off at the strategically important port of Dakar, the former capital of French West Africa, which de Gaulle hoped would offer a base. Instead, the Free French and the 13th came under heavy shore fire as they approached and were forced to retreat. Dakar was clearly a Vichy puppet.

They moved on to the Cameroons, which had already announced its support for de Gaulle, and remained inactive for weeks on end, until December when two battalions sailed around the Cape of Good Hope to the east coast of Africa to join a combined British force preparing an attack on Italian Eritrea. They first engaged the Italians in a mountainous region and dug in for eight days of tough fighting before the enemy broke and surrendered in large numbers. They suddenly acquired 1,000 prisoners.

They moved on to Massawa, Eritrea's principal port on the Red Sea, defended by a strong Italian force behind heavy fortification. After the British loosened the masonry with heavy artillery fire, the 13th Demi-Brigade moved in to scale the fort walls and the Italians gave up. The legionnaires also had to eject machine-gunners carefully positioned in the surrounding hills. Several throats were cut and hearts bayoneted before the area was finally secure, and by early evening on 10 April

1941, Colonel Magrin-Verneret, using the pseudonym Montclar for the safety of his family, was driving ahead of a couple of trucks full of legionnaires into Massawa. De Gaulle had his first piece of territory, although officially it was in Allied hands.

There seemed no hurry by the Allies to engage the large Vichy armies in North Africa, and months passed without confrontation. The French Army of the Levant had kept a substantial presence, principally in Syria and the Lebanon, since 1920. Its overall commander, General Henri Dentz, with around 50,000 men to call upon, was unwavering in his loyalty to the Vichy government, a stance which was only strengthened when the British navy sank the French fleet at Oran, killing many Frenchmen in the process.

The garrison in Syria included the 6th Regiment of the Foreign Legion, under the command of Colonel Fernand Barre, who also believed that the best way to keep the French empire from British hands was to honour the Armistice. The notion that Britain was still not at war with Vichy France, however, prevailed until the Germans began using Syrian bases under French control to launch attacks on Allied positions in neighbouring Iraq. The stance of the French generals made confrontation with the Allies inevitable, especially as Rommel's Afrika Corps moved on Egypt from the west. Finally, the moment had arrived: Free French against Vichy French, Legion against Legion.

On Sunday, 8 June 1941, four Allied divisions moved into Syria, made up of British, Australian and Indian troops, plus a small Jewish contingent. They were joined by the Free French which included the 13th Demi-Brigade, Senegalese Tirailleurs, North African saphis, and a group of Cossack Muslims who had settled in Syria years earlier. At the last minute, de Gaulle tried to persuade the Legion's 6th Regiment in Syria to join him. An exchange of intelligence soon made it clear that Colonel Barre was resolute in his loyalty to Vichy.

The Free French and the multi-national Allied troops crossed the Syrian frontier from Palestine. The 13th Demi-Brigade was initially to be held in reserve, behind the 5th Indian Brigade and the 7th Australian Division. They rattled across the desert in a collection of commandeered vehicles, rusty old trucks, ancient cars and buses, in fact anything that would move. The legionnaires were assigned familiar terrain of dusty hills around Damascus. Vicious infantry fire opened up as the Free French cut a path towards southern Damascus and on the approaches the 13th was engaged in a fierce battle, in which they lost twenty men. On the outskirts of the city the 13th finally and apprehensively reached the spot where their brothers of the 6th were known to be dug in. Colonel Montclar, commander of the 13th, stood down, unable to face the prospect of legionnaires fighting each other. As Legion historian Anthony Mockler noted: 'He could not go against the unwritten rule that the Legion should never fight the Legion.' His decision hit morale in the 13th, but it was quickly revived by his replacement, Lieutenant Colonel Dimitri Amilakvari, a suave White Russian prince aged 36 who had joined the Legion in the 1920s and like his hero, General Rollet, never swapped his kepi for a steel helmet.

The 13th probed the 6th with a patrol which was promptly fired upon. Both sides postured and a man from each was shot and killed. Then, the two units presented arms and pulled back and never engaged in a head to head, nor would they. When the real fight for Damascus and the Lebanon began, the confrontation was a blur of Allied troops. The Free French became an integral part of the overall Allied force which took on the Vichy French Army of the Levant. The Legion's 6th Regiment matched the Australian division which at times had the 13th at its side but according to most reliable reports, the two Legion regiments were kept apart. The Vichy Legion in a hard fought battle with the Australians and elsewhere lost 130 men with 720 wounded. The 13th suffered far less, with only twenty-two dead and fewer than fifty injured.

The Vichy-loyal Army of the Levant fought on for a month and each side, by then, had lost around 1,000 casualties. A local armistice, signed on 14 July 1941, gave the Vichy troops the opportunity to join the Free French, though there was still no great enthusiasm to do so. Those who did not wish to join de Gaulle would be repatriated to France; the remainder would be expected to stay and fight.

They made their choice by marching through a tent; the direction they turned at the end of it signified the side they elected to support.

Less than 3,000 men from the ranks of the Vichy army chose to go with de Gaulle and only 670 legionnaires from the 6th Regiment changed sides and joined to the 13th Demi-Brigade, in spite of a determined propaganda effort by de Gaulle's officers. With other volunteers from Allied PoW camps, plus 39 officers and 328 NCOs from the Levant, de Gaulle virtually doubled his tiny army although it was still fewer than 8,000 men in total. Those being repatriated and, at that time, still loyal to the Vichy numbered in excess of 30,000. The dead of both sides were buried together. Legionnaires remaining loyal to the 6th's commander, Colonel Barre, and all but a half dozen of his officers, amounted to fewer than 1,500 – all that now remained of an original force exceeding 6,000. They were shipped back to Sidi-bel-Abbès where they sat out the war until the Allied invasion of North Africa under Operation Torch on 7 November 1942. Re-equipped by the US Army, Legion units went on to fight the Germans in Tunisia, Italy and France.

The reinforced 13th was posted immediately to support the over-stretched British Eighth Army in the Western Desert, along with the enlarged Free French Brigade. With its recruits from the 6th and other volunteers, the 13th now fielded 1,700 men who were grouped into three battalions of around 500 men each. The British re-armed them as best they could, although there were only enough vehicles to equip two of the Legion battalions in their newly-created role as mechanized infantry.

In January 1942, Rommel's panzers raced forward to attack British positions south of Benghazi, in Libya, penetrating 150 miles eastwards towards Egypt. On 29 January disaster struck when German and Italian troops took Benghazi, a port full of supplies for the British attack on Tripolitania. In the next two weeks, the British began to regroup and reorganize their defences across thirty-five miles of terrain leading into the sparsest desert in the whole of Libya, south from El Ghazalah on the Mediterranean coast. The line was to be held with a solid minefield stretching from the coast, southward into the desert, manned at intervals by a fortified 'box' of troops who could defend attacks from any direction. Each box was surrounded by mines and barbed wire. Towards the end of February, two battalions of the 13th joined a Free French unit to take over the defence of the most extreme of these defensive positions, at a desolate place called Bir Hakeim. Surrounding it, and as far as the eye could see, was windblown desert, devoid of vegetation and providing no protection from the scorching heat by day, the coldness of the nights and the biting grit of the sandstorms. To this desert wilderness, the British commanders sent a polyglot force of Free French, numbering in total 3,720 men and one woman. She was Miss Susan Travers, the first female ever to be formally attached to the Legion. A tall and attractive 31-year-old Englishwoman, Miss Travers, as she was universally known (La Miss to the French), was the daughter of a Royal Navy captain and his wife who had retired to the south of France in the late 1920s. She had attended finishing school in Florence, played championship tennis at Wimbledon in the 1930s and at the outbreak of war, she had volunteered to the French Ambulance Service.

She graduated to driver for Colonel Lotte, a divisional medical officer, and joined the French expedition to Norway in 1940. She returned to England at the time of the evacuation and continued on with the Free French as de Gaulle began his African tour. Sometime during the attack on Massawa, she found herself attached to the 13th Demi-Brigade as driver for General Pierre Koenig, a former Legion officer who was now commander of the French Forces in the desert. As such, she would hear of nothing less than driving him at the head of his column of assorted fighting men heading for Bir Hakeim. She was not the only woman travelling with the Free French. They had their own medical contingent which included female nurses but none remained with them for the latter stages of the Bir Hakeim battle. The 13th Demi-Brigade contributed just short of 1,000 men to the Bir Hakeim garrison, and in the coming three months they became specialists in laying the vast minefields around the desert compound and running the reconnaissance missions to map out the surrounding territory for hides. The battle for Bir Hakeim became one of the desert classics, in many ways mirroring the Legion's own Battle of Camerone, only on a scale magnified 1,000 times.

Attack after attack was driven off and the enemy was harassed with hit-and-run tactics, principally by legionnaires. In one day alone, raiding parties returned with four captured enemy vehicles, a 1,000 litre tanker of water, 153 Italian and 125 German prisoners, along with 654

British and Indian soldiers freed from a makeshift PoW camp. The extra personnel put an additional strain on the garrison, until the enemy prisoners and most of the exhausted Indian troops were removed by a Free French supply convoy, along with fifty-four wounded French. One day, two Italian officers arrived waving a white flag and invited the Allied commanders in Bir Hakeim to surrender. Like his Legion ancestors at Camerone, he politely but firmly rejected their offer and returned the two Italians to their Jeep.

A fresh axis onslaught raged for the next three days and the little desert fortress came under nonstop bombardment by ground and air forces. Combined attacks by enemy tanks and infantry were countered by hour upon hour of response from French 75mm cannon. In total, the Bir Hakeim gunners fired more than 40,000 shells during the time of the siege. The Germans sent in the Luftwaffe with a clear mandate to blow the French garrison off the face of the earth. More than twenty Stuka dive-bombers and a dozen Junkers heavy bombers flew 1,400 missions and pounded the French position with 1,500 tons of explosives. In between, the RAF were flying up to 200 retaliatory missions a day with Spitfires to hit German supply lines and artillery positions. They also had to make many drops of supplies into the Bir Hakeim garrison, including water which ran out several times. Koenig radioed headquarters on 9 June: 'Water and ammunition virtually exhausted. Cannot hold out much longer.' Soon after dawn the following day, an enemy artillery barrage opened up and continued all morning, followed immediately by dive-bombers. At 3 p.m., a full-blown attack by German infantry began and twelve legionnaires were taken prisoner and several were killed before it could be repulsed. By the end of the day, there were no shells left for the 75mm cannon.

At six that evening, Koenig called his officers together to discuss a daring plan in which the Legion was to figure prominently. Under cover of darkness, they would make a run for it – quit the compound and try to get to the British lines. It would be a mass breakout, not a soul would be left behind. Losses during the siege had been remarkably light, fewer than 100 wounded and 28 dead. The Legion's 13th had itself lost 17 dead and 40 or so wounded. Now, Koenig faced the seemingly impossible task of sneaking past the German positions with a roaring convoy of assorted vehicles and weaponry, along with more than 3,500 personnel.

The plan was for legionnaires, along with a small British contingent still in their midst, to lead the charge. They would draw the fire of the enemy, heading towards their positions with Bren guns blazing. Next, General Koenig and Legion commander Lieutenant Colonel Amilak-vari would lead the convoy out of the compound in a staff car driven by Susan Travers. Finally, a second contingent of legionnaires would bring up the rear. The route out unavoidably took the fleeing garrison over a track crossing the minefields they themselves had laid. Inevitably, the night sky was suddenly lit by explosion after explosion as the mines were struck by the thundering herd, as trucks and Jeeps became blazing coffins for those who did not manage to jump clear. The Germans added to the fireworks with multi-coloured tracer and flares, zig-zagging across the dark sky. Along the way, legionnaires and others fought running firefights with German troops and it was nothing short of a miracle that the flight, albeit a shambolic race, did not end in total disaster. In the event, it was only a small calamity. By seven that evening, 2,500 reached the relative safety of the British lines. Three days later, stragglers were still coming in, mostly on foot. The final tally listed in the official log of the Free French was 72 dead, 763 missing presumed captured and 21 wounded. The Legion was worst hit, with 11 killed, 32 wounded and 37 known to have been captured. Another 152 were listed as missing and it was likely they had met Koenig's worst fears of being interrogated in PoW camps. The two battalions of the 13th Demi-Brigade who went to Bir Hacheim were left with 650 men, and lost most of their equipment, abandoned with the rest at Bir Hakeim. They were the heroes of the hour, acting as protectors for the escaping majority. It was not all glory for the 13th, however. They made a mess of a major task, a diversionary action assigned to them by Field Marshal Montgomery in the Battle of El Alamein, and were not called back to the front until the final stages of the Tunisian campaign. There, they were side by side with remaining North African regiments. The gulf that existed between them was very evident.

Later in Italy, the 13th restored its credibility and was awarded the

Croix de Guerre for heroic efforts at Monte Cassino and in France as part of Operation Anvil to reclaim the south of the country. Rows between the 13th and Legion headquarters continued almost to the last. The 13th took more than 1,000 casualties, almost half its strength, in last ditch battles in Alsace and its officers formally complained to the war minister that Vichy loyalists in Sidi-bel-Abbès sought to destroy the Gaullist 13th through perpetual engagements and withholding recruits and supplies. As Douglas Porch uncovered from regimental diaries, they received an angry response from the French high command, deploring the fact that the 13th 'pretend that their action alone saved the French army from disaster and liberated Belfort and Mulhouse'.

To end the quarrel, said Porch, the war ministry disengaged the 13th and sent the entire unit to the Alps for a quiet conclusion to the hostilities. As a footnote to the above, there was a happier note to record. Susan Travers was formally appointed to the 13th Demi-Brigade with the rank of adjutant, equivalent to sergeant major. She subsequently joined the 13th on its forthcoming journey to Indo-China. In 1947, she married legionnaire Nicolas Schlegelmilch, who had served in the 6th Regiment in Syria and then transferred to the 13th. He had also been at Bir Hakeim. They concluded their service in Morocco and moved with their two sons to a small town near Paris. Susan collected a number of medals, including the *Croix de Guerre* for Bir Hakeim, the *Médaille Militaire* and the Colonial War Medal.

13

1945–1954: INDO-CHINA, THE FINAL IGNOMINY

'Shellfire rained down on the weakest of the fortified positions ...
trenches and dugouts exploded around them, many who were not
hit by the bombardment were buried alive in the mud and slime.'

THE ACTION switched to the Far East. On 9
March 1945, Japanese military commanders, who had effectively been
calling the shots in Indo-China since Vichy France gave them free
access in 1940, made their move. The Japanese invited the French
military commander in Lang Son, General Lemonnier, and his
civilian counterpart to dinner to discuss the situation. Once inside the
Japanese base, 150 miles from Hanoi, the two Frenchmen were
arrested. Simultaneously, Japanese troops surrounded French military
bases manned by legionnaires. The first, with a smaller guard, led by
Sergeant Müller, a German, was quickly over-run and all inside were
killed. At the second, with a larger and more troublesome Legion
presence, the Japanese bombed the compound with mustard gas and
sat back and waited. With the majority of the fort's manpower
knocked out, the Japanese troops moved forward and captured the
survivors. They were lined up against a wall and machine-gunned;
sixty-five were killed.

On 12 March the two officials arrested in Lang Son were executed by decapitation with the sword, along with their bodyguard, a Greek legionnaire, Sergeant Tsarkiropolous. The Japanese then began rounding up all French civilian officials and locking up the French *gendarmes* in their own jails. A new administration of Vietnam was formed by Emperor Bao Dai, under the protection of Japan. French military commanders were ordered to lay down their arms and surrender immediately. Within three days, more than 60,000 prisoners were taken.

At the Legion's frontier garrison at Ha Giang, in the far north of the country, legionnaires fought to the last round of ammunition, waved a white flag and were mown down by Japanese machine-gunners as they marched out. Remnants of the Legion's 5th Regiment, which had remained loyal to Vichy France, scattered. Around 3,000 reassembled by the Black River. They marched out of Indo-China, through northern Thailand and into the safety of China – a journey of some 550 miles, during which they regularly came under attack from both Japanese troops and the nationalist guerrillas of the Viet Minh who were just as vicious as the occupation forces. When the march ended, and they returned to Vietnam after the surrender of Japan in August 1945, fewer than 1,000 of them had survived, and their regiment, which had largely remained loyal to the Vichy regime, was disbanded. It did not appear again for another four years.

The nationalist movement which tracked them had begun to field its guerrilla force as a resistance movement two years earlier. At its head was one of the country's leading political figures, Nguyen Hai Quoc – now known as Ho Chi Minh (He Who Lights The Way) – who had been a member of the French Communist Party and one of the founders of the League for the Independence of Vietnam. They wanted all foreigners out of Vietnam.

The Vietnamese leader also had a score to even with the French settlers. Their arrogant colonial administration had left some embarrassing human rights issues from pre-1940 days and the Foreign Legion, in its role of colonial policeman, supporting the Sûreté, had some nasty incidents to live down.

Indo-China was for years regarded as a choice posting in the Legion and was generally looked upon as a reward for excellent service elsewhere. The overseas pay bounty (paid with each posting abroad) was higher, the region was spectacular, the barracks and off-camp accommodation for officers were among the best anywhere, there were ample servants for the garrison, to do every duty from cleaning boots to cooking and, above all, the local women were very available. Some even married, had half-caste children and quite often sold their women when they moved on. But, as in many places where life becomes too comfortable, the system was heavy-handedly applied and often abused. Many legionnaires were known associates of criminal mafias, some even joined them and settled in Indo-China to make their fortunes. Revolutionaries began to stir reaction against the increasingly shoddy French rule, in which human rights were ignored and atrocities occurred by the week.

French planes once bombed a group of 15,000 peasants who were marching on Vinh. Legionnaires were regularly called upon to perform summary executions of resistance leaders: at its peak 1,000 Vietnamese were shot and more than 4,000 were imprisoned by the French in one year alone. A pamphlet campaign directed against the Legion by the nationalists accused it of being an 'unbridled army out of control; a rabble, raping, stealing and killing . . . men, young people, are arrested and shot in cold blood, without trial by this troop of pirates which has been set loose on the country . . .'

The Vietnamese prepared for their own uprising when World War II ended. For the Vietnamese, the end of the war was merely a beginning, and on 16 August 1945, Ho Chi Minh seized control.

De Gaulle sought help from Britain and America in reclaiming the country for France. On 22 August, a battalion of Gurkhas and a company of Free French were landed in Saigon by the British to ensure the safety of de Gaulle's personal representative, Colonel Jean Cedile, who was to set up shop in Saigon. Ho's Viet Minh army withdrew to the North, and began establishing an effective stronghold for future operations. Within the month, 100 Westerners had been slaughtered and dozens more taken hostage. On 26 September, the commander of the American Office of Strategic Studies in Saigon was shot dead. 'So began the Indo-China War . . . and American blood was shed in its opening hours,' stated US secret service reports written at the time.

France was already preparing to make a forced entry into the North when international mediation intervened. The partition of Vietnam, as set forth in the Treaty of Paris on 6 March 1946, allowed 15,000 French troops to be quartered north of the 16th Parallel. The tenuous peace lasted only a few months. By December, France and the Viet Minh were at war – a bloody, dirty, brutal conflict that was to last almost nine years. Within months, the Legion had 15,000 men in Vietnam and was recruiting at the rate of 10,000 a year. They used up 150,000 volunteers over the period of the war, amid serious protests from Germany where tens of thousands were said to have been recruited.

Out in the country, the French strategy of dispersing legionnaires and regular troops into small garrisons was soon found to be immensely dangerous to both manpower and, more importantly, to equipment. Far-flung outposts were sitting ducks and supply lines across hostile, often near inaccessible landscapes were constantly ambushed. The Legion took the brunt of these attacks, especially in the northern territory close to the Chinese border. The only way to provide fast relief to troops under siege was by air, except that there were few airstrips either. Back in Algeria, the Legion commandant asked for volunteers to create the first parachute battalions. The call was heavily over-subscribed. The Legion had many men with airborne experience in other armies, especially among the Germans.

Among those who stepped forward was a medical orderly, a corporal who had been a lieutenant in the German army and later in a para-chute company. He reluctantly confessed that he was one of the German para commandos who made a glider assault on the mountain hotel to free Italian dictator Mussolini in July 1943, after his capture by the Allies. A large number of German parachutists were now available to the Legion's Captain Segretain, the jump school's first commander, and they swiftly prepared the first batch of 350 legionnaires who passed the course ready for service in Vietnam at the dawn of 1949. While more Legion paras began training – 'to commit suicide' according to recent volunteer journalist Alan Liddell-Hart – they in turn took additional recruits locally, training volunteers from the forces already in Vietnam and men drawn from Indo-Chinese troops. The process was on-going, and self-feeding. Legion paratroopers took part in many small company- and battalion-size combat jumps during the first phase of the war. Colonel Raspeguy described to Jean Larteguy one he had himself witnessed:

> Two battalions of legionnaires were attacking a Viet position and I was to support them from the rear with my para-troops. At a given signal the legionnaires emerged from the trenches en masse. They advanced, on line, step by step, as though a drum was beating out the time, like a loud death march under a heavy, overcast sky. The legionnaires kept advancing at the same pace, bolt upright, without lengthening or shortening their stride. They did not even turn around when one of their number fell beside them, his guts spilling out or his head smashed to a pulp. With their sub-machine-guns under their arms, stopping now and then to fire a well aimed burst, they went on step-by-step, a blank expression on their faces. There were quite a lot of Germans among them; they were the ones who set the pace. The Viets were firing as hard as they could, like mad men. The legionnaires marched on and reached the Viet lines, impassive as ever, still moving at the same steady pace, firing their bursts and hurling hand grenades with mechanical precision into the trenches. The Viets were seized with panic; they threw down their arms and tried to run, but the legion-aires bowled them over like pins, not with hatred, but something worse then hatred, this slow, inexorable advance. It was several minutes before the legionnaires assumed a human expression, before a little blood came back into their cheeks, before the icy demon left them. Then some of them began to collapse, they had not even realised they had been wounded. Half of them were killed.

If the Viet Minh suffered from battle nerves in early exchanges, the condition was soon knocked out of them. Mao Tse Tung's final victory in China in 1949 provided Ho Chi Minh's forces with an instant safe haven in which to train whole divisions of men, heavily equipped by China and the Soviets, and ready to be turned out for battle. Legion forts in the far north of Vietnam, between Lang Son and the Chinese border, were most vulnerable. Viet Minh commander General Giap was stepping up his campaign with almost classic set-piece attacks. Sergeant Tom McVeigh, in the Legion's 3rd Regiment, described a typical confrontation, staged at a carefully selected point in the track where the Legion convoy out of Lang Son had to negotiate a narrow gorge:

> As we reached it, there was a massive explosion. A mine exploded after armoured cars at the front had passed by, splitting the convoy in two. A couple of dozen invisible machine-gunners, hidden in the undergrowth of the cliffs immediately above, opened fire. Then came a barrage of grenades, hurled with precision by Viet troops swarming down the embankment. In the space of just two or three minutes – no more – every truck was knocked out and blazing.
>
> Legionnaires who survived that bombardment, jumped from their trucks and grouped together forming a square on the embankment, attempting to defend themselves from a wave of Vietnamese who split into sections. While one group went from truck to truck picking up abandoned arms and supplies, the others fought the legionnaires, hand-to-hand in this reciprocal slaughterhouse, with the Viets being directed everywhere by very calm political commissars.

One sergeant escaped into the forest nearby and hid in bushes fifty yards from the road. He heard several shots nearby. They came not from the Viet Minh but from two legionnaires who had been discovered and who blew their brains out before they could be taken prisoner and subjected to the torture tactics of their would-be captors.

Into this bloodbath stepped Robert Diffey, a Londoner who had joined the Legion in search of travel and adventure on 15 November 1949, a few months after his 18th birthday. He had used the money he received in gifts from the family get-together to finance his trip to Paris from whence he sent them a card: 'Dear All: I've joined the Foreign Legion. Don't worry. See you in five years . . . Bob.'

Diffey had a hard job getting to Vietnam. He had all the attributes of what his colleagues called 'a good legionnaire'. He passed through the training regime with flying colours and became exceedingly efficient in the play-acting of guerrilla warfare training. He'd also had a good tutor. Legion veteran, Chief Adjutant Stengler, had just returned from his own stint in the jungles and swamplands and was regarded as a specialist. Stengler took Diffey under his wing and passed on his skills, to the extent that the pupil was rapidly made up to corporal/instructor for each new intake of volunteers.

Diffey was anxious to see active service but his company commander reckoned he was too valuable training others. He was undoubtedly saving lives, and promoted him to sergeant kept him sweet. Diffey, still only 20, kept up the pressure and was finally allowed to sample the real thing. Like many legionnaires, he kept a journal of noteworthy events. In the beginning, as he joined combat duties with his regiment in the Annam and the Tonkin delta sectors, he was writing about his pay, £80 a month, far better than he'd have been earning in London. He mentioned too that he had 'acquired' a .50 calibre Browning machine-gun which he kept with him for the duration of his tour and fitted it to all the vehicles and amphibious craft that he used, instead of the standard issue .303s. Jim Worden researched Diffey's story for his own archives, from which the following extract is taken:

Robert Diffey was a very bright young man, well above average. He came to the Legion full of enthusiasm and keen to do well. He was emboldened not by drink or the smell of action, but by a lively adventurous spirit. He was just a kid and his journal reflected the excitement of the experience. This was soon to change. Like many young legionnaires posted to Indo-China, and indeed those thousands of young Americans who followed a few years later, he possessed a fairly carefree attitude in the beginning. It was to his great delight, for instance, that he was given a fast motor launch for his patrols on which he mounted his .50 machine-gun, acquired through a bit of judicious bribery of the adjutant.

He was also made a section chief, of the 4th Squadron of the 1st

Regiment of Cavalry. He even got hold of a French naval officer's white cap which he wore when out of sight of his commanding officer, and did not object when the members of his crew called him 'Captain Bligh'.

Quite quickly, however, the youthful spirit of Bob Diffey was overtaken by the sheer awe of the carnage he was witnessing. He was forced to look upon sights that he had never imagined possible, and nothing in his very expert training could have prepared him for it – not even the warning words of Sergeant Stengler. On one occasion his section came upon a group of legionnaires who had been captured by the Viet Minh. They had been crucified, nailed to trees, their ears and private parts slashed off by machete, and their skin raked with knives, probably while they were still alive, and honey smeared upon them to attract ants and other passing wildlife. He saw the mutilated bodies of women and children in villages opposed to the Viet Minh. He also lost a number of his men when his section was ambushed by the guerillas at Thanh Luong.

On that day the adventurous young man himself became a dedicated killer, not interested in taking prisoners. The bright eyes and cheerful face were dulled by the horror; his whole persona changed and there was a sense of real purpose when he shot up the banks of the rivers with his .50 calibre machine-gun. Enemy troops were cut down as Diffey reduced the trees lining the rivers to matchwood. And he learned another hardening lesson, that atrocity was to be met with atrocity in this exceedingly dirty war. When they went ashore to treat his own wounded, he and his lieutenant carried out a body count of the enemy dead. For the loss of three legionnaires, his *équipe* had accounted for more than sixty of the enemy. While searching the jungle, they found three guerillas still alive, but seriously wounded. When a body is struck by a heavy calibre machine-gun bullet, it does not leave a small neat hole. The copper jacketed lead can take off an arm or leg. If it strikes in the stomach or chest, then the contents of these will spill out in the cavity left by the exit wound.

Diffey was on the verge of firing a bullet into the head of one of these injured souls to put him out of his suffering when he was restrained by a veteran *sous officier*. The act was not out of compassion, as he first thought. Gaston went on to demonstrate the art of knee-capping by firing his pistol into the centre of each knee. He explained that by leaving a few wounded enemy for his friends to collect when they returned to bury their dead, they would see that the Legion was prepared to inflict the same suffering on prisoners that they themselves were giving out to captured members of the French forces. It was the kind of ridiculous logic that escalated the terrible events of a war that on occasions made legionnaires put a bullet through their own brain rather than risk torture if caught.

Not one of those three wounded Viet Minh troops would ever walk again, none would ever again spill the blood of a legionnaire and it would be more than likely that rather than carry the body of one of their compatriots, they would execute them themselves. For his bravery in this operation, Robert Diffey received the first of several decorations, the *Croix de Guerre*. He was honest enough to say that it gave him no pleasure.

Still only 22 years of age, he realized he had become a hard-bitten legionnaire and trained killer. The following month, in August 1952, his unit moved forty kilometres south to Hue. They travelled by rail and should have arrived in little more than an hour. But the line had been sabotaged every five kilometres, the rails levered from their beds and tossed into the undergrowth. Each time they stopped to repair the track, they were ambushed, giving covering fire while other legionnaires made the necessary repairs. When he eventually arrived in Hue, he had lost 40 per cent of his force.

On return to base, another notch in his career was hewn. He was promoted to Chief Sergeant, a rank seldom attained in such a short career. By then, he had stopped the repetitive entries of combat in his journal, making notes only of the names of his friends who had died, and clearly suffering mental anguish. Instead of writing about combat, he had begun to talk of his pet dog Zouzou, or of his visit to the dentist where he had been obliged to have a tooth extracted without anaesthetic, and that the female dentist had been a Vietnamese operating under primitive and unhygenic conditions and who charged him at least twenty times the normal price.

Though mentally scarred, Robert Diffey himself survived dozens of combat missions without a scratch, and in March 1954, he returned to Algeria, looking forward to a long leave and spending some of the cash bounty that had been stored up for him in the Legion bank. The irony was he used the money to buy a new car before travelling home to England where he was to have been best man at his sister's wedding. There was a crash . . . Diffey who had all the 'Magic of Baraka' in Indo-China was killed on the road from Oudja to Casablanca. His body lies in the Legion cemetery at Oudja.

The humiliation of the French and the near annihilation of two regiments of the Foreign Legion in Vietnam came in two stages. The first was in the summer of 1950 in a remote valley of North Vietnam. It was a watershed year in many respects, not least with the realization by military and civilian leaders that certain parts of the country had become no-go areas. Far-flung Legion outposts were evacuated and a particular area in the north of the country, known as Cao Bang, was beyond the means of effective defence. It was located at the intersection of the two principal roads serving the north, the RC3 and RC4. There, a township opposed to the Viet Minh was defended by 1,126 legionnaires of the 3rd Regiment of Infantry and 680 Moroccans from the *Armée d'Afrique*. The only route out for this convoy of men, machines and civilians was over a very exposed main road.

It was a death trap, lending itself admirably to the ambush tactics of the Viet Minh. As Giap turned up the heat with more attacks on their supply lines, the newly appointed French commander in chief, General Marcel Carpentier, resurrected an earlier plan – rejected at the time because of the shame of retreat – to extract the community of Cao Bang. It was a two-phase operation, first requiring the convoy to march thirty-eight kilometres to the fort at Dong Khe which had since been taken over by two companies of the Legion's 3rd Regiment. There the party would be taken under the protection of an escort group consisting of legionnaires, Moroccan soldiers and the Legion's paras of 1BEP, almost 5,000 men in all.

The Cao Bang rescue mission, originally discussed a year earlier, had become a priority but Giap's intelligence network was as good as ever. On 16 September, the key factor in Carpentier's evacuation plan was torpedoed. The rendezvous fort at Dong Khe came under heavy mortar bombardment and after a two-day struggle, the Legion's two companies were overwhelmed. Only one officer and thirty-one legionnaires managed to escape and they emerged out of the jungle at the Legion's That Khe garrison eleven miles away several days later.

Even as the defeated legionnaires arrived, the Cao Bang convoy under the command of Lieutenant Colonel Charton had set off along route RC4 to make their rendezvous at the now abandoned fort. In Saigon, Carpentier and his commanders moved to Plan B. They would airlift a battalion of Moroccans to strengthen the Cao Bang convoy. In the meantime, they assembled three battalions of Moroccans and another from the Legion's 1BEP, 3,500 men in all, at the That Khe garrison. Under the command of Lieutenant Colonel Marcel Le Page, they were to march to Dong Khe on the night of 30 September and repossess the fort. The rendezvous with Colonel Charton and his evacuation column could then go ahead as planned on 3 October. The Legion's para commander and one of their most famous officers, Captain Pierre Jeanpierre, pleaded to be allowed to take his 1BEP on ahead and make a pre-emptive strike, but Le Page refused. He wanted his full force to attack simultaneously and overcome the Viet Minh by the element of surprise.

It was no surprise. Their respective columns were heading towards a huge reception party planned by Giap, courtesy of his exceedingly efficient espionage department. Some historians have since estimated that he had moved 30,000 Viet Minh troops with artillery and mortar support into the area. Dong Khe itself had been heavily reinforced, so Le Page's column was ordered to bypass the town and head directly to the RC4 and link up with Charton at a new rendezvous point, a valley known as Coc Xa.

Giap had covered that possibility too. Le Page's column cut off the road on to a track which, according to his map, should have taken him to the valley but ultimately led to a wall of dense jungle and tangled vines. The Viet Minh opened fire. Waves of troops attacked and the Legion paras and a battalion of Moroccans held the rear while the main body tried to hack a path forward. By 3 October they were still far away from the valley. Le Page ordered the destruction of their mules and heavy equipment to help speed up his progress. The attacks from the Viet Minh intensified. Dozens fell by the wayside and legionnaires at the rear were being snatched and individually butchered by squads of Viet Minh. In one night, negotiating a steep pass, the Legion lost 100 men. Their screams could be heard ringing through the jungle. It was all too much for the Moroccans who fled en masse into the undergrowth as the column reached the valley. Approaching from the opposite direction was Colonel Charton with his motley convoy which included men of the Legion's 3rd Regiment, several hundred civilians, including the town's prostitutes and camp followers, and the Moroccan escort. As they approached and heard the sound of distant cannon, the Moroccans also panicked and many fled into the jungle where they were soon caught and killed, or taken prisoner.

Giap's troops converged on the two columns, who were trapped in what was effectively a blind canyon with no way out. Waves of Viet ground troops were backed by incessant artillery fire which dragged on for a further two days until the Cao Bang rescue mission – a military fiasco – collapsed finally into an horrendous bloodbath: 7,000 men killed or captured, most of the civilians slaughtered. The Legion's 1BEP was given the task of attempting to force a path out of the valley for Le Page's group. It was a murderous job, fought in hand-to-hand combat with the Viet Minh. Those who did escape through this brief and temporary exit passage did so literally over the bodies of the Legion paras, some still moaning on the ground as their lives ebbed away with the blood flowing from their wounds, others shot to pieces by machine-gun fire. The 1BEP contingent was annihilated – fewer than a dozen paras survived.

Many of those captured were to remain in the appalling Viet Minh prison camps for almost four years, including Colonel Charton, veteran Legion officer since 1928. The carnage was the first phase of Ho Chi Minh's successful onslaught to rid his country of the French. As of that moment, North Vietnam was in his hands although the French refused to admit it. They appointed a new High Commissioner and military commander whose task was to reappraise the French situation in Indo-China and convince everyone, and most of all the government itself, that victory against the Viet Minh could be achieved, although many of the generals did not themselves believe it.

One of the first improvements was to increase the strength of paratroopers. By the end of 1950, 1 and 2BEP were reinforced and brought up to 5,600 men. They were virtually doubled again the following year. They were to form the shock troops of the French army and their expansion coincided with a reversal of the previous policy of shutting outposts of French military in territory where the Viet Minh were most active. The new policy was to rapidly build larger fortresses within that territory which could be supplied by air and used for attacks and intelligence missions and as centres for those groups who supported the French.

The BEP and the Legion's 3rd Regiment were constantly at the forefront of these plans and of the on-going war which, in conditions of jungle and swamp confrontations, reached a stalemate of continuous running firefights. French war managers pleaded for more and more troops. The French government, facing hostile public and international opinion at a war that was going nowhere, refused to comply, sending less than 25 per cent of the numbers requested. Even so, it wasn't all one way traffic. The French inflicted some major reverses for the Viet Minh, particularly in a number of spectacular battles involving legionnaires and BEP paras in the northern territories.

For large numbers of troops in posts and garrisons in the southern regions of Vietnam, life was more even, a combination of nervous tension on active patrol combined with duties in the garrison which could be tedious and boring. Henry Ainley, who was in a small post thirty miles from Saigon, set up largely to guard a French-owned rubber plantation, reckoned that legionnaires were brilliant at two things: killing and dying well, and did both frequently. They generally had no interest in hearts and minds issues, or the clearly failing missions of pacification by political re-education and religion. So when legionnaires returned to base, there was little to do other than drink, watch or participate in the barrack-room fights which rose from heat and liquor, especially on a Sunday, or to have sexual intercourse with the *congaies* from the local villages who occasionally doubled as spies for the Viet Minh, topics which were summed up by Ainley in his description of a typical Sunday:

> Gradually the morning disintegrated and the afternoon pattern began to form under the increasing weight of the heat ... in the sergeant's mess, Smedlow, Rossini and Moinea were indulging in their usual after lunch fight, plates flying, bottles breaking and the Annamite boy screaming like a stuck pig just for the fun of it. Hartz and I sipped our brandy and ducked the flying crockery. A few huts away we could hear Sergeant de Perre quietly and methodically beating up his *congaie* who was crying in a soft, penetrating, brain-piercing note. From the captain's bungalow we could hear him explaining to the planter's *congaie* how much he was loved by his men and admired by his superiors ... just another Sunday, no different to many others.

In places away from the war, the Legion had secured for itself a bad name once again. Allegations of rape were never seriously denied. They also had a tendency to steal whatever items of value fell into their path, such as a small herd of cattle which could be rounded up and sold to a meat trader. All money would go to the much diminished company funds. It was accepted practice, said Ainley, to carry off everything moveable and saleable that was found during operations or patrols in the non-pacified areas.

This stalemate situation continued for some time, with the war bobbing along through peaks and troughs of military activity and fluctuating levels of reciprocal horror. Some said General Giap was content to wait for the right place and the moment in history to snuff out the French invaders once and for all. If that was so, then all that he planned now fell into place ... piece by piece.

In the autumn of 1953, Giap began to show interest in territory around the border with French-controlled Laos. When intelligence reports suggested that he was about to launch a full-scale invasion through a previously unheard of place called Dien Bien Phu, the French prepared to pre-empt him by preparing to move thirteen battalions totalling 15,000 men – virtually their entire force in North Vietnam – to a completely new frontier.

Located 145 kilometres west of Hanoi, Dien Bien Phu straddled the route into Laos and represented a substantial area, around seventy square kilometres of jungle-clad hills surrounding a valley plateau with a river and an airstrip, native villages and rice paddies. On the night of 29 November, the French launched Operation Castor, flying in four battalions of paras to secure the airstrip and surrounding area at Dien Bien Phu. In the skirmish that followed, sixty communists were killed and the paras lost fourteen men. The Viet Minh were well aware of French plans. French commander, General Henri Navarre, who had been openly pessimistic about winning the guerrilla war, told newsmen he believed the move into Dien Bien Phu was the most important action by the French in months. The general believed he could defend the area with mobile columns radiating out from the airport. They would then thwart the communists' seasonal offensives and the base would serve as a centre for pro-French resistance fighters, and prevent General Giap from increasing his recent gains in Laos.

The French commanders had convinced themselves that with their superiority in the air, and the large number of Legion paras at their disposal, they would have little trouble halting any Viet Minh incursion. There was no way either, they argued, that Giap's artillery could get close enough to do any serious damage to the base and the eight fortified positions protecting the Dien Bien Phu which were to be set up in the surrounding hills.

The French ground force who followed the paras in were drawn almost entirely from non-French units: five battalions of legionnaires from the 13th Demi-Brigade, the 3rd and 5th Regiments and a battalion of Legion paras as mobile reserves to reinforce any position. There were four other units from the *Armée d'Afrique*, two battalions of Thais and Senegalese, plus contingents of Vietnamese and French paras.

The Viet Minh watched from afar as the French strengthened their fortifications and built underground mortar-proof caverns covered by felled trees and earth. Among the facilities was a fully equipped hospital unit with an emergency room, operating theatres and around forty beds. The complex also included the airstrip and the equipment stores for Legion pioneers and a *foyer* for off-duty soldiers. Although the base became a labyrinth of dugouts and trenches surrounded by minefields and barbed wire, the French did not even bother to camoflauge it because they thought it beyond Viet Minh attack capabilities.

Military historians, with the benefit of analytical hindsight, have quietly applauded the strategy of General Giap which now began to unfold though, of course, abhoring the end result. The French had fallen into the biggest ambush in modern military history. The Viet Minh made enough attacking sorties in the region to keep the French occupied in the weeks and months leading up to the cataclysmic events that followed, ensuring that they not only remained in the area but continued to build up their manpower. Soon, it would become clear that the communists were prepared to risk the destruction of the major part of their army to defeat the French.

While the French were engaged in building their base, the communists employed between 50 and 60,000 engineers, pioneers and coolies to drag hundreds of tons of heavy artillery, including 200 105s, into position on the hills above the French fortress and its own elevated defensive positions. The pioneer force moved only at night under cover of forest trees, invisible from the air. The gun emplacements were positioned with great accuracy, with Giap's experts on site to set the ranges directly to pre-determined targets. Next, they put in place a line of anti-aircraft cannon to hit incoming French aircraft and parachutists. Now, they moved a thousand tons of munitions to the gun sites, burying the stores in bunkers around the batteries ready for use. Finally the coolies dug the first line of trenches and tunnels to carry the attack forward, and early in the new year, the infantry began arriving by the same method, silently travelling by night through the jungle. In all, Giap amassed four infantry divisions, eventually calling upon 50,000 men. Unknown to the French, even the roads leading from communist strongholds in the north were being resurfaced to run in supplies from China and the Soviets.

The Battle of Dien Bien Phu began on 13 March. The monsoon season also started early. Torrential storms sent oceans of water down the hills and turned the French positions into a quagmire. Shellfire rained down on the weakest of the fortified positions, held by the

Legion's 13th Demi-Brigade contingent. Their trenches and dugouts exploded around them. Many who were not hit by the bombardment were buried alive in the mud and slime. Within eight hours, the position lost contact with base. The few legion survivors managed to scramble back to the French lines the following day: 326 men were killed or captured.

History records the calamity that was overtaking the French – a brutal, relentless attack by an army which outnumbered the French four to one, and whose equipment was so well placed that no effective counter attack could be mounted. At the end of the first week, the French artillery chief, Colonel Charles Piroth, devastated by their lack of intelligence on Viet Minh firepower, pulled the pin on a hand grenade and killed himself. The second of the eight fortified positions, held by infantry units of the *Armée d'Afrique*, was crushed the same day and two days later another defended by Thai soldiers fell.

Yet the casualty figures were far greater among the Viet Minh. Legionnaires reported that they had killed hundreds as the Viets came through the undergrowth in waves following the artillery bombardment. 'The ground before us was covered in bodies, but they just kept coming and eventually we stacked them on top of each other to form a protective shield,' said a Legion sergeant who scrambled back to base clutching the stump of his handless left arm.

By the end of the second week, the main road that ran through Dien Bien Phu was blocked at both ends by constant shelling. In one more week, the airstrip which provided the beleagued French troops with their only route to the outside world was pitted with deep craters and out of action. The last aircraft, carrying some of the vast numbers of wounded back to French military hospitals in Hanoi, was hit by shellfire as it tried to take off and all on board perished. There was no way out ... and the only way in for reinforcements and the 150 tons of supplies and ammunition needed each day to sustain the French action was by parachute, usually under the cover of darkness. Much of it fell behind enemy lines and the Viet Minh gratefully accepted the ammo delivered to the wrong address to kill more French soldiers.

This was not entirely the fault of the French air force who responded almost from day one with napalm attacks on Viet Ming positions.

They were themselves being shot to pieces by the barrage of anti-aircraft fire as they approached the drop zones.

Unable to get the wounded out of the battle area, Dr Paul Grauwin's underground hospital became a desperate scene compared by many to a field hospital in World War 1 ... an incredible, bloody stomach churning horror story of rows of mutilated bodies on whom he and his staff were operating around the clock, sewing up and cutting off damaged pieces. Many became double amputees, had their faces half shot away, blinded, charred ... and dozens just died before they could receive attention. Overhead, the shells continued their continuous downpour. In his book, *Doctor at Dien Bien Phu*, Grauwin recounts stories of true heroism and bravery. What seemed to impress him most was the way legionnaires, injured once, twice, perhaps even three times, rejoined the battle as soon as they could. Even those with amputations and the partially blinded returned ... one-armed men would say they could still throw grenades ... men who had lost a leg would stumble back, prop themselves against a tree and pick up machine-guns ... the man who had lost an eye would say: 'It's easier now ... I don't have to close one eye.' Grauwin wrote:

> So I had to send back to their fighting positions hundreds of wounded who were well on the way to being cured – abdominal cases, amputations, limbs in plaster, muscular wounds, thorax wounds and those who had lost an eye. Nearly all these were wounded a second time, and I am sure that a third of them were killed in the blockhouses in the course of the final week.

Occasionally there were lapses in the ground attacks from the Viet Minh, sometimes lasting up to two weeks, because of their own heavy losses. And then, thousands of fresh soldiers would arrive, swarming over the hills and through the trees and into the trenches that were encroaching ever closer to the French positions.

Another of the remarkable heroics that occurred at Dien Bien Phu was the arrival of the parachutists who descended in waves from the Legion's 2BEP on 10 April to join their comrades of 1BEP which had been the mobile reserve from the beginning and had taken heavy losses. With them came 750 legionnaires from the 3rd and 5th Regiments who had to parachute into the action, although most of them had no previous para training. Many died on the way down. By then, the drop zone was small as the main body of French troops retreated further into their compound, and many paras floated outside and into Viet Minh lines. They were shot as they came down, or were slaughtered as they became entangled in trees.

There were sufficient numbers, however, to launch a counter-offensive, spearheaded by 2BEP. Again, the paras were repulsed and took heavy losses under the continuing artillery fire. There were enough survivors of 2BEP for a combined attack to recover two remaining defensive positions. In a pitched battle in which the French were met by 3,000 Viet Minh, the paras stood their ground in fierce hand-to-hand fighting. Once again, the dead of both sides were counted in their hundreds. On the night of 7 May, the surviving troops of the French had been pushed back into a desolate, body-strewn patch pitted with smoking craters in the centre of Dien Bien Phu, and one remaining Legion outpost, codenamed Isabelle, remained.

Word of the French collapse came in a dramatic radio report to Hanoi from the French commander Brigadier General Christian de Castries:

> After twenty hours of fighting without respite, including hand-to-hand fighting, the enemy has infiltrated the whole centre. We are out of ammunition. We can no longer do anything, but we will not surrender. The Viet Minh are now within a few metres from the radio transmitter where I am speaking. They are everywhere. I have told the Legion gunners at Isabelle to open fire on this command post with their heavy artillery if the enemy break through.

A few moments later, the radio went dead. Around 350 Legion survivors at Isabelle attempted to battle their way out and escape into the jungle. Fewer than 100 reached French lines. The siege of Dien Bien

Phu, in which the French had endured fifty-five days of sheer hell, was over. The battle cost them more than 6,000 killed, and all but a handful of the remainder of the 16,000 who came to Dien Bien Phu were wounded, missing or taken prisoner. The Viet Minh suffered far higher losses; some estimates put their dead at 12,000. That day, French radio stations played solemn music; all theatres and cinemas were closed and those citizens who had turned their backs on the Legion and the colonial forces who bore the brunt of this war had already begun to feel guilt, if not pain.

On 21 July 1954, the two sides met under international mediation in Geneva, to agree a pact formally ending the Indo-China war. The nation of Vietnam would be split in two. Ho Chi Minh would become president of the Republic of North Vietnam while the south would remain under Emperor Bao Dai. In Washington, Senator Knowland, Republican leader of the US Senate, said: 'We may live to regret that such an agreement has been forced upon the French.'

14

1954: ALGERIA GROWS RESTLESS

'The boot, or perhaps a fist landing in the solar plexus,
directed the recruit's attention to what the sergeant
was saying.'

WHEN WORD of the disaster in Indo-China
reached Legion headquarters in Algeria, the remaining force assembled
on the parade ground at Sidi-bel-Abbès. The Legion had lost 10,000 men
in the nine-year struggle, with thousands more still in the rotting hell of
Viet Minh prison camps. Officers and other ranks stood bolt upright to
attention as the Legion trumpets sounded *Aux Morts*, and their commanding officer, Colonel Jean Gardy, read the eulogy to the fallen:

> We are gathered here to commemorate the heroes who were
> lost in epic combat. Let us present the colours of our units
> who have disappeared in battle ... the 13th Demi-Brigade along
> with its service units and 1st and 3rd Battalions, the 1st and 2nd
> Legion Infantry, the 1st and 2nd Legion Parachute Battalions, the
> mortar companies of the 3rd and 5th Regiments and the coura-
> geous non-para volunteers from other Foreign Legion units dropped
> into the fortress during the siege.

Seldom had there been such emotion as the Legion band played *Le*

Boudin. Gardy's voice faltered as he read the eulogy; he, the senior officer and before long to become Inspector General of the Legion, took
several minutes to recover his composure.

In the weeks and months ahead, the war zones, the French bases and
hospitals in Vietnam were cleared, the injured survivors brought home
and the prisoners released under the truce agreements. Frail and shattered men came back and for a few months, the Legion was quietly
licking its wounds, fattening up those who chose to continue Legion
service, as many did, and beginning the process of rebuilding its decimated and weakened regiments with new recruits. Barely had they
begun the process, however, when the shout went up: '*Come on you
bastards . . . pull yourselves together. There's another war . . .*'

Inspired by the communists' success in Vietnam, Ahmed Ben Bella,
a former sergeant in the French army, and eight other Algerian
revolutionaries in hiding in Cairo, formed what was to become known
as the *Front de Libération Nationale* (FLN). On 1 November 1954, it
launched its first strike in the campaign for Algerian independence,
killing six Europeans in the remote Aures mountains. It was the
beginning of yet another catastrophic chapter in the turmoil of French
colonialism. After more than a century of haphazard and often
uncontrolled administration of its overseas territories, the French
dream of a huge and glorious empire was incontrovertibly collapsing
around their ears. The jewel in their crown, Algeria, with its vast
natural resources of oil and minerals and historical connections, would
be next to sail away. It had been a province of France since 1936 and a
colony since 1836. As such, when the native population began to rise
up, the French government sent in their troops as a 'police action' to
quell subversives, protect French sovereignty and the 1.5 million
European settlers.

The revolutionary council of the FLN did not see it as such and, in
David and Goliath style, put its tiny *Armée de Libération Nationale* on
a war footing. Beginning with just a few thousand men trained in
Egypt and given sanctuary in Tunisia (which the French were also giving up to home rule) the ALN grew to a force of 50,000 men, better
armed and equipped and more organized than the Arabs and Berbers
the Legion had been fighting in North Africa, on and off, for more

than a century. They were deployed in a region whose landscape, like Indo-China, strongly favoured guerrilla tactics, beyond even the hammer blows of an eventual French force of 350,000 troops.

In a confrontation lasting from 1954 to 1962, the dead were again counted in their tens of thousands. Violence, torture and murder on a huge scale came from what developed into a three-handed action of Arabs, anti-nationalists and French troops, eventually striking at the very heart of the mainland and in the process bringing France to the brink of civil war, and the Foreign Legion to the point of total disbandment.

The race to bolster the Legion's depleted effective fighting force began immediately the ALN launched its first attack. The parachute regiments which would, with French regular para units, form the back-bone of the forthcoming engagement with the Algerian nationalists, were most in need of revitalization. The Legion's 1st para regiment, known as 1REP, was based at Zeralda, a superb barracks close to Algiers, while 2REP was stationed at Philippeville, on the Mediter-ranean coast close to the Tunisian frontier. The training facilities first established to provide a rapid reaction force for the Indo-China war were upgraded and expanded, while all other aspects of training remained firmly in line with Legion traditions.

The need to produce fresh fighting units in double-quick time seems also to have produced the side-effect of a far more heavy-handed regime than had been the case in recent times.

Jim Worden was an unusual recruit to the Legion, because of his age. He was almost 40 when he stepped through the portals of the recruiting office at the Chateau Vincennes in Paris, hankering after a life he had experienced years earlier as an RAF pilot in World War II. Forty is push-ing it, but not only did he withstand the rigours of training as a legion-naire, he went on to raise his profile even higher as a member of the elite 2REP. Worden became one of the Legion's characters of the time, renowned for his card schools, an expert poker player and one who cre-ated something of a record in the Legion by going his whole service without serving a term in prison, not an easy feat. In typical tongue-in-cheek mode, with the smirk masking the seriousness of any situation, Worden described his early days in the Legion with sardonic wit. Like everyone else in those times, he had gone through the acceptance stage in Paris, boarded the ferry to Oran and attempted to comprehend the commands of a band of NCOs who between them knew about as much English as he knew French, which in his words was 'absolutely zilch'. He went on:

With the inevitable aid of the boot brought into contact with the arse, it took only three months to memorize enough French nouns to identify by name each and every item in the barrack block and the contents of my very large kitbag. I could name each piece of the weapons which required instant recall of twenty-seven different parts. However, despite having an exceedingly sore arse, I was still unsure whether or not it was correct to say *'la bayonette'* or *'le bayonette'*. Each time I was questioned on this piece of weaponry (which during the whole of my service, was used only for removing the top from a bottle of beer, opening a can of food or probing for suspected mines), if I replied to Instructor A *'le bayonette'*, I received a swift boot but when questioned about the same item by Instructor B, and I responded *'la bayonette'*, I received yet another swift boot! Nothing was more frustrating when, at a later date, I was asked by a German sergeant to identify the object he was holding aloft in his hand and, remembering my previous errors, responded *'ein bayonette'*. That cost me a further boot plus four days fatigues. This, as the good sergeant explained, was for speaking pidgin German.

The boot, or perhaps a fist landing in the solar plexus causing the knees to buckle and the body to slither slowly to the ground whereupon it would be raised again by a sharp kick to the arse, directed the recruit's attention to what the sergeant was saying, in a language he could not understand. This method of tuition was varied occasionally by requests from the instructors for the recruit to demonstrate the number of press-ups it was possible to complete prior to total collapse. On commencement of the instruction, most recruits as unfit as myself – there were not all that many – would normally collapse after a nominal ten.

Nothing was more astonishing at the completion of my training than to find I could complete fifty, and further, that at the same time I could sing the Legion song *Le Boudin*. There was an alternative to the ordinary press-ups, probably devised by a sadist. This was to complete the same exercise *avec musique*. This did not require the recruit to sing, merely to demonstrate the agility to clap his hands between each press-up, while in the prone position. Unless the recruit is extremely proficient at this, his face strikes the ground before the hands prevent impact. This could become more difficult, and somewhat of a handicap, whilst wearing a rucsac on your back. But, if your instructor was of a sympathetic nature, he would not insist that the rucsac be filled with rocks; very few were sympathetic.

I think it was the bruising of many Legion recruits' faces, caused by their inefficiency at carrying out these press-ups *avec musique*, consequently allowing their faces to strike the ground repeatedly, that gave rise to the vile rumours that they had been beaten up by their corporals and sergeants. A Legion recruit can, of course, always take action against his sergeant or corporal should he wish. If the recruit objects to receiving a kick up the arse or a smack across the mouth, and the recruit is fairly tall and considers it anti-social to be treated in such a manner by a diminutive little shit of a corporal, he has the option of challenging the corporal to a fight on 'equal' terms. Whereupon, even if it be in the middle of the parade ground, the corporal instructor will remove his jacket and gleefully pound the dumb recruit near to death. It is thus that he demonstrates to the other recruits, all of whom have equal opportunity of challenging him but who have been sensibly discreet, the value of the Legion's training in unarmed combat, and the advisability for all in the future of carrying out his slightest wishes.

Meanwhile, the dumb recruit who has been damn near beaten to death, resigns himself to the fact that a bruised arse is much better than a mouth without any teeth. (I was once that dumb recruit.) Basic training in the Foreign Legion must have been a regular subject for discussion in the sergeants' mess to discover new ways of providing entertainment for the poor bloody recruits. And like all

The certificate 'Commando Guyane' awarded to Carl ('Jacko') Jackson.

Legionnaires leaving for the Front, September 1914.

Legionnaires in action in North Africa during World War II.

A typical camp fire scene of legionnaires on patrol.

Waiting for action: inside their tented city during the Gulf War, 1991.

The Camerone hacienda near Puebla, Mexico, where the Legion fought one of its greatest battles.

BELOW Members of the Foreign Legion Association of Great Britain commemorate Camerone Day in 1998. Legion veteran Jim Worden (centre) is presented with an Illuminated Address for his service to the Foreign Legion.

senior NCOs at Legion training establishments, being of a kind and loving nature, these sergeants would have been discussing ways to eliminate the recruit's homesickness, like perhaps making him walk barefoot on broken glass or crawl through a roll of barbed wire instead of under it. However, they were limited by the rules. General Rollet, father of the Legion, as far back as 1925, laid down a code of conduct concerning the treatment of subordinates. The problem was that General Rollet had died during World War II and some of the bastards had thrown away the code of conduct.

On the nightly inspections of our barracks, for example, there was only one safe place to be and that was in bed. If you were not sleeping, act your heart out and pretend to be asleep. Only two men were required to be suitably dressed and standing to attention at the entrance of the inspecting sergeant. One was the *chef de chambre*, the corporal in charge of the room, the other the *garde chambre*, the poor slob responsible for the cleanliness of the room that day who took the kicks if an inspecting sergeant happened to find a piece of fly shit on the table. The legionnaires would be safely sleeping (or acting) like thirty-five corpses, their individual *paquetage* [kit] spotlessly clean and meticulously arranged on the shelf above their heads. Their knife, fork and spoon brilliantly polished and standing to attention, boots cleaned, beneath the beds, fully laced and also standing to attention. Then the inspecting sergeant would make his slow tour around the room. If he was Spanish and there happened to be two Spanish recruits in the room, the only sound that would be heard would be that of the Spanish recruits beautifully arranged *paquetage* being thrown the length of the room. If they happened to be sleeping (or acting), near a window, then out it went. If the inspecting sergeant happened to be Italian, and there were Italian recruits in the room – boom! – the same treatment. In my room were twenty-two German recruits. After a visit by a German sergeant, it took no longer than a couple of hours groping around by candlelight for the troops to identify their possessions and remake their *paquetage* for *reveille* the next morning. Such demonstrations were obviously to prove that national favouritism was non-existent. For almost two months I was the happiest recruit for there were no

British sergeants. But those evil sods in the sergeants' mess had obviously got their heads together and decided that they would become naturalized Englishmen, lest I felt lonely. I had my *paquetage* tossed out of the window ten days in a row until they had all had their turn. The remainder of the room had ten nights of peace. This is only to emphasize that the main qualifications for a sergeant in the Foreign Legion is to have a mother but no father.

I survived the three months at Saïda, and was relieved to discover I had been passed for specialist training at Sidi-bel-Abbès. My relief turned to shock. It was like standing outside the gates of Heaven, taking a step forward and finding yourself in Hell. I would have settled for the infantry. I'd have settled for anything, even a transfer to the Salvation Army, rather than that bastion of the Legion, Sidi-bel-Abbès.

The stories I had been told by many veteran legionnaires of its discipline and regimentation, and of it being a short-cut to the road heading for 'Company Discipline', the 'Penal Battalion' and even 'Devil's Island', did nothing to make me feel anything less than dejected. I was not a young boy easily influenced by stories exaggerated out of all proportion to the truth, but a doubt was nagging at my mind as I recalled the favourite expression of my granny, 'Where there's smoke, there's fire'. Sidi-bel-Abbès was decidedly not my idea of 'home from home'.

The above, Worden points out, is factually accurate and told as it happened. It was merely the Sunday School, a flippant taste of the proper stuff which was to come later when he joined the parachute regiment. In the meantime, there was a war going on and Worden and his pals in the infantry were soon in the thick of it. Two types of warfare confronted legionnaires in their skirmishes with the ALN or the Fell as they were more readily known. In the towns and cities, the nationalists made indiscriminate use of plastic explosives, planted in hotels, bars, shops and even schools. The devices were often transported by the female elements of the ALN and planted at targets in busy areas of the European sectors. Outrage followed outrage, and there was no discrimination among the dead, men, women and children.

The second 'front' was in the hills and the mountains of Algeria where the Fell used hit-and-run tactics against the European settlers and the French military. Most of the Legion forces along with the specialist regular para units of the French army spent weeks at a time out on patrol tracking down and, according to Worden, 'exterminating those Fell who had entered Algeria through the frontiers of Tunisia or Morocco'. He went on:

Firefights with the Fell were not a daily occurrence. Tracking them down and getting them to fight was exceedingly difficult. The vast undulating landscape provided brilliant cover for them, and for us when we chose to use it. Our missions were 'search and destroy' and that meant a hell of a lot of marching, and some of it in a near vertical direction over the never-ending mountain ranges which, incidentally, are also some of the most beautiful scenery in the world.

Although I served in a company of the regiment and within that company as part of a section, my only close acquaintances were those members of my own *equipe* – a small team of five men.

It would be rare indeed if a group of more than a dozen or perhaps twenty Fell were ever encountered. Then, after a few bursts of fire, they would disappear into the wilderness having tried to inflict as many casualties as possible. They had learned the tactics of the guerrilla well: hit hard, hit quick and run like hell. Usually, the first indication of Fell in the area would be when one of your comrades had fallen to the ground with a look of surprise on his face. *Then* would come the sound of the shot.

The Legion units would commence their unified and meticulous tracking and extermination tactics. The only time we got the chance to shoot first was when we set up the ambushes, often at night. It was a scene to behold. The ambush was usually set up along the side of a track used by the Fell, just before we prepared to bed down for the night. We always assumed that although we had not seen 'them' during the day, 'they' may well have been tracking us. There was nothing more embarrassing for five legionnaires setting up an ambush to be ambushed themselves. It happened. Rules of conduct were: select your own place and make sure you know the location of the rest of the team; no smoking – cough during the night and the man nearest to you had permission to cut your throat. Then the final injunction from the *Chef d'equipe*, 'For the love of God, don't shoot in my direction'.

Challenges on ambushes were a thing of the past. Words of the instructors rang in the ears of legionnaires: 'Shoot the bastards as they approach, or else you'll end up shooting each other'. Kill or be killed.

Shooting the enemy at close range at night without moonlight when one can distinguish neither face nor outline brings no qualms of conscience or guilt. It can be likened to the shooting of an inanimate object. The later check and body count actually brought a sense of disappointment if only one dead body was on the track. Gratitude came from the fact that he was dead and not wounded, thus foregoing the usual mouthful of abuse from your *chef d'equipe* for being a lousy shot. In daytime, between the fruitless searches, boredom set in after you had reflected upon the training you had received, and how bloody glad you were that those bastards had made you fit and unfeeling. Who can you cry to? No one. You do the business, or you shoot yourself, or you run away. Once, after such a day, I recorded in my journal that a young sergeant deserted while we were in the hills near the Tunisian frontier. He had been foolish enough to have taken his weapon with him. The rules were strict on this; he must be traced. If intercepted by the Fell, his weapon would be used to kill other legionnaires. He himself would have welcomed death if caught, because they were not kindly people. His own section was sent to find him and bring him back. This they did. He foolishly opened fire as they approached and was consequently killed. They then had the onerous task of carrying his body back as evidence of the completion of their mission. The rucsack of the sergeant contained his letters, family photographs, a slab of chocolate purchased from a *souk* and a spare water bottle. He had therefore planned his departure. When offered, I declined to share the chocolate.

I also wrote in my journal of 'Black Thursday' and the reluctant

Fell. I witnessed the incident only because I had escorted a lieutenant from my own section situated two kilometres away. A group of a dozen Fell had been intercepted by members of the 5th Company, and three of them had been killed in the fight. In the first flurry of fire, the remainder had thrown down their weapons and surrendered. Prisoners in the almost inaccessible heights of Algeria can be neither fed nor watered. Nor did the rules of the Geneva Convention apply between the Fell and their enemy, which was us. Captured legionnaires would pray for death to come swiftly. After being interrogated, for which purpose my lieutenant had come, the captured Fell were searched and relieved of all their possessions. Looking somewhat dejected and miserable, they sat crouching and squatting about ten metres away, their hands firmly clasped on their heads. No effort was made at guarding them. The section responsible for their capture was sitting drinking coffee, and I was invited to join them. The section sergeant approached the Fell and told them to piss off, but none showed any inclination to depart, despite his repeated shouts, and it required none too gentle kicks even to get them on their feet. Then, rather reluctantly, they began to edge away. None of the legionnaires sitting drinking had a weapon in his hands; all were only interested in making the most of the break offered. At a distance of thirty to forty metres, the poor bloody Fell broke into a panic-ridden stampede for what they mistakenly thought would be their freedom. Without even standing up, the group of legionnaires with whom I had been sitting simply picked up the weapons lying by their sides and opened fire. None of the Fell survived. None gained a greater distance than sixty metres. All were reported as killed whilst trying to escape.

I had not taken part in the shooting. That was not because of my high principles as an Englishman. John, whom I had joined, was far more English than me. He had higher principles and had demonstrated them, and his marksmanship, by shooting with only his right hand, while still holding firmly on to his coffee with his left. I had not opened fire because it was not my party, and I had not been invited to shoot. I was happy that I had not participated in the pigeon shoot, and I slept well that night.

Yet another incident recorded in my journal: a legionnaire who had deserted from the 13th Demi-Brigade almost six months earlier. He was picked up by one of the sections who had intercepted some Fell. He had been with the enemy for the whole period since his absence from the Legion. He was court-martialled, prosecuted and defended by the same captain within thirty minutes of being captured. All legionnaires were called close to witness the execution which was carried out by the same captain. He was made to kneel, given two minutes to make his peace with God and shot in the back of the head with a revolver.

The bodies of the Fell were never buried, at any time, but the concession to this ex-legionnaire was that at least he was buried, albeit in an unmarked grave. He had been a fool, he had made a mistake, he had been executed, but he was buried by his family. At one time he had been a legionnaire – one of us.

15

1957–1961: ALGERIAN REBELLION

'They were split into four teams deployed to assassinate
de Gaulle during his visit, on the basis that one out of the
four would surely succeed.'

THE DEATH toll on both sides mounted. Cities
were under attack from the ALN's urban guerrillas and Algiers, once the
most beautiful of North African capitals, became an ugly place in mood
and appearance. In 1956, the French Socialist Premier, Guy Mollet,
sent for General Raoul Salan, a 56-year-old white-haired veteran of a
dozen French wars. Pinned to his chest were thirty-six decorations for
military action. Mollet told him: 'Get us out of this'. The third hand in
the bloody Algerian war came into play. The European settlers were
convinced Salan came on a sell-out ticket to smooth the way for independence, and within two months of his arrival in Algiers one of their
leaders, Philippe Castille, tried to assassinate him with a bazooka. But
Salan was definitely on the side of the settlers – of keeping Algeria
French. About a quarter of the settlers were of French origin. The rest
were descendants of immigrants from Spain, Italy, Sicily, Greece,
Malta, Corsica and other parts of the Mediterranean area.

Out of this melting pot emerged the '*Pieds Noirs*', or 'Black Feet',
supposedly because most of their ancestors had arrived without shoes.
They stood apart from the French in style and attitude, combining
Italian exuberance with Sicilian guile and Spanish poise. As instructed,

Salan cracked down hard on the Algerian nationalists. He brought in the 10th Paratroop Division to which was added the Legion's own 1REP and 2REP. They were engaged on two fronts: in the towns, predominantly Algiers; and in the hinterland and the regions close to the borders with Tunisia and Morocco. The ALN's urban campaign was hard to counter.

The ALN brought a reign of terror to Algiers. In January 1957, twenty people were killed and dozens injured by three ALN bombs in the busy shopping streets of the capital. The next weekend, another twenty-eight were blown up. In the same month, a rowdy general strike by the Algerian nationalists brought a brisk and robust response from General Jacques Massu, in charge of the 10th Paratroop Division. He was ordered by the civilian governor to restore order by 'whatever means necessary', and did so by turning out 3,000 heavily armed troops at dawn the next day. They flooded the streets of Algiers' Arab districts and threw a ring of barbed wire around the Casbah, home to around 100,000 Muslims, from where the bombers launched their missions. The paras patrolled in groups, searching houses, forcing employees of the utility companies back to work at gunpoint. Anyone who resisted was arrested or if they had a weapon, shot. There were ample claims of unprovoked violence and widespread torture by the paras among the 2,000 taken captive to get information about the enemy. In Paris, left-wingers who supported the Algerian nationalists screamed blue murder. From then on, and for the next four years, the bomb attacks were seldom out of the headlines and very soon it moved into its three-handed stage, when the *Pieds Noirs* set up their own militia.

In the spring of 1958, the legionnaires of 1REP took heavy losses in action. In a four-month campaign of almost continuous fighting in Algiers, the Sahara and north towards the coast, they killed or captured more than 2,000 Fell, while 1REP itself lost 123 dead and 350 wounded out of a force of 1,200. Among them was 1REP's commander, one of the Legion's heroes and an immensely popular and respected veteran, Lieutenant Colonel Pierre Jeanpierre. He had been commander of the Regiment for fourteen months, since February 1957, and had been engaged in action ever since. A founder of the

French Resistance, a former prisoner of war, and latterly the collector of many medals for bravery in Indo-China, his helicopter was shot down by smallarms fire while scanning Fell positions. His death was deeply mourned by the Regiment, and it was a watershed in the resolve of its officers to throw their weight behind the cause of defeating the nationalists and retaining Algeria as a possession of France.

The ratio of casualties in these battles strongly favoured the Legion paras but it was, as Tony Geraghty pointed out, no slaughter of the innocents. The Fell were masterly in combat and even better at choosing their battlefield, which invariably put the legionnaires in a defensive position. But the Legion had superior weaponry, including artillery and napalm, and better mobility with the fleets of helicopters at their disposal. More often than not, the Fell continued to win the deadly game of hide-and-seek.

French troops in the field were increased and on the borders, east and west, with Morocco and Tunisia, massive fortifications were built, manned by legionnaires to try to stop the Fell coming into Algeria by way of those two countries. Britisher Simon Murray, one of Jim Worden's friends when they came together in 2REP, was detailed to a patrol on the Tunisian side. He described them as:

> an amazing sight ... a network of barbed wire and mines which run from the northern coast the full length of the Algerian frontier with Tunisia, deep into the Sahara in the south. On the western borders of Algeria, a similar barrage runs along the frontier with Morocco.

The Arabs frequently broke through the barrages by using bangalores – long tubes stuffed with explosives fed under the wire. When they exploded, they set off the mines and cut a way through. They then quickly dispersed into the hills. Legion patrols tried to anticipate where they would break through then ambush them. Murray also described a typical 'day of action'. They had begun first thing in the morning, on a patrol in the Chelia mountains in the east of Algeria. There were three companies out in the peaks, and 2nd Company came under fire. Reinforcements for the paras arrived within minutes by helicopter, and as they came in machine-gun fire and hand grenades exploded around the landing zone. Attempts were made to drop a company on the hill where the Arabs were installed, but as it came down a burst of machine-gun fire sprayed the sides. The chopper managed to get away, but not before one man had jumped and found himself alone against a hail of enemy fire. He had five hand grenades on his webbing and by throwing them in every direction, dashed for cover until he could be rescued. 2nd Company took a bad hit in the first barrage of Arab fire: five men killed and fifteen wounded. One of them, a sergeant, met a particularly horrific end when a bullet exploded a hand grenade hanging from his webbing and blew him to pieces. That day, after a succession of firefights in the hills, fifty-three Arabs lay dead. 'There were no prisoners today,' Murray commented, 'Geneva's hands do not soothe insults at this distance, and the feeling is mutual.'

The Legion counted nine dead and thirty wounded. Arms captured from the Arabs included twenty sub-machine-guns, half a dozen light machine-guns, Brens and German '42s, and several rifles. As they were coming in, helicopter spotters radioed a sighting of three Arabs 100 yards ahead of the line.

Once again the sound of machine-guns echoed across the hills as the company leaders fired off in the direction of the enemy. In the bushes were three young Arabs, riddled with bullets. They were well equipped: two Enfield rifles and a British Sten gun, binoculars, compasses, and good boots. In their *musettes* they each had shaving kit, a toothbrush and a blanket. The bodies were left where they lay, minus their weapons and the new boots, the latter being purloined by one of the legionnaires. What happened next was perhaps the most gruesome part of an already bloodstained day.

Down in the valley, Murray's company came upon a section of the 13th Demi-Brigade who told them an intelligence officer of the *Deuxième Bureau* was interested in the Arabs they had just shot in the hills. They were currently searching for Arab regulars of a French colonial unit who had shot and killed their officers in a mountain fort and deserted with large amounts of stores and weapons. Murray's section leader was ordered to send three volunteers back to the cadavers and remove their heads for possible identification. Murray and two others were sent on the mission. One of them, Dornach:

> ... got to work on the heads with a small, sharp penknife, cutting across the necks. I was numb inside and felt nothing as I watched Dornach hack away, with bloodied hands, like something out of *Macbeth*. He didn't turn a hair and could well have been skinning a rabbit.

They retrieved only two heads, as the third was so shot up as to be unrecognizable. They returned to base where the *Deuxième* officer had arrived to photograph the heads, illuminated by the headlights of a Jeep, and then Murray was told to dispose of them. He did so carrying them by their blood-soaked hair, one in each hand, and throwing them into the bushes. The climax of Murray's story is:

> There then followed an incident that I will recall to my dying day with a shudder. Some Spaniards in the 2nd Section had prepared a cauldron of soup for their supper, and there appeared to be plenty left ... so they called over a German and invited him to fill his tin mug. Just as he was about to put the cup to his lips one of the Spaniards, with a mighty guffaw, reached his hand into the cauldron and pulled out one of the Arab's heads by its hair. The Spaniard stood there with the ghastly head, dripping soup, while the German stood aghast, white as a sheet, frozen for a second, and then promptly turned and threw up. This gave rise to another guffaw from the Spaniard and his chums. There is no accounting for people's 'sense of humour'.

The awfulness of life in the wilds of Algiers ran parallel with the fiasco of leadership and collapsing governments in Paris. Three administrations in as many years came and went until the chaotic Fourth Republic entered its final death throes. The war in Algeria edged towards its triple-sided catastrophe. The settlers still jeered at Salan as the 'republican general' but in private talks with the Europeans, he surprised them all by announcing he was on their side. On 13 May, after three French prisoners had been executed for their crimes, 40,000 *Pieds-Noirs* took matters into their own hands and stormed government buildings in Algiers. General Salan went public and, in an emotional speech from the balcony of the Forum, announced: 'Algerians, I am one of you. I have provisionally taken into my hands the destiny of French Algeria.' He concluded his speech with '*Vive de Gaulle!* The crowd, like Salan, believed only De Gaulle could keep Algeria French, and broke into pandemonium.

The *Pieds Noirs* formed their own militia under the guise of a Public Safety Committee, and General Massu, still head of 10 Para, made his own remarkable declaration: 'The Army is behind you.' He became chairman of the committee and by his own position had allied the paras with the settlers of Algeria. To the Legion's 1REP, it was like a bond of blood-brotherhood. They were already spiritually tied to Algeria and the Legion graveyards were full of their dead. But it went much deeper – a regiment of men following a collection of officers who believed that for the honour of France, the sell-out of Algeria was one humiliation too many. All the lands they had sacrificed their men for – Indo-China, Morocco, Tunisia – had now all been given back or lost. They were not going to let it happen in Algeria. The air now was filled with heavy politics, a revolution against the revolution.

De Gaulle became Premier of France in June 1958, and President upon the inauguration of the Fifth Republic in December. To the Algerian settlers and to the generals who wanted Algeria to remain French, he proved a bitter disappointment. In the months ahead, he spoke more and more of Algeria's self-determination, and even of a ceasefire with the ALN and the release of prisoners. Then came what the *Pieds Noirs* saw as one more betrayal. To their disgust, General Salan was recalled to Paris by de Gaulle who rightly believed that he was an obstacle to a settlement with the nationalists. A year or so later, General Massu, head of 10 Paratroop Division, was moved away to Metz after giving a newspaper interview stating he would not necessarily obey orders to fire on *Pieds Noirs*. Soon afterwards, Salan's replacement as supreme commander, General Maurice Challe, was also removed and left the service but, like Salan, had no intention of quitting the Algerian cause. Salan himself retired in 1960 and was soon delivering flaming speeches, urging war veterans 'to take justice into your own hands'.

The following month, July 1960, one of the senior commanders of 1REP was at the heart of a plot to capture and imprison President de Gaulle on Bastille Day. The plan was aborted only because the Paris end of the conspiracy was not ready to proceed. In October, Salan eluded Gaullist security guards assigned to watch him, and slipped across the border to Spain. From a Madrid hotel room, he set up links with co-conspirators in Algiers and other anti-Gaullist exiles joined his court. Every day, at noon, Salan phoned his wife Lucienne, living with their daughter Dominique in the Salan villa in Algiers. Meanwhile, de Gaulle's plans to give Algeria its independence were moving irrevocably towards conclusion.

In December 1960, it was announced that de Gaulle would tour Algeria, including the Legion headquarters at Sidi-bel-Abbès, to explain that there was no going back. Two days before his arrival, a handful of legionnaires led by Lieutenant Roger Degueldre and his right-hand man, a tough Yugoslav, Sergeant Bobby Dovecar, absented themselves from the Legion's 1REP headquarters at Zerelda, taking six others with them. They were split into four teams deployed to assassinate de Gaulle during his visit, on the basis that one out of the four would surely succeed. They were foiled, however, when de Gaulle's security advisers changed his itinerary and his routes at the last minute, and cut Algiers from the schedule completely.

From that moment, the countdown to a rebellion, a mutiny and an attempted *coup d'état* had begun, starting out in the streets of Algiers where the *Pieds Noirs* extremists clashed with the FLN; 120 people were killed. In January 1961, a referendum gave de Gaulle a massive majority for Algerian independence. Coded messages were flying between Salan and his co-conspirators in Paris, Algiers and Madrid. Rumours flew in equal profusion and even the FLN warned Paris of talk of a *coup d'état*. De Gaulle had dispatched plane-loads of intelligence officers to monitor the situation but the possibility of insurrection led by French generals seemed to have been discounted. But it was already at an advanced stage of planning. Although by no means exclusively Legion based, officers and men of 1REP provided the core of its proposed military strength.

In late January 1961, the OAS, the secret army organization founded the previous November, opened its account by assassinating a liberal *Pieds Noirs* lawyer. Roger Degueldre and other more senior militants were forcing the pace, and demanding action. At last, the putsch generals put the plotters on alert and they themselves gathered in Algiers on the night of 20 April under the leadership of General Maurice Challe himself. At 1.30 a.m. a plane touched down at Maison Blanche airport, outside Algiers, and out stepped Raoul Salan. Rushing to his villa in Hydra, Salan kissed his wife, put on his uniform and all thirty-six of his decorations. They were ready to move. Salan joined Generals Challe, André Zeller and Edmond Jouhaud, who were to lead the putsch attempt in Algeria. Soon after midnight, the commanding officer of 10 Paratroop Division, General Saint Hillier, a loyal Gaullist, was placed under arrest.

At the same time, 1REP was mustered at its Zerelda barracks. The legionnaires were informed that General Challe was assuming military control of Algeria and all appropriate buildings were to be secured by the Legion paras, supported by other military units, taking certain key targets during the night, such as the radio station, *gendarmerie*, civil government buildings and the principal military headquarters. The action was no surprise to the men of 1REP. Many were apprehensive, but all moved out in the convoys, joined by paras of two other regiments of 10 Para. They quickly achieved their targets without opposition, except from an army sergeant guarding the radio station. He was shot. By dawn, the first phase of the putsch was complete and the *Pieds Noirs* gleefully broadcast the news that French Algeria was saved. The settlers swarmed on to the streets.

By mid-day, the generals' euphoria was descending into deep gloom. The rebellion had gone well in Algiers; all key targets had been taken except the telephone exchange, which meant that those loyal to de Gaulle were in constant contact. But the only support they could definitely count on was from *some* of the officers and men of the paras. The rest of the armed forces in Algeria were either in opposition or sitting on the fence. The man whom they most expected would join them, Colonel Albert Brothier, of the Legion's high command, refused. Although simultaneously expressing some sympathy with the officers of 1REP, he kept the main forces of the Legion out of it. Furthermore, the great swathe of military leaders they had hoped would fall in behind them for a bloodless *coup d'etat* hadn't materialized.

In Paris, de Gaulle moved swiftly and declared a State of Emergency. Fearing an airborne invasion by the para units from Algeria at any moment, he mustered a scratch army, 10,000 strong, made up of republican guards and CRS riot police. They were deployed to strategic points in the city and Sherman tanks moved to surround the Presidential Palace. The two Paris airports were blocked by military trucks and buses and de Gaulle ordered an immediate sea blockade of Algeria. Eight generals on the French mainland whom he believed might join the plotters were arrested. It was still doubtful if the little army could withstand an attack by 3,000 crack paratroopers and, unsure of the extent of the rebellion, de Gaulle made an emotional broadcast to the nation. 'French men and women ... I appeal to you ... help me', he said. 'In the name of France I order all means, I repeat, all means to bar the route to these men until they are defeated.' He laid into the quartet of retired generals behind the threat to the republic as 'prejudiced, ambitious and fanatical'.

Challe and Salan spent the next twenty-four hours on the telephone, attempting to persuade senior figures in the military to join them. As the hours wore on, it became apparent that it wasn't going to happen. Legion commanders at Sidi-bel-Abbès refused to talk to Challe's emissary. Both the Air Force and the Navy were confrontational in their response. Navy chiefs sent a French cruiser to a spot one mile offshore and ranged its 16-inch guns on the 1REP base at Zerelda. Air Force generals ordered all transport planes based in Algeria into the air and once airborne their pilots were given instructions to fly to France. They put their fighter squadrons on alert and warned that they would shoot down any aircraft attempting to land paras on the Champs Elysees.

The Air Force decision was relayed directly to Challe, who had insisted all along that the *coup* should be without bloodshed. It was the final straw, and he collapsed. Salan made a last effort to keep the Revolt of the Generals going, again by addressing the crowds from a balcony overlooking the Forum, where a supercharged Algiers mob was screaming that it had been betrayed. Salan's words could not be heard; someone had cut the microphone wires. In one last attempt, one of the rebel officers, Captain Pierre Sergent, went to the radio station and made a broadcast calling upon all soldiers of the French army to support the cause and live up to their responsibilities. There was no response, not even from other Legion regiments. The rebellion had run its course.

At dawn, a newsman asked Salan if he were going to surrender. Curtly the general answered, 'No!' Weeping, Lucienne Salan tied a silk scarf about her husband's neck in a farewell gesture. Generals Challe and Zeller surrendered themselves, and several others returned to France as prisoners. Legionnaires of 1REP returned to their base at Zeralda and set fire to all records and blew up three rooms. Generals Salan and Jouhaud, with 180 deserters from the 1st Foreign Legion Paratroop Regiment, disappeared into the underground. The barracks were surrounded and the remainder of 1REP were taken away in trucks and buses, singing the Edith Piaf song, *Je ne regrette rien!* while the *Pieds Noirs* threw flowers in their path. The Regiment was disbanded instantly. Officers who had joined the putsch were taken into custody, some legionnaires were discharged, others were dispersed into other regiments.

Soon afterwards, General Salan broke his silence with a press statement – he was now chief of the Secret Army Organization, the OAS. Lieutenant Roger Degueldre and his Legion sidekick, Sergeant Bobby Dovecar, who along with others had deserted 1REP on 11 April, were also to play leading roles, running Commando Delta, the operational wing of the OAS, manned by between forty and fifty men, mainly Legion deserters, most of whom were German.

They were to become, as events would soon prove, the bombers, the snipers, the assassins in the OAS terrorist war, while above them was a larger army of all-embracing anti-Gaullists, ranging from *Pieds Noirs* activists, the National Front and even a group of French monarchists who supplied volunteers to the cause. Ahead lay months of turmoil, and thousands more deaths at the hands of both nationalists and the OAS, and from Degueldre's assassination squads in particular.

16

PUNISHMENTS, LEGION STYLE

'Deserters were put through hell. Legion punishment
stretched a man's physical and mental endurance to the
absolute limit.'

ALTHOUGH they did not join the rebellion,
most legionnaires, with the possible exception of the 13th Demi-
Brigade, were not without sympathy for 1REP. Twice wiped out in
recent years through bravery in action, sharp-end players in every
Legion action since its formation in 1947 and especially in the Algerian crisis, the Paratroop regiment had a past full of accolades. Campfire
discussions raged for months: what would any one of them have done
if their commanding officer had said: 'Join me, Legionnaire!'? Would
they really have considered the reasons or the consequences, or would
they have blindly followed, as they had been disciplined and taught to
do, to the point of death if necessary? Sympathy was tempered only by
the fact that the officers and men of 1REP who supported the putsch
had put the Foreign Legion in jeopardy. A furious de Gaulle, never a
fan of the Legion despite the 13th Demi-Brigade's support in the war,
now wanted to get rid of it entirely. He was dissuaded from doing so
by one of those original 13th Demi-Brigade members, Pierre Messmer,
who had fought at Bir Hakiem, and tactfully reminded him that the
Legion had formed the backbone of the Free French army that gave
him a platform in the first place. The Legion was saved, but there were

many in its service who harboured what was nothing short of a hatred of de Gaulle, a hatred strong enough for many of them to support an assassination plot.

Elsewhere among the paras, especially in 2REP, morale was at a low ebb and desertions were on the increase, according to Simon Murray who had joined the Regiment a year before the attempted putsch. He found that the punishment for deserters, especially in the smaller Legion camps, was incredibly harsh, even before the rebellion. It would be all too easy to explain it away by linking the brutality of NCOs and officers to the general pressures surrounding the Legion at the time, and Murray makes no attempt to do that. Indeed, it was an ongoing feature of training, as it always had been, and continued long after the events in Algeria had been posted to history.

Murray's experience of the punishments dealt out to deserters was first gleaned at the Legion farm of Sully. There were two sections, around forty men in converted barns. The camp commandant, Captain Glasser, looked a tough no-bloody-nonsense officer, and he was.

Six days after Murray arrived at the camp, two of his colleagues, Lefevre and Aboine, deserted. They were caught two days later by a unit of the regular army, and Murray, who was on guard duty, went with the company adjutant, Chief Sergeant Westhof, and Sergeant Wissmann to fetch them back. On their arrival at the regular's camp, the prisoners were dragged forward and Westhof staggered all present by pulling out his pistol and dropping both of them to ground with a blow to the head with the butt of his gun. Murray recalls that Lefevre's head started to bleed heavily. They were then bundled into the Jeep, watched by regular French soldiers whose faces were overtaken by a mixture of horror and astonishment. In Murray's words:

> We returned to Sully and the two prisoners were paraded in front of Captain Glasser in his office. I was on guard duty outside the room. He beat the living daylights out of them . . .

After that, the deserters were put through hell. First they were given three hours of *la pelote* – a long-established ritual of Legion punishment which was banned in 1984. The reasons are obvious: it stretched a man's physical and mental endurance to the absolute limit. It often began with the prisoner being given a sack of rocks, tied to his back by wire shoulder straps. A helmet without its padded interior banged against his head. He had to run, while a sergeant blew a whistle – an instruction for the man to perform tricks, such as crawling on his stomach, doing press-ups, or marching with bent knees. If he slowed or collapsed, he was beaten with a knotted rope. The final indignation came when he was made to crawl on his belly back to the barrack-room where his colleagues were standing to attention. The prisoner, covered in filth and slime, no longer resembled a human being – a lesson to all present. For Lefevre and Aboine, their *la pelote* went on for days. Murray recorded:

> Aboine, a Negro, seemed to be standing up to it quite well . . . Lefevre on the other hand looks like a dying man and he is completely devoid of human spirit, just a moving wreck . . . a man with no will to live. I hope he pulls through.

Lefevre did pull through and rejoined the unit on the completion of his sentence. Nine months later, he was dead – a bullet to the brain from a Fell marksman while on patrol in the Chélia mountains.

Another who witnessed *la pelote* was Bob Wilson, who enlisted in the Legion at the age of 21, at the beginning of the 1960s, and who stayed for almost eighteen years, rising to the rank of adjutant and completing his service in the Legion's secret police.

Today, a quiet, unassuming man living in Blackpool, Wilson described with obvious candour his life in the Legion, which spanned two important decades of change. He had just completed his National Service, with a commission in the 22nd Light Anti-Aircraft Regiment, Royal Artillery. He liked army life, but at the time the pay wasn't good and he couldn't afford to stay in. Ironically, soon after he'd joined the Legion, a letter was forwarded on to him announcing that he'd been promoted to lieutenant on reserve.

First impressions for Wilson were not good. The château which formed a barracks for the Legion in Paris was a beautiful building on the outside. Inside, it was primitive: steel beds three high in rooms that offered not the slightest hint of design for modern living. They were kept there for a few days while other volunteers were collected in and then taken to Fort St Nicholas in Marseille where they went through the medical tests and screening by the Legion police before being shipped fourth class to Sidi-bel-Abbès. They looked like hobos in awful thick uniforms. Wilson recalls:

As we entered the ferry boat for our journey to Algeria, we were each given a deckchair and directed to a place next to the engine-room, where we sat for the next thirty-six hours and not allowed to do anything except go for a pee and eat the pigswill they called food.

To that point, our entry into the Legion had been rather disappointing. Quite a few chaps might have been tempted to have gone home had they been given the opportunity. At Oran, we perked up. The Legion buildings there were more spacious, whiter. They had a good selection of food, salads, fruit and wine on tap. When we moved on to Sidi-bel-Abbès, it was back to square one, and we were once again wondering what we had done. The barracks were crap. We were to be there for ten days before being transferred to our training regiment. The place was awash with intrigue. Politics was everything in Algeria at the time. We were marched in the evenings to the local cinema under armed guard, not to stop us deserting, but to protect us from hot heads among the local population who weren't very keen on having the Legion around.

Then they stuck us in trucks and we rattled our way along the dusty roads to a place near Mascara. Our destination was a rough 19th century barracks where we would begin our training. I spent my first Christmas in the Legion there. It was awful. I hated it and have done ever since. Not Christmas itself, not the festivities, but they had the business in the Legion of preparing a crib of the nativity scene. It was amazing. I couldn't believe that we, the supposed future elite of the Foreign Legion, were being ordered upon pain of death to build a crib – 'and it had better be brilliant because we want to win'. There was a competition between sections to judge who'd made the best one. With four sections to each company in a regiment, plus headquarters, you were looking at something like twenty or more cribs being made for the Christmas festivities. It seemed an absolutely unmilitary activity! While we were training for the finer points of warfare, like slitting a man's throat in hand-to-hand combat, we could return to barracks and start building a bloody crib, for God's sake!

The chaplain and the colonel's wife, or other top brass, marked them with points. That Christmas, our Yugoslavian staff sergeant decided to base our crib on Roman ruins. There were plenty of materials around in Algeria so it was a popular theme. We used to plunder them for all kinds of things, if archaeologists knew half of it, they'd weep for days. Anyway, the judging was completed and the colonel's wife announced that the prize would go the section with a stone sculpture, carved by a Spaniard. Our staff sergeant, a temperamental bugger at the best of times, was so mad at not winning that he proceeded to smash up our entry. No sooner had he done that, than the judges announced that because it had been such a close run thing, they'd have a second look at all the entries the following day – and we were up all night rebuilding it! That's why I hated Christmas, or at least that part of it. I was with a guy named Kenny, the only other Englishman in my section. Kenny's real name was Donald. I was with him for the whole of the first five year engagement. He'd served in the British Parachute Regiment and the SAS. Kenny and myself went down for our first Christmas Day in the Legion, and it was terrific. Every man was given a Christmas gift, not a cheap present but quite a decent thing like a watch or a camera. The tables were laden with food and drink of every description, first-class stuff.

It was a brief respite. Those of us who volunteered for para training were kitted up with another uniform. We experienced another routine altogether, testing our fitness with incessant press-ups and eight kilometre runs down concrete roads with a full pack on your back. Kenny knew about these runs. He told me to hold back, so we trotted early on and let the others dash off ahead. He was right; we kept a steady pace and were soon over-taking the early leaders. We came in quite high up in the line which set us up for para training.

They were transferred to a Legion farm not far from Sidi-bel-Abbès, where parachutists did their basic training. The instructors came from the disbanded 1REP. These guys meant business, said Bob Wilson. It was a farm on its own well away from the general Legion activities. They were really out to make something of the recruits in their charge and the methods of instruction changed dramatically. As Wilson recalled:

You got belted and kicked, sworn at and insulted. We were lodged in a wine cave which had two-tier bunks. No heating, of course. I'd seen one or two examples of brutality by Legion NCOs, although generally it wasn't as bad as some people would have you believe.

It was at the para farm that it was revealed to me that they were not playing games. We'd heard that two Spaniards from another detachment had deserted, with their weapons. They were caught by the *gendarmerie*, brought back and tied to the flagpole in the court-yard of the farm, totally nude. They got belted and kicked by the NCOs who came out of the mess, and were left there all night. The following morning, the captain stood at the top of some concrete steps which led to his office. The two Spaniards were made to crawl on the ground and up the steps, one after the other. When they reached the top, the captain took the stance of a penalty shooter and kicked the first one in the face. He fell back. The second one had to crawl on to receive the same treatment. They were subse-quently given sixty days in the guardhouse.

We had a German sergeant major who was a bastard. He decided he wanted a well dug. The two Spaniards were selected for this task. The routine was that one of them stood in the hole digging and the other carted the sand and rock away. This went on for some time and eventually they were both in the hole and another prisoner was carting the stuff away. They went down and down without hitting water. The hole got bigger and bigger, without any supports at the sides, and eventually you couldn't see the Spaniards. They went so deep, that one night they just stayed down there. What happened after that was the subject of rumour. The sides of the well collapsed, and no one ever saw the Spaniards again. The sergeant major posted them as having deserted for a second time, which given the circumstances was pretty near impossible. We all came to the conclusion that the Spaniards were in the hole when the sides caved in and they were left there. That was that. No one ever challenged his version of events.

That was a watershed for me. It was an example to everyone. We moved on back to Mascara for further training for which we combined with the French paras, and later to the drop zone at Blida, not far from Algiers. We were now in the hands of the French Red Berets, about thirty of us in a class of around 100. We had a few incidents. The only guy who could speak both perfect English and French was a young Belgian-American, Hepps, and he did the translations which were beyond many of us, especially those who could speak neither language, like an Italian named Scapelli. When eventually we went up to do our first jumps, it was all quite relaxed and one by one we went out of the aircraft over a very nice drop zone, all except Scapelli who froze at the exit point. So the Red Berets unhooked him and sent him back to sit down.

That night, the Red Beret monitors went into the NCOs mess and made a few disparaging remarks about the Legion to three of our own instructors, and told the story of Scapelli. Our NCOs went bananas. We were all in the cinema that night when they stopped the film and made an announcement: 'Would Legionnaire Scapelli kindly go to the front entrance'. Blida was a vast camp, and there were about 400 people in the cinema, all watching as Scapelli got up and left. Outside, he was confronted by four Legion NCOs, two sergeants and two corporals who dragged him off to the entrance to the camp where there was some kind of statue with water around it. They gave him a beating that went on for a long time, with Scapelli howling and screaming. We never saw him again. He was thrown off the course and sent to the infantry. Unofficial punishments like this tended to be of an extreme nature and infrequent – although on this occasion, there was another not long afterwards. As part of the training aids they had the fuselages of old Atlas aircraft up on stilts to provide a realistic setting for jump preparation. A legionnaire had overheard the Red Berets talking about a party they planned to hold in one of these old planes that night, with girls coming up from the village. This guy decided he was going to gatecrash and managed to get through several picket lines and guards posts and out of the camp. He apparently picked up one of the women and screwed her. He then hit a Red Beret monitor who discovered him and darted off into the night. He apparently left something behind – his own beret.

The following day we were mustered for our fourth jump. We had with us a couple of Red Beret monitors who took particular interest in our headgear when we arrived. We were all wearing our helmets ready for the jump but they made us take them off and put on our berets. There was one guy, the party gatecrasher who did not have his with him. Questioned, he admitted he had lost it the night before. Questioned further, along with threats of nasty consequences, he confessed to having picked up one of the girls.

They did things to him that were diabolical. That night, he was put in the shower room and each one of us had to come in and give him a cold shower every fifteen minutes. When that was done, the *caporal-chef* invited us all to the shower room and said: 'Right give it to him.' We were all a bit reluctant, no one made a move and the *caporal* was getting rather angry with the rest of us, about thirty in all. So, I thought, a lesson in how to save your skin . . . I stepped forward and belted him. That took the cork out of the bottle and everyone followed suit, so the legionnaire took a real duffing up, with the final humiliation of parading about nude with his underpants on his head. Next day, he'd gone from the course, so that was another we lost.

Wilson's group had a Sunday out at the end of training when they had received their wings. They went to the beach at Zeralda, just down the coast from Algiers, in a convoy of seven trucks. The legionnaires were in the last truck because they did not have walking out uniforms with them, just their camouflage suits. They also took their weapons hidden in the bottom of the wagons, just in case of trouble. Algerian peace talks were in progress but there was still a good deal of trouble about. The weapons were fairly ancient. The corporals had MAT 49s, the 9mm sub-machine-guns, and the legionnaires were equipped with 7.5mm guns which took five cartridges. They were returning from Zeralda around 4 p.m. when they were ambushed by the Fell. The whole convoy was sprayed with machine-gun fire and all seven trucks drove into the trench at the side of the road. The legionnaires were the only section with weapons and engaged the Fell while the rest took cover. Wilson recalls:

Our *caporal-chef* stood on the bonnet of our Jeep and spotted the emplacement. He ordered us all out, fix bayonets, which were like needles, and march up the road, stop and open fire. This we did. A couple of the guys were hit; Hepps, who had been the most useful man in our section doing all the translations, was killed. We ran forward to the top of the hill, guns blazing, but the emplacement was vacant. They'd scarpered. The other paras had by now pulled their trucks out of the trench and they were hurrying on home. We loaded Hepps into the back of the truck and went back to base. When we reached the front entrance, we placed his body on a groundsheet which was carried by a legionnaire at each corner and we marched into base singing. They had the guard out to receive him.

After that the Red Berets couldn't do enough for us. We gave Hepps a good send off at a cemetery in Algiers where many legionnaires are buried. I was among those posted to the Legion parachute regiment, 2REP, which was then based at Telergma, in eastern Algeria close to the Tunisian frontier. Just before we were due to leave I was admitted to a local hospital run by nuns, with an infected hand. It needed to be operated on and I was placed in a bed on the first floor beside a window overlooking the Arab quarter of the town. The second night I was there, I was awoken by a commotion outside. A corporal and a couple of legionnaires were involved in a fracas at the brothel. They'd had a row with a local Arab over money. The corporal went outside, grabbed a sub-machine-gun from a passing *gendarme* and went back into the brothel with the intention of sorting them out. The brothel manager had called the Military Police and a truck load of Redcaps weighed in whacking everyone in sight.

It was summer when I arrived at the camp in Telergma, but already the talk was we wouldn't be there for long. The French were pulling out.

17

1962: ALGERIAN INDEPENDENCE

'It was agreed that Sam should be paid £40,000 for
shooting De Gaulle at a time and a place of his own
choosing.'

FOR A WHILE, after the failed rebellion in Alge-
ria, recruitment to the Legion was halted, but was restored again in
1962, with the apparent reluctance of President de Gaulle. It remained
an embarrassment to the Legion's high command that former officers
and men of 1REP had become key figures in the OAS campaign of
bombings and assassinations which spread murderously through the
major cities of Algeria and to Paris as talks proceeded to conclude independence for Algeria.

Discussion of the Legion's role in the failed putsch had also become
the topic of open debate, especially in the media. Left-wing commenta-
tors accused French officers who led soldiers of multi-national origin
into mutiny of an abhorrent crime. It was argued that they had taken
advantage of men whose loyalty was traditionally to its officers and used
them in a dispute which was very definitely a French affair, albeit
involving French colonialists and the indigenous populations. Men of
the Foreign Legion, said the critics, would do anything, go anywhere
and if necessary commit murder at the command of an officer because
that is what they had been trained, if not brainwashed, to do. They were
brought up on a diet of discipline that expressly forbade the discussion

183

of politics and, importantly, had at its very core the instruction, ignored on pain of death, that ALL ORDERS MUST BE OBEYED.

That piece of Legion indoctrination, as Jim Worden points out, is chanted endlessly in the training of legionnaires and 'is inscribed indelibly on the hearts and in the minds of all Legion recruits, not only for the remainder of their service but for the rest of their lives: the creed of *La Base de la Discipline*.'

The French people themselves, exhausted by the continuing crisis of collapsing governments, had elected their so-called saviour, General de Gaulle, and that in itself had given way to a developing sub-plot which materialized by way of a succession of plots to assassinate him, two of which involved British legionnaires.

The OAS, meanwhile, attempted to bomb its way into public perception. While ex-general Salan chaired the ruling council made up of military and *Pieds Noirs* civilians, General Yves Godard, a paratrooper and former Resistance leader in France, was chief of operations. His single most famous success was to smash a 100-strong commando unit sent to Algeria by de Gaulle to end the OAS attacks. At the heart of the military operation was Commando Delta, the enforcement wing of the OAS run by Legion deserter Lieutenant Roger Degueldre, and his devoted sidekick Bobby Dovecar.

Degueldre claimed French nationality but in the blur of post-war prison camps from which he emerged, the truth became indeterminable. He was said to have been born in Louvril, northern France, in 1925. During the war, he joined the Resistance movement but was captured and thrown into Matthausen. There he met the then Captain Pierre Jeanpierre who, with the liberation of the prison camps, resumed his military career as an officer of the *Bureau Securité de Légion Étrangère*. Among the first recruits he signed up for the Legion was Roger Degueldre who used an assumed name, stating his nationality was Belgian.

In Indo-China he established a reputation for being one of those constantly at the front of the pack in skirmishes with the Viet Minh. He gained rapid promotion to chief sergeant and after rescuing a colonel from certain death, he rose further to adjutant chief. He volunteered for the paras, still following in the footsteps of Legion hero

Pierre Jeanpierre whose own exploits in Indo-China were spectacular. Degueldre became one of the most decorated sergeants in the Legion and received direct promotion to lieutenant in the field, one of only two field commissions granted, and the only one secured by a legionnaire.

Never far away in Algeria was Bobby Dovecar, a young man with only three years Legion service. He was of Yugoslavian birth and an exceptionally good legionnaire, as indicated by the short space of time it took him to make the rank of sergeant. The only reason he was fighting for the OAS was his utter devotion to Degueldre. Degueldre demanded loyalty, just as he and all officers in the Legion had done. If he was unsure, he would ask for a demonstration, like a Mafia boss, for the man to prove himself, as he did when he ordered a former Legion lieutenant on his team to murder his best friend, whose child was the assassin's godson, as a proof of his loyalty.

Commando Force, not to put too fine a point on it, was about killing people and around the hub of Degueldre's organization was a coterie of young legionnaire deserters who were willing to do his bidding without hesitation. They began their 'reign of terror' even before the rebellion was lost, financed by a horde of cash, courtesy of right-wing supporters in mainland France and of the wealthy Algerian settlers. They were able to buy modern accoutrements for their forthcoming bombing campaign which tore at Algiers and other principal cities, as well as Paris itself.

The targets were initially prominent Arabs, a response to the FLN/ALN bombing campaign against *Pieds Noirs*, along with supporters of the nationalists' campaign for the Independence of Algeria. Later, well known left-wing opponents of the OAS in France were targeted, along with government officials, ministers and, as ever, de Gaulle himself for whom the hatred among the settlers and the renegade army mounted as each month of talks and negotiations with the Arab nationalists progressed towards a settlement.

The OAS campaign was a new kind of urban warfare, devastatingly accurate in its execution. *Plastique* was the principal weapon. Looking like putty, it could be rolled into a ball, could be cut, kicked, and carried in a bag.

Expert teams fully trained in the use of *plastiques* were deployed by the OAS from early 1961. In addition, Commando Delta had formed its own assassination squads. Dovecar's team consisted of two young ex-legionnaires and three OAS militiamen. One of the group's early killings was on 31 May 1961 when they broke into the apartment of Algerian Police Commissioner Roger Gavoury and knifed him to death. By the year's end, more than 3,000 killings of Muslim men and women in Algerian cities were attributed to the OAS, and 300 or more specifically to Degueldre himself.

The death toll rose dramatically in the early months of 1962 as peace talks proceeded and the French government reached agreement with the provisional FLN government of Algeria for a settlement. The countdown to Algerian independence and the end of French rule was marked with a final burst of desperate and bloody opposition by the OAS. In January 1962 alone, 364 people were killed and 624 wounded in an OAS killing spree, aimed at wrecking the peace plan by causing a full-scale uprising of the Arabs against *Pieds Noirs* and in turn forcing the French army to protect the Europeans.

On 23 January, ten OAS bombs exploded in daylight in Paris to mark the anniversary of the settlers' revolt in Algiers, hitting the homes of politicians and journalists. One of them, intended for the writer Andre Malraux who was also Minister of Culture, wounded and disfigured a four-year-old child, causing outrage in the city. De Gaulle announced new measures, banning all newspapers from publishing OAS communiqués and increasing the presence of armed troops on the streets of Paris, bringing the total to more than 25,000. On 8 February, eight people were killed after a banned march organized by the communists clashed with riot police. On 28 February, de Gaulle ordered 40,000 more troops into Algiers to crush the OAS terrorists after they shot and killed a dozen Algerians in one day. In addition, a secret French intelligence force known as C-Group stepped up its activities. At its head was Michel Hacq, who brought with him just 200 men from the mainland *Gendarmerie Mobile*, a police force within the armed forces. They operated from their own anonymous barracks and were instructed to stay clear of contact with any established law enforcement agencies or army units in Algeria. By the end of February, the force had rounded up more than 600 OAS men and bagged 642 automatic firearms, 10,000 rounds of ammunition and a cache of documents.

At the beginning of March, the provisional Algerian government under its communist/Muslim leaders formally signed what became known as the Evian Peace Agreement under which France effectively relinquished its authority over the country and promised a phased withdrawal of its troops. General Salan responded by declaring a state of 'civil war' with both French forces and Arab nationalists. For days on end, indiscriminate executions of Arabs were carried out by gangs roaming the city streets. Algiers and Oran turned into urban battle-fields.

On 26 March, the French army launched a ruthless offensive after seven French army conscripts were shot dead and eleven were wounded when the OAS ambushed their patrol. Their first success was to capture ex-General Edmond Jouhaud, one of the four OAS supreme commanders, after a seven-hour battle between infantry and tanks of the French army on an OAS stronghold. Then 100 *Pieds Noirs*, many of them taking no part in the battle, were killed and another 200 wounded when French troops opened fire on what was supposed to be a peaceful demonstration.

Another OAS team, consisting of nine ex-Legion officers and eighty-six of their men, retreated into the mountains where they came under attack from FLN ground forces and French fighters before they surrendered. The net was closing. In the first three weeks of April, the three most sought after men in the OAS were captured – Dovecar was caught in a villa of a wealthy Algerian and Degueldre was trapped by his own arrogance. Convinced that he would never be taken, he calmly relied upon false identity papers when he was arrested by police. He made no attempt to escape and, still claiming mistaken identity, was taken to police headquarters in Algiers where he was immediately rec-ognized. Finally, on 20 April, Raoul Salan was arrested in a first-floor apartment in Algiers. His wife, Lucienne, was with him, along with their daughter and his faithful ADC, ex-Captain Ferrandi. He had been betrayed by one of his own men.

Bobby Dovecar, three times honoured by the French for bravery in action as a serving legionnaire, was brought quickly before a military tribunal and sentenced to death by firing squad at Fort Trou d'Enfer. His last defiant shout as his executioners took aim was: '*Vive la Légion*'.

Much to the amazement and indignation of most of France, Raoul Salan, regarded as the man who had brought his country to the brink of civil war, escaped the death sentence. He stood trial before a Paris military tribunal and was represented by the ultra-right barrister Maitre Tixier-Vignancour who had also defended Marshal Pétain after the war. The OAS issued a statement warning they would kill the judges if he was executed. On 23 May, the military tribunal ruled that in view of extenuating circumstances – which were curiously never explained, and perhaps never can be – he was sentenced to life imprisonment. He wept as the sentence was announced, and as the realization dawned, he broke into uncontrolled hysterical laughter.

The killings went on. On 8 June, OAS terrorists blew up Algerian oilfields at Hassi Touareg, deep in the Sahara. Then they firebombed Algiers University and magnificent public buildings in Oran in a vain scorched-earth attempt to halt the final acts of the drama. On 3 July, 132 years of French rule was formally ended after a referendum in Algeria, which enfranchised both Muslim and French citizens, voted 99 per cent in favour of an independent Algeria. The exodus of Europeans began immediately, and even as they prepared to leave they came under fire from the Arabs; hundreds were massacred as they gathered at Oran on 5 July, and in the months ahead thousands died in revenge attacks by Arab gunmen. If it wasn't already a contender for the title, Algeria would in time become one of the most dangerous places on earth for Europeans, a reputation which it still holds today.

By the time Roger Degueldre faced his trial, the battle for Algeria was all but over, and he was to be de Gaulle's symbolic offering to the peace process. Refusing to accept the legitimacy of the military tribunal, Degueldre remained silent throughout the hearing, with his steely, piercing eyes fixed on the tribunal head, General de Larminat. But after the second day of the hearing, De Larminat shot himself, presumably unable to face the fact that the decision of the court had already been made in a higher place . . . the presidential palace.

Legion Lieutenant Degueldre was ordered to be shot. General

Jouhard, the fourth of the original generals who commanded the putsch attempt in Algeria, was also sentenced to death but was reprieved after 299 days in the condemned cell. No others directly involved in the OAS uprising or the putsch were executed. Most were given early releases from their sentences, some receiving amnesty as early as 1968, and others in a general amnesty in 1975. Quite a few members of the OAS Delta Force escaped arrest in 1962–64 by rejoining the Legion under fictitious names. The Legion, in spite of all the turmoil, still looked after its own.

The death sentence on 36-year-old Degueldre was carried out on the morning of 6 July 1962, in the main courtyard of Fort d'Ivry, a grey, imposing military compound on a hill overlooking the southern approaches to Paris. The prisoner waited in his cell, paying little regard to the priest who prayed for his soul. The firing squad was drawn to attention and eight rifle bolts sent echoing rattles through the silent precincts of Fort d'Ivry as the soldiers tested, charged and cocked their rifles.

Under the watchful eyes of military officialdom, in accord with convention, Degueldre was taken to the stake, the priest following with his unheard readings. An NCO marched the eight members of the firing squad to their positions. He was an apparently 'worried man' by the name of Prideaux, a regular army sergeant, who had taken the place of commanding the squad normally filled by an officer. Degueldre, wearing his old Legion camouflage uniform, was shackled and blindfolded. He faced death with a cool calm. An arrogant smile flickered across his mouth.

Prideaux barked his order: 'Take aim . . .'

The carbines were raised to shoulder height.

Degueldre responded by loudly proclaiming to his executioners the unnerving instruction: 'Do your duty.'

This calculated distraction was only enhanced as he began to sing *The Marseillaise.*

Sergeant Prideaux did not wait for him to finish.

'FIRE!'

The volley of shots rang out, echoing around the courtyard. Degueldre slumped forward and in doing so defiantly tossed his head and laughed as he realized he wasn't yet dead. Given the conflicting emotions, no one ought to have been surprised that he had been hit by only *one* of the eight bullets, which ripped into his shoulder, providing a nasty but certainly not fatal, wound. But how could seven fine army marksmen miss such a sitting duck? It was simple. They aimed to miss. It was left to the NCO, Sergeant Prideaux, to deliver the 'mercy' shots from his own pistol to ensure swift passage to the other side ... or at least it should have done.

Prideaux also tackled the task with a degree of uncertainty. His first bullet hit Degueldre in the opposite shoulder. This too failed to kill him, as did the next, and the next. In fact, he fired five more shots before Degueldre was pronounced dead by the attending medic – ten minutes after the first shot had been fired.

Precise details of the execution were never revealed but word of the botched-up killing spread through the Legion like wildfire. Thus, at a meeting of like-minded men at the Chez Vania restaurant in Paris, early in August 1962, Sergeant Prideaux was himself sentenced to death by this kangaroo court, a sentence which was in due course carried out by a British legionnaire. And, it was also a Briton who would join those determined to do what Degueldre had not managed – to assassinate De Gaulle. At that meeting in Chez Vania, the vow was re-affirmed.

A British legionnaire, identified only as 'Sam', was a brilliant marksman and sniper. Using a rifle with a telescopic sight, he was capable of placing three shots in as many seconds into a regulation US steel helmet at a distance of 300 metres. The wound, to a human head, would be a tiny hole going in, but the exit would would leave a jagged tear coated with brain tissue. Sam's abilities were made known to the OAS as early as November 1960, when Salan was still in Madrid.

Subsequently, a deal was arranged by one of the OAS leaders. It was agreed that Sam should be paid £40,000 for shooting de Gaulle at a time and a place of his own choosing, which as one of their number pointed out, although a small fortune at the time, was still a bargain-basement price. Sam was handed half the agreed sum in advance, and departed the Legion with his nest egg. Sam's movements then became blurred by the activities of the OAS. He went home to England for a while, and then returned to France where he had hidden his weapon. He checked into a hotel on the outskirts of Paris. With a small Citroën van, he set up the disguise of being a window cleaner, apparently utilizing the tools of that trade to carry his rifle. What is known is that Sam made an attempt to kill de Gaulle on two occasions, in the hope of claiming the second part of his fee. But he failed in his mission, and was not seen again.

The second plot to kill de Gaulle, also involving a British legionnaire, was hatched after the meeting in the Chez Vania restaurant, when the death sentence was passed by kangaroo court on Sergeant Prideaux, the man who had made such a hash of Degueldre's execution. Prideaux was duly executed with a bullet to the brain, on the night of 22/23 January 1964. The same legionnaire who undertook that execution (for a fee of £2,000, which was never paid because the moneyman skipped to Italy) was involved with former legionnaires in another attempt to assassinate de Gaulle. The moment arrived when Winston Churchill died in January 1965. The legionnaires sprang to action. Initially they considered an assassination attempt during de Gaulle's visit to London for Churchill's funeral. This scheme was scrapped when de Gaulle himself announced that a memorial service to his great wartime friend would be held in Paris a week later. A detailed synopsis of the assassination of President John F. Kennedy, two years earlier, was called for. The would-be assassins considered locations and an escape route, but in the end were foiled by the security net surrounding de Gaulle, and the fact that for years after the Algerian crisis his movements were so carefully planned and monitored that it was virtually impossible for any sniper to get a shot at him.

18

1970: GOODBYE ALGERIA

'Negotiations between France and Algeria about the
future presence of our bases in this country have
broken down. The base will be evacuated immediately.'

WHEN THE peace agreements were signed, the
local armies were no longer required. Across North Africa, France
demobilized around 150,000 men from units of the *Armée d'Afrique*.
Very few of these soldiers were given the opportunity to settle in mainland France, and thousands were subsequently massacred in their
homeland. The retribution in North Africa that resulted from France's
treatment of the anti-communist Algerian soldiers was a final despica-
ble chapter in the whole affair. France not only left the country it had
plundered for more than a century in bloody disarray, but betrayed
those among the indigenous population who had supported French
rule to the last, and who were now killed for doing so.

The Foreign Legion, synonymous with Algeria since its foundation
in 1831, was given little time to clear out. It was to be but one of their
concerns at that time. De Gaulle took his own very personal revenge on
the French military by axing two elite para divisions, along with airborne commandos. He ordered what amounted to a personal vetting of
thousands of individual soldiers and, especially, a complete 'detoxifica-
tion' of the Foreign Legion. The cure entailed the breaking up of known
cliques in the officer corps. Men were posted to other regiments at a

moment's notice, sent far away from their families, passed over for promotion, given early retirement or put under fairly overt surveillance. What particularly angered Foreign Legion rank-and-file was that during the purge of its hierarchy, de Gaulle freed around 6,000 communist ALN prisoners, a not unexpected move in the process of peace among two warring nations. Except that, in this case, the Legion had been told all the way along that it was not at war.

For this reason, the campaign medal struck for the final piece of action in North Africa was a *Croix de Valeur* rather than a *Croix de Guerre*. And so, more than a century of history came to an abrupt end with the minimum of ceremony. The Sidi-bel-Abbès base was stripped of its past, its monuments and its ghosts, packed up and shipped to France to be re-installed at its replacement headquarters at Aubagne in the hills of Provence – the first time in its long history that the Legion had been allowed a permanent base in mainland France. The move was completed with such speed that it was four years before the new headquarters became fully operational. In the meantime, regiments were dispersed to French interests abroad, across central Africa, the French Sahara, French Guyana, Madagascar and French Polynesia.

For the time-being, 2REP remained in Algeria until its new base in Corsica was ready. It was sent to a desolate place down the coast from Oran, as one of the garrisons guarding the last remaining French territory around oil installations and the huge French naval base at Mers el-Kébir. Around twenty-eight kilometres beyond that was the small town of Aïn el-Turck. But even this was not the place of 2REP's new headquarters. It was fifteen kilometres beyond that, at Bou-Sfer, a ghost town, once the beach resort of French colonialists of Oran.

The Legion paras, tails between their legs, set up their new base camp which, for the time-being, was under canvas. A support company had gone on ahead to begin erecting the tented accommodation. The move was more or less the last stepping stone to the final retreat of 2REP, along with the rest of the Legion, from Algeria. Under the independence deal, the French had leased the naval yard at Mers el-Kébir for five years and were building a vast electrified barrage around this piece of territory that was to be the last base. Bob Wilson recalls:

How long we would be there was anybody's guess. The French Pioneer Corps were doing the work with machines and bulldozers. You could see for miles where they had ripped out a deep trench up hill and down dale, mile upon mile, to put in double fencing covered with barbed wire and electrified cables. Talk about the Berlin Wall. All the entries and exits were controlled by guard posts. Our new camp was a tented enclave which went up where, but a few weeks ago, lay a countryside of old vines run wild, with roots deep in the soil. They had bulldozed it flat to make room for a village of 900 or so paras in four companies and a headquarters' company. The final site preparation had to be done by hand, 200 men shoulder to shoulder with pick and shovel. When the groundwork was completed, the tents went up – rows of canvas, twelve men to a tent, and the bare earth as the floor. There was no mess hall. The cookhouse was in an old farm building and each company sent a truck to collect their food at mealtimes, and brought it back to their tents in containers, and the wine. The latrines were primitive, just trenches basically, and the showers were of the tin and string variety. In the future, we were told, there would be tarmac roads and modern barracks. Some of us had our doubts, given the current political situation and the mood of the nationalists.

Mother Nature added to the confusion. The Regiment had barely been there a month when it started raining. It rained and it rained, three days solid from the end of October and then intermittently through to the middle of November, when winter came gushing in. Only now did they realize that the place selected for this last oasis of French colonialism was in a natural depression. During periods of rain, it filled with water to form a lake which became the habitat of migrating geese. They had to dig trenches around each of the tents with an outlet point for the water to drain away. Soon they were encircled by rain-filled trenches surrounding the twelve-man tents for a regiment of 900 men. It was, as Wilson described it, 'a total nightmare, mud and slime everywhere'.

The Regiment worked its guts out for eighteen months or more building the new base. There were a good many desertions – around 140 in the last quarter of 1962. Morale was appalling and there was a lot of tension in the wake of the failed putsch.

The new year was going to see a lot of changes, however. In the spring of 1963, the Regiment's commanding officer, Colonel Channel, left and his replacement, Colonel Cailloud, came in with the task of reshaping the whole of 2REP to the needs of the moment. It was in line with what was happening in the rest of the Legion. 'It was a watershed,' said Bob Wilson, who went on to add:

> Rifle companies, engaged in search-and-hold, ambushing, long patrols policing the countryside were all to go. There was no need for them any more. With vast chunks of its colonial empire diminishing, France's reliance on the Legion was to be less in terms of manpower but more in the way of specialist units. To begin with, no one took it seriously. It was soon apparent, however, that Cailloud meant business. We were all going to specialists of one kind or another: No. 1 Company became reconnaissance and anti-tank; 2nd Company would specialize as mountain troops, climbing and ski-ing, 3rd Company became amphibious, while 4th Company became a general company and a sorting house for new recruits. We were, it transpired, just part of the wider scheme of things, for an overall pattern of Rapid Reaction Deployment that emerged in the mid-1970s.

Wilson himself was up for promotion to corporal and that meant his participation in the dreaded *peloton*. This is the name given to the famous, if not infamous, NCOs' course which makes the initiation into the Legion look like a Sunday School tea-party. The course was conducted away from the main body of the regiment, at a camp called Lindless, 2,000 feet up in the hills. It was outside of the secure fencing, but was itself fully protected. Ahead lay six months of fieldwork and in-house examinations. There was prestige in passing out at the end of it as a corporal, and some decent rewards. All the candidates were rated and the one who came first was considered for immediate promotion to chief corporal which gave him the right to wear a black kepi, and it also doubled his pay. The *peloton* had always had a reputation for testing a man's endurance to the limit. Anything experienced in the past was supposed to be kid's stuff compared with corporal training. The course, said Wilson, was incredibly harsh:

What they were showing us was how to make life hell for new legionnaires. They did it by example. Nasty stuff that corporals and sergeants dream up when they're feeling mean, like while you're out on a twenty mile run with full pack, you stagger back to find the barracks have been wrecked and all your kit and all your bedclothes are piled in the middle of the room and hosed down and have to be shipshape again in thirty minutes for inspection. The key to it, as ever, was the deprivation of sleep. We were doing classroom work at 8 p.m. after a very full day. Then, just when you thought you'd finished for the day, they would say report back in one hour with all gear – that meant full kit and pack and rifle for inspection. They'd give you a bit of a mauling and then it was back to the barrack room for lights out. We were just closing our eyes when in came the staff sergeants, furious that torchlights and cigarettes had been seen through the windows after lights out. Having given us a bollocking for that, we were ordered back to bed like a bunch of kids. I fell into the deepest sleep I had ever had and awoke to the sound of music – a bugler playing reveille in the middle of the barracks. I looked at my watch. It was 11.15 p.m. I'd had three-quarters of an hour's sleep! The sergeants were shouting *Alert! Alert!* Full kit, packs and rifles, into the briefing room and the captain came in to send us off on some mock emergency. That was the pattern for the whole of the course. You were half dead from lack of sleep, but fitter than you'd ever been and doing things you never knew you were capable of doing. I was a glutton for punishment. I finished first and instead of being made a corporal, I moved up straight away to chief corporal and spent another three months at Lindless for specialist training in sabotage and survival.

Wilson remained at Bou-Sfer for the rest of his time with 2REP, which in the wake of all that had happened in the previous few years, was a relatively peaceful time. The action had come into his busy training for higher rank and in the general routine of Legion business; there had been little time for anything else apart from nights in the camp *foyer*, wary visits to town, and brief encounters with the camp followers. Through this, he saw out the completion of his first five years with the Legion and thoughts of home came into his head:

A moment arrived to jolt my thoughts back to England. I had had no contact with my family since I joined the Legion, apart from letters. When I left England, my mother had contacted just about every missing persons bureau in the western hemisphere before discovering I had joined the Foreign Legion. In those early days, during training, contact with the outside world is virtually impossible. Eventually, letters flowed back and forth. I even sent my mother the pawn ticket for my gold watch, which she retrieved. I still have it today.

I had left Scotland with my mother and the man who was to be my stepfather at the age of seven. My natural father remained in Glasgow and I had little contact with him. One day, a couple of years after I had joined the Legion, I was called to see the company captain who told me they had received a letter through the Red Cross, informing me that my father in Scotland was dying of cancer of the throat and had probably less than three weeks to live. He had asked to see his two sons. I was the youngest, and frankly I would have liked to have seen him before he died. I told the captain that they would have my assurance and word of honour that I would return.

The captain said that this possibility had already been considered. The answer was no, I could not go back. I refused to accept it and asked to see the colonel of the Regiment. The captain said it would not alter the situation because the colonel himself had made the decision. I still wanted to see the colonel and eventually I was standing in front of him pleading my case. I made the point that if I could not go back with official sanction I might have to look for another method. I was thinking of diplomatic pressure, possibly through the British Consulate in Algiers. The colonel assumed I was talking about desertion and immediately put me under extreme surveillance.

The next I heard was when they pulled me out and told me my father had died; they gave me twenty-four hours exempt duty. To be honest, when I thought it through, I did not feel too badly done by. At the time, I was not far into my contract; desertion rates were running high because of the situation in Algeria. This situation came back to haunt me some years later. By then, I was an adjutant in the 13th Demi-Brigade, based in Djibouti. Adjutants in the Legion are not like a sergeant major in the British army; they actually take command of troops going to the front and have authority over their men. At the time, I was in a little fort commanded by a captain. He had received a message concerning a corporal in my platoon. His brother had been killed in a road accident and his mother, a widow, had asked for her other son to have leave to return for the funeral and to comfort her. Recalling what had happened to me, I said, 'No, he could not have leave'. The captain obviously had more compassion than my colonel and overruled me. He gave the corporal two weeks' leave. I even had to advance him his air fare to Paris via Air France because he had no money. To give him his due, he came back and repaid the money. There was a sting in the tail of this story, however. The brother was driving the getaway car in a bank hold-up and was shot dead by the police. I had great pleasure in telling the captain.

In the four-and-a-half years since he joined the Legion, Bob Wilson had had no extended leave. He had accumulated seventy days which could be subtracted from his five year contract. He was reaching the end of his time and as the date to leave came closer, he was called in for a discussion about his future. The captain offered the carrot of promotion to sergeant if he stayed on. Wilson declined. He'd had enough, he said, and wanted to go home to the UK. He said his goodbyes, attended several drunken farewell parties and made his way back to

London with the intention of applying to go back into the British army. Armed with a letter which confirmed he had been promoted to lieutenant before he joined the Legion, he made his application and received all kinds of excuses as to why this was not possible. Thus, he was standing on the street corner with no job, aspirations shot to pieces and feeling a touch gloomy. Finally, he said 'What the hell?', packed up his belongings and caught the next plane to Paris.

I arrived at a new recruiting office, Fort Nugent, and discovered that because I had been out of the Legion for more than three months, I would have to re-apply. The black kepi denoting rank of chief corporal was replaced with a white kepi, for a second-class legionnaire. I found myself doing menial duties and, sadistic bastards that they are, they assigned me to duties as a server in the mess hall of the *caporal-chefs* until eventually the authorities in Aubagne agreed that I could return at my former level, and I went into the mess not as a server but a recipient.

Wilson was sent on to Aubagne to a holding regiment, and at Christmas 1966, he was sent to Corti, in Corsica, to complete a five-month sergeant's course. Since he was no longer automatically attached to 2REP, he was given a choice of postings. Tahiti sounded inviting, until he realized that the Legion base was in a remote station 2,000 miles from anywhere, so he took Madagascar where he spent a fairly uneventful couple of years. He was promoted to staff sergeant and moved into a new regiment, 1REC, which was starting up a 4th Company based at Orange. It was through this attachment that Bob Wilson found himself supervising the last exit of the Legion, and the rest of the French military, from Algeria. The company had been moved back to Algeria to replace a company of Red Berets, ostensibly for a three-month posting. The company arrived in Algeria with a hefty order programme of guard duty, interrupted only by the preparations for Christmas 1970, and the crib-making competition.

On Christmas Eve an Air Force general, newly arrived in Algeria, ordered all officers and *sous-officiers* over staff sergeant to assemble in the cinema. It soon became obvious he was not there to dispense Christmas cheer. The general and his staff marched rapidly down the aisle of the cinema and on to the stage, from where he made an immediate announcement:

> Gentlemen: Negotiations between France and Algeria about the future presence of our bases in this country have broken down. The base will be evacuated immediately. An air bridge has been established and flights will commence tomorrow, 25 December, and the evacuation must be completed by 1800 hours, 28 December. The Legion will continue to be responsible for security and aid the evacuation. They will leave last.

Service personnel from other units, such as the Air Force, and civilian staff who had been there for some time had pressing questions about personal possessions. Many of them had motor cars. The general re-iterated, everyone out by 1800 hours on 28 December. What could not be carried could not be taken. All military equipment would be removed, but only essential personal belongings would be allowed. With that, the general closed the meeting and left. They had one last fling, a brief and unusually drink-free Christmas meal and even the cribs were judged. Then they started to evacuate.

The departure was fraught and when, finally, there was only the Legion left, the captain hauled down the French flag and the Legion flag and gave them both to Bob Wilson. They marched off to the airport for the flight back. The captain was later brought before the top brass for failing to formally hand over the French base to the Algerian authorities. The Legion's transport aircraft was waiting on the runway, ready to go. Wilson was the last man in, and before the doors slammed shut, he said goodbye to Algeria with a symbolic gesture: he smashed a bottle of Kronenborg on the tarmac. And then they flew away.

19

1970s: DJIBOUTI

'Many were killed in their attempt to get past the barrage ...
2REP was under orders to warn those who attempted to cross to
retreat, and if they did not we would shoot them, which we did.'

AFTER ALMOST a decade of reconciliation and
change, the next generation of legionnaires faced a whole new arena
which demanded new techniques and, to a degree, moderation to
accommodate the changing political scene. The legion became part of
the Rapid Reaction Deployment forces in a defence policy which combined the needs of France with commitments to NATO and the
United Nations. While on the one hand Cold War tensions dominated
the military strategy of European nations, it was still necessary for the
French to police and protect its various commercial and intelligence-
gathering interests around the world, along with support for the
leaders of its former and existing protectorates.

By the mid-1970s, the Legion had units forming part of the French
military presence across central Africa, Madagascar, Mayotte in the
Indian Ocean, Tahiti and Mururoa in the Pacific, and French Guyana
on the mainland of South America, as well as its permanent bases on
Corsica and in the south of France.

Parachute operations were increasingly to the fore and 2REP moved
to its new camp at Calvi, on the island of Corsica, where it built up its
strength and re-established itself as a key component of French military

capability. The legion's command and management was by then centred at its superb new base at Aubagne, with large contingents of 1 REC quartered at Orange, guarding the Mirage nuclear bomber base and missile silos on the Albion Plateau. Elsewhere, they were standing watch over the first nuclear test site at Reggane, in French Sahara, and later the Pacific nuclear test site in French Polynesia, both of which demanded a strong Legion presence.

For the time-being, however, live action was derived from their role as guardians of French communities overseas, and none more so than in the former French colonies of Central and East Africa. It was here that the Legion found itself in almost continuous action for the next two decades, while at the same time France maintained its policy that young conscripts could not be sent to any military action overseas.

The 1960s dash by European nations to extract themselves from volatile colonies across the African continent had left in its wake a chaotic disarray of warring governments and *coups d'état*. France had a greater interest, and responsibility, than most in Central Africa and often her troops found themselves propping up dubious governments or leaders under threat from communist-backed infiltrators.

The Republic of Chad was the largest nation in the former French Equatorial Africa, bounded by Libya, Sudan and the Central African Republic. For years, there was continuing animosity between northerners and southerners as a result of Muslim slave-raiding in the south before the French conquest. France gave Chad its independence in August 1960 under President N'Garta Tombalbaye's one-party rule, and when the French army pulled out in 1964, old enmities between them flared up. Northern Islamic communities were discriminated against, and a near neighbour, Colonel Gaddafi in Libya, later joined in giving the north backing in a long-running campaign against the Tombalbaye regime.

The adventure introduced the Legion to a different kind of combat, confronted by running battles with large marauding bands of inexperienced yet heavily armed soldiers, often including children as young as 11 or 12. The Legion had to be seen as a buffer, rather an an aggressor. Theirs was supposed to be a kind of expanded law enforcement operation against rebel forces whose incursions more often than not degenerated into massacre and pillage. From the Legion's point-of-view, it was a very unsatisfactory intervention especially as it was often difficult to distinguish between the armies of friend or foe. Further, there were few bases from which the Legion could operate. The days of distant forts were over. Long-range patrols went out for days at a time and often supplies had to be dropped by air. The shortage of food, fuel, parts for vehicles which constantly broke down in the heat, undrinkable water, and disease such as hepatitis, drew comparisons with conditions the Legion had encountered in the dim and distant past. Chad was a bleak policing operation that was quelled by the early-1970s but would later come to the fore again as Gadaffi made expansionist moves.

Next came Djibouti, another of France's annexations from the turn of the century which had become the permanent home of the 13th Demi-Brigade, supported by rotational postings from other Legion and French army units. The tiny nation and its capital city of the same name was the former French Territory of the Afars and Issas, bounded by Somalia, Ethiopia and Eritrea. It had a recorded population of less than 400,000, half of whom lived in Djibouti city itself. Since agriculture was limited to a few oasis areas, it was a desperately poor nation whose national economy depended upon the port of Djibouti, linked by rail to Addis Ababa. Like Chad, it was also on the brink of independence, under its president Hassan Gouled Aptidon whom the French had promised to protect and support, while keeping his railway line open too.

The Legion was required to maintain a continuous presence to help stop wholesale incursions from neighbouring Somalia. Among the few local treasures in the Legion's possession was an old fort at Hol Hol, guarding the one-metre gauge railway that runs between Djibouti and Addis Ababa, and a very large viaduct. The 13th Demi-Brigade also provided the guard for a massive barrage which the Legion helped build along the entire length of the border with Somalia to halt the flow of subversives, asylum seekers and starving refugees. Thousands were camped on the other side of the line with families and animals.

The 13th Demi-Brigade was supported by other Legion and French army units on the various positions which had to be covered. The order was clear enough: keep the frontier sealed by whatever means. There were watchtowers every quarter of a mile or so. Each one was staffed by one legionnaire, armed with rifle, field telephone and search-light. Guards were given a four-stage standing order to be employed if anyone approached the border. The legionnaire should:

1 Shout a warning at 200 metres, telling them to go away.
2 Fire a single round aimed at the ground nearby if the person disregarded the warning.
3 Fire to wound if he persisted.
4 Shoot to kill.

'I don't know who wrote the orders,' Bob Wilson who came to the posting newly promoted to adjutant recalled, 'but it sounded like something out of *Monty Python*. The last option was not to be taken lightly. The *gendarmerie* always got involved and there was an inquiry.' One afternoon, around 2 p.m., a shot rang out on his section and he learned that an intruder had been shot dead by a legionnaire manning one of the watchtowers. Wilson went out to do an on-the-spot investigation. True enough, a Somali lay dead. The legionnaire, a German, looked sheepish and Wilson said: 'Well done.' The *gendarmerie* came down and as was usual in these cases, they gave the police a couple of cartridges and said these were the ones that had been fired as warning shots. He took away the body and that was that. Four days later, the same thing happened; same legionnaire, another dead Somali. Once is normal, twice becomes suspicious, said Wilson. The German legionnaire was relieved of his post and was sent off to another base before he had the chance to shoot anyone else.

Djibouti city tended to provide more action for the legionnaires than manning the watchtowers. In the hot climate, 90°F in the shade, tensions ran high, much drink was taken and fights and rugby were regular sport. It could also be a soul-destroying place if the legionnaire was not keen on any of the local facilities. The place was pretty dire and dangerous to health and body. It was full of bars and brothels but the Legion liked to keep control of the sexual pleasures of its soldiers. The camp brothel was run under strict medical supervision. It was staffed mainly by Somali girls, although at one stage the Legion answered the requests of its men for a change of scenery and brought in half a dozen Ethiopian girls. As Wilson noted:

All hell broke loose. The Ethiopians were really classy and even though they were jet black, they had European features. When we mixed the two races . . . mayhem! It was something we had not considered in advance but should have done. It was open warfare. As soon as they were put together, the Somalis declared war on them, out came the knives, literally, and they were stabbing each other. Disharmony in the brothel was quite serious. In such a climate, and with so little other entertainment, the men could easily get bored and then the alcohol intake goes up.

As adjutant at the fort, Wilson suffered a bad few months. He had to investigate two suicides and the curious death of one of his close Legion pals. The first was just before six one evening when they were changing the guard. They were approaching the railway viaduct which his men were guarding and as they neared one of the sentries, a shot rang out and they saw him fall. He'd put his rifle under his chin and pulled the trigger, blowing the front of his head off. In Wilson's words:

I never did like recording a death as suicide, for the sake of his record and his relatives. I tried to submit – and I think I had a good case in this instance – that it was probably accidental, caused when the guy going off duty pulled out the magazine and worked the bolt action to check the breach was empty before standing down. It was possible that he had a round up the spout. It didn't wash. I was overruled and the verdict was suicide. We got a coffin and took the body down to Djibouti for a church service. The stigma of suicide was all too evident. Apart from myself, the pallbearers and the priest, there was only one other person present, the colonel's wife who was a particularly sensitive lady, the mothering kind. It was a poor show. Even a chap killed in a motor accident would get a few of the dignitaries turn up for his funeral.

Not long afterwards, again at six in the evening, one of the corporals who worked in the infirmary came running in. A young legionnaire who had only recently arrived from France had gone into the hospital and while the corporal was attending one of the patients, he'd broken open a cupboard and swallowed all the pills he could lay his hands on. By the time I arrived, the legionnaire looked pretty rotten. We stuck a funnel in his mouth and tipped a saltwater solution down him to try to make him vomit. He got worse and worse and so we sent for a helicopter to take him to a civilian hospital. The doctor on board gave him on-the-spot treatment, but he died in Djibouti.

The third death, and probably the worst from my point of view, was my second in command, Daniel, who had been in the Legion a long time and was an expert with every kind of weaponry. He was a former para who had also won many shooting competitions run by the French military. He had all the qualifications as an instructor on ammunition and explosives. In fact, one of his jobs in the fort was to look after all the ammo and ordnance. He was running a lesson for legionnaires on how to booby-trap a grenade. Daniel went through this procedure, as he'd done dozens of times, and put his legionnaire observers on a ridge overlooking the valley where he would perform his demonstration. There were two curiosities. First, instead of using a normal practice grenade, he used a shrapnel grenade. Second, the booby trap is normally set by running trip wire *to* the grenade, and then setting the mechanism in position. On this occasion, he attached the wire first and began unravelling it, walking backwards. He had gone only half a pace when the wire pulled the pin and the shrapnel grenade exploded under him. Of course, the legionnaires were stunned by this, and no wonder. When we went to recover his body, he must have had about sixty wounds on his upper torso. His right forearm was never found, it was probably taken by an animal. We had lost a terrific guy, well liked and a Legion stalwart.

Another task which hit international headlines for the Legion and the French army involved the rescue of forty-two children who had been taken hostage by Somali terrorists trying to escape across the border. They were the children of French air force personnel, normally picked up at various stops in the Djibouti camp around 7 a.m. That morning, six armed Somali terrorists had forced their way on board and ordered the military driver to head towards the frontier post.

There was only one official checkpoint which gave entry and exit over the barrage to the general public, controlled by the *gendarmerie*. Another opening was used only by the military for patrols. It was manned by a small detachment. The terrorists chose the military control for their crossing, knowing full well they would be warned in advance of the delicacy of the situation. The bus charged the checkpoint and forced its way through. A Legion corporal fired at the bus as it went speeding on its way, holing the diesel tank. It ran out of fuel just 100 yards on the other side of the border, on the ridge line. Bob Wilson takes up the story:

I was in the alert company, and we followed the bus towards the point it halted. A French artillery general took control and ordered us back towards Hol Hol, in case the hostage-taking was a diversion to a planned invasion by the Somalis. The general meanwhile had ordered the Legion to line up a squadron of light tanks in a semi-circle towards the bus. Then a company from the Legion's 2REP who were also on a tour of Djibouti was called in to act as the assault force, with six ace snipers and spotters standing by to do the business. As soon as they all had the terrorists in their sights, they were to open fire on command. The assault troops would then converge and get the children out through the windows of the bus. The general dithered at the key moment of the plan's execution – the order to fire. He could not be sure that all the terrorists would be shot or that the children would get out unharmed. Either way, it was a risky business and as they all stood waiting in the burning heat and the tension, the Legion's Colonel Ladre jumped on to the bonnet of his Jeep and ordered: 'Fire!'. Six terrorists were shot dead, but when the assault troops hurled themselves at the bus, they found a seventh not previously spotted. He opened fire as a corporal from 2REP jumped onto the bus, killing two of the children and wounding another two. The Legion corporal shot him dead with one bullet to the head. The majority of the children escaped unhurt. The Legion and other French forces stayed on high alert for a week afterwards. It was always a tense situation at the frontier. They had tried every possible type of barrier to try to prevent the Somalis getting in, but somehow they still kept coming.

Kevin Arthur, to use his Legion name, had barely completed his training in 2REP when he learned he was being posted to Djibouti. He was just a lad of 19 then, and said with all innocence: 'Djibouti ... where the fuck's Djibouti?' Travel information was still not regarded as a need-to-know ingredient of Legion operations. Born in 1956, Arthur, as he became universally known, had lived all his life in Brentford. He had no memory of his real father and in due course his mother married again when he was four. Ten years later, when he was 14, his stepfather also left. Soon afterwards he discovered his real father had lived just 200 yards away from the family all that time. They met and got on well. By then, Arthur was already something of a local tearaway, without any real discipline in his life. He got into a fight in Shepherd's Bush and hurt someone very badly. He was sent to Borstal, the then detention centre for young offenders, and got out after a year. He couldn't get a job with his record and reverted to the same style of life that put him in there in the first place, which was thieving and fighting. Arthur went on:

I told myself I had to do something about the future otherwise I would end up back inside. Quite a few members of my family were in the British army. I fancied the Royal Marines. No go there, because of my record, so I decided that the next best thing was to get away, out of the country if necessary. I was talking to someone and the French Foreign Legion came up. I liked the sound of that, so I borrowed fifty quid and trotted off to Paris. I decided to have a look around first, get to know the city a bit and the French. I got mixed up with some prostitutes who needed a bit of protection and hung around for a month or so until the time came I finally decided I would go and knock on the Legion's door. From asking around, I knew they were involved in quite a bit of action at the time. In fact, the Legion was the only army that was doing anything. I went to Fort Nugent in Paris and was greeted by a Swedish sergeant who I learned later had served in Vietnam in the American army. He spoke perfect English and chatted away. He made a point of asking me several times, 'Are you sure you want to join the Legion?'

I said 'yes' each time, without hesitation. A Jamaican Englishman from North London and an Irishman arrived. We all said we were going for it and wanted to sign up. We were brought before a captain, a German who was once in the Hitler Youth, and then on to the preliminary screening process where they check if you're wanted by the police. I was lying through my teeth about my past, but it didn't matter anyway. They'd have found out my life story before they shipped me out. I signed the five-year contract which they pointed out did not mean I was in the Legion yet. It meant that I accepted the code of the Legion and allegiance to France, but they had a get-out clause that allowed them to send me home if I was no bloody good.

After a week at Fort Nugent I was taken by train to Marseille, to the mother camp of 1RE. There I went through all the tests and checks, including the interview with the 'Gestapo'. The interrogator was a South African who spoke perfect English, and he went through much the same detail as in Paris. I was quite sure by then they knew everything there was to know about me, and incidentally they gave me a new name, Kevin Arthur, a fictitious birthdate and place of birth. I had nothing to hide, but it suited me just the same.

After my four-month basic training, they told me I would be sent to Corsica to join the para regiment. I had no idea then that 2REP was the elite of the Legion for which only the top ten of any batch of new recruits gets selected. And there we began our para training. Now, as I speak, having served twenty-one-and-a-half years in the Legion, I can't exaggerate. It can only be a statement of what happened to me in reality.

The Legion was a brutal outfit, and 2REP more brutal than most. But I reckoned that you actually had to analyze the situation. Of course, it came as a bit of a shock to suddenly get a punch in your solar plexus or a whack across the mouth for nothing at all.

Although I was only a kid, I was saying to myself, 'Why the fuck are they doing this to me?' All the way down the line I was looking at the punishment, and then trying to correct the crime. So when I was kicked or punched for the most minor of offences, like failing to understand a command in French, I decided to make sure I knew it next time. I came to realize it was necessary. I can't say I enjoyed it. Of course I didn't, although you do take on board some of the finer points of sadism.

You learn things quickly. The other thing was London pride. I came from England, from Brentford, and I decided I was going to take whatever shit they threw at me. You had to come to terms with that. If I was hit because I wasn't listening or didn't understand, that was my fault. You got your punishment, and that's how it should be. I decided I wasn't going to show I was hurting, even though my guts had just caved in. The alternatives were not for me. There were four suicides while I was in basic training, one of them on the first day I arrived, and a couple of desertions. You looked at their situation afterwards, and you say to yourself those people shouldn't have been where they were. I had come to join the Legion and I was going to make damn certain that I came through it.

I'm talking now about the mid-1970s, and all the NCOs and officers commanding then had fought in some campaign or other. They had all been in the wars, alongside legionnaires upon whom they relied. A lot was made of that. You had to be able to rely on the bloke next to you, if it came to the crunch. There's no point having someone who's going to break down and cry for his mother. They'd done the business and I looked at it this way: if I was getting hit, it was for a reason, and basically for my own good. It would be too late to learn it when we were being charged by ten thousand rebel tribesmen.

They actually asked you: 'What do you feel like now?' And it was best if you replied: 'I enjoyed the punishment and can I have some more please.' There was no answer to that. They respected that kind of attitude.

Arthur reckoned they wanted to see spirit in a guy, and a legionnaire's reaction to punishment was one way of judging it. So the legionnaire did his punishment and got on with the job. If he didn't he was finished, or at the very least the process would take longer and thus be more painful. It was better to get it over and done with. Either way, and with all the language difficulties, it was hard and a lot of recruits found it beyond them. Arthur maintains he could match the reaction to punishment and training rituals to the reasons why a legionnaire had joined in the first place.

According to his assessment there were basically three types:

1 The guy who had woman trouble, rejected in love or in a bad relationship; he's the guy who is emotionally unstable, most likely to crack and commit suicide or desert.
2 The criminal or guy escaping from some bad thing in his life. If they've come to the Legion to hide away for five years, the problem won't go away. There's something inside that means he's always trying to escape and perhaps Legion life actually exacerbates his problem. He might also desert.
3 The soldier or the adventurer; the guy who wants to do something with his life, achieve an ambition that is perhaps not available to him in his own country. He was usually the most committed, the one who was most likely to come through it pretty well unscathed.

The type-casting could never be hard and fast – the disappointed lover might become a great legionnaire.

Another of Arthur's theories – and one which General Rollet used to drum in to new recruits – was that there were many lessons to be learned from the *anciens*. These are the legionnaires who have done their time and reached the grade of first-class or corporal. They never made senior NCO rank, or if they did had been busted. But they were vastly experienced. Arthur said:

> I soon learned that these were the people to watch. It was very important and I latched on to a guy who had seen it all. He was a German named Mishkin. He had been in the original 1 REP and had served four years when the 1961 putsch came along. He was among those who were prepared to jump into France in support

of the putsch leaders and, consequently, he left the Legion when it failed. The amazing thing was that fifteen years later, he came back as a legionnaire, which was bottom of the ladder again. This man taught me everything, most of the time just by watching him and quite often, it's the stupid little things that make life easier. Quite early on, we went on a week's march in the mountains of Corsica and I saw him putting five tins of boot polish in his bag. I asked him why. We weren't going to stop and buff up our boots were we? Well, as it happened, yes we were. We'd stop marching at, say, 3 a.m. and then we'd have to clean our boots ready to be walking again by six. But that wasn't the only reason he took so many tins. He also used it to light a fire. Even damp wood smeared with polish would catch alight very quickly. It was pretty basic really, but when you put a lot of these things together it becomes part of the technique of survival, not only of the elements but of the Legion itself.

Basic training in the 1970s was probably more gruelling than it is today. Also, the weaponry and equipment was fairly unsophisticated. The Foreign Legion was still the poor relation of the French military, and expendable, which meant we were badly equipped. We had to take great care of our gear and make it last. The leather webbing I first used was, believe it or not, World War I vintage. Arms were also fairly ancient when I joined. They had a rifle which was a treasured antique – the MAS36, which was a wooden semi-automatic, capable of ten rounds, with a long, thin bayonet which clipped under the barrel. It was called the toothpick. It was a good rifle and everyone loved it, but it was ancient.

It was when you got into field training that you realized why the discipline was harsh. Legion training was very realistic, often using live ammo. Combat sections were divided into two, assault and cover, and we had to master the commands which were given in French. Training continued in the rudiments of jumping out of a plane into action. We had a week's training on the ground before they took us up to the drop zone. We were told you just get up there and jump out, simple as that. I had never been in a plane in my life and on my first ride I had to jump out! The plane hardly filled you with confidence either. It was an old, very old, Atlas and you could see the bolts falling out as it rattled and banged its way along the runway and into the sky.

There were thirty of us in two lines, all nervous as hell, waiting for the word, *Allez!* We were scared because there were so many things to do – get down on the ground, fold your parachute, get back to the assembly point with your parachute perfectly folded and laid out in perfect lines. There were no pats on the back, or any praise. You did the morning jump and then a night jump, and it wasn't until you had completed your programme that the jump master said, 'Well done lads'. You had to adore him. You had to obey the man. At the end of it, he changed completely. We had hot wine with sugar in it. It was the start of a pattern that emerged throughout training. Once you had done what you had to do, you were admired. There's no other word for it.

We camped out close to the drop zone that night, getting to bed about 2 a.m. and were woken at 5 a.m. We had to clean our boots, clean our combat outfits, clean and oil our guns all in pitch black darkness. By six, we were lined up and ready to go. We climbed aboard the trucks and were driven back to the 2REP camp at Calvi. The colonel and officers were waiting for us. We were lined up and the colonel came up to us one by one and presented us with our wings. Until you received those, you were considered shit. Once you'd got your para wings, that was it. You were one of the family . . . 2REP, the greatest unit in the Foreign Legion.

At that point I had been in the Legion seven months. That night we were allowed out for the first time. We marched into town with the officers for a drink. That was the night I was really proud of myself. This was when I decided the Legion was for me. It wasn't about money; no way. The pay at that time was £53 a month, including jump pay. It was about achievement and pride. Sounds corny but that is how it was for most of us who'd got our wings that day. I swore to God that night I'd stay and do my five years, no matter what happened.

Two months later, in October 1976, Arthur was ready for live action when 2REP were posted to Djibouti. The country was preparing for independence in June 1977 and opponents were shaping up for trouble. The Legion paras were to patrol a section thirty-five miles from Djibouti city, close to the frontier with Somalia. The job of 2REP was two pronged. They were to provide protection for French expatriates and bolster internal security at a time when the situation looked fragile. There was an airport at Djibouti city and the paras could jump rapidly into wherever they were needed in the country. They were also under orders to provide close-quarter protection for the President of Djibouti, Hassan Gouled Aptidon. They linked up with 13th Demi-Brigade to block all access from Somalia into Djibouti, and especially from the 20,000 refugees who were crowding into a shanty town which had built up not far from the frontier. The situation described by Bob Wilson among the refugees had deteriorated, as Kevin Arthur recalls:

> Unfortunately, many were killed in their attempt to get past the barrage. I will not go so far as to say atrocities were committed, but 2REP was under orders to warn those who attempted to cross to retreat, and if they did not we would shoot them, which we did. It was already a difficult situation which is why 2REP was called in. By the time we arrived, the barrage across the frontier had been strengthened. It consisted of an electrified fence of barbed wire, under which had been placed anti-personnel mines at every metre or so, and on the Somali side there was about 200 yards of broken glass. It did not stop them. They would get to the glass, strip off naked and lay their clothes over it and crawl across to the fence. Then they would dig underneath the barbed wire, dodge the mines, and get through to the other side. Up and down the barrage the watchtowers and patrols kept observation twenty-four hours a day. This was combined with routine training operations and jumps which meant that sometimes we barely got any sleep for two days at a time. The blacks trying to cross the barrage seemed to be aware of this and there were times when they would try and catch us offguard.

One of the patrol leaders, a German sergeant, devised a particular way of warning them. He strung victims who were shot or blown up at the barrage to the wire as a warning to others. It was stopped after local protests. Another of the Legion's tasks was to assist the local *gendarmerie* in rounding up illegal immigrants who were already in Djibouti. They would be stopped and searched and if they did not have the right papers, or no papers at all, they would be put into wagons and driven to Post Six and put back over the frontier. It was not unknown for those with papers to be shunted over as well.

For Arthur, a new boy, Djibouti had been a beginning. For Bob Wilson it was one of his last overseas tours. His final term in the Legion was in 'the Gestapo', the Legion's secret police force. Bob, promoted again to chief adjutant, had come full circle and ended his Legion days on the team at Aubagne that vetted all new recruits.

20

1978: KOLWEZI INCIDENT, ZAIRE

'Many whites had been massacred, and if former powers who
once controlled the region had intervened earlier, a lot of lives
could have been saved. We went storming in, guns blazing . . .'

ARTHUR SPOTTED even then what was to
become the pattern of the future for 2REP, and to some extent, the
Legion as a whole. France's military requirements, linked with international commitments, called for greater mobility of troops. They were
required to be reactive to international events, dropping in at the troublespots and move on to the next when the immediate problems had
been resolved or calmed. The Legion's paras soon demonstrated their
adeptness at this role, and by 1978 were on permanent standby for
quick response activity. International armies of the West were all
moving towards rapid reaction solutions, with greater reliance on the
specialist groups within them to take on any situation, any terrain and
any terrorist activity.

While the French military followed its own course, the British and
the Americans were in the process of building up their special forces
units, like the US Seals, and the British SAS and SBS. The Foreign
Legion was, at the dawn of the 1980s, shaping up to become an all-
embracing unit, with its own regiments and specialist companies capable of meeting any military requirement. Already versatile, the Legion
was enhanced by its diversity and since its regiments were linked and,

to some extent, interchangeable, they offered a far more unique service to the French military commanders than standard regiments or specialist forces.

This was now being recognized by the military commanders. Whereas the Legion had been, as Arthur said, 'the poor relation in terms of equipment', this was quickly remedied once the appreciation of the Legion's RR capability was realized. By 1978, 2REP had become the spearhead unit of the French 11th Paratroop Division. It was the same story elsewhere. The Legion was leading the way in on virtually every assault engagement from the 1970s to the present day.

Arthur, for example, was on the move again with 2REP only five months after returning from Djibouti. Now turned 19, he headed across the Atlantic to French Guyana, on the north-east coast of South America. Settled in the early 17th century, French Guyana is the oldest of the overseas possessions of France and the only French territory on the mainland of the Americas. The capital and main port, Cayenne, has a population of 40,000. The country is famous for two other reasons – Devil's Island, dating to the days when it was a French penal colony (which was closed in 1938), and Kourou, the satellite launch base. The country is also one of the finest locations for jungle warfare training, with rich undergrowth and dense, impenetrable terrain which is visited by specialist forces from around the world.

The Legion had a long-standing connection with French Guyana. It was generally adequately looked after by 3REI but in the late 1970s, neighbouring Surinam, granted independence by the Dutch in 1975, was having trouble with a group known as Robinson's Rebels who were attempting a *coup d'état*. The rebels were eluding government forces by crossing the border into Guyana, and 3REI was under pressure, covering the vast territory of difficult terrain. Arthur was with the 2REP unit which was flown in with the one specific task of rounding up the rebels in French territory. 'We operated in the jungle,' said Arthur, 'and we were there for exactly one month when, having made our contribution, we returned to Corsica.'

Barely had 2REP had a chance to settle to their new training schedule mapped out for them in Calvi, than another urgent situation arose in Africa – one that had echoes of the darkest days of the old Belgian Congo when, in 1960, the country gained its independence and disintegrated into bloody civil war. Thousands were massacred, including many white hostages, in the breakaway state of Katanga. In May 1978, the feud re-emerged when around 2,500 Katangan irregulars known as Tigers, heavily armed with Soviet-made hand weapons, mortars, machine-guns and rocket launchers, broke out of exile in Angola where they had been in training with Cuban advisers. They drove in a convoy of Jeeps and trucks to the border town of Kolwezi in their former province, where they engaged upon an orgy of killing, looting and rape. More than 2,500 Europeans, mostly Belgians and French, were trapped and the international media pondered upon their possible fate.

While the Belgians dithered, the French answered Zaire's plea for help by sending in the Legion's 2REP, ever-ready to put on another show of France's willingness to go-it-alone in the international policeman stakes if necessary. It was just possible that they were rushing at the gate in a rather foolhardy manner, and as the paras were quick to note, the last occasion in which the French had parachuted into operation was in Algeria in the 1960s when it was not an altogether qualified success, and previously it was into the disaster of Dien Bien Phu. Arthur was, however, ecstatic then and in his recall exactly twenty years later: 'For us, the Kolwezi affair and our jump into it was the ultimate, a classic of those times,' he insisted. 'And, it was exactly what I had joined the Legion to do.'

The 1st, 2nd and 4th Companies were flown from Corsica in commandeered DC-8s; 638 men in all. They landed under a strict security blanket at Kinshasa. There, they were to transfer to five C-130 Hercules from the Zaire Air Force and two French Transall troop-carriers, seven planes in all. The paras had arrived in the middle of the night, twenty-four hours after they had been placed on standby, and were expecting to set off towards the drop zone by 9 a.m. except that one of the Hercules did not turn up, another developed a fault and one of the Transalls had a flat tyre. In the end, five vastly overcrowded planes got into the air for the three-hour journey to the assault zone. Arthur recalls:

Each Company had specific objectives, progressively gaining control. It was an ambitious project for a total force of just 406 men who were in the first wave but our officers were in no doubt that it could be achieved. Unbeknown to us, the Belgians had sent out a recce team of around twenty-five men who had jumped a couple of nights earlier. I believe they were all wiped out. We saw the bodies of some of them when we jumped, many of them still hanging in the trees. We moved towards our objectives in Kolwezi only to discover that the Belgian army was already in position on the perimeter of the action area but their commanders had been unable to get permission to advance, presumably the Belgian government was still awaiting developments. They refused to tell our officers what they intended to do, so the order came down from on high that we should walk over them, literally, and continue with our own pre-arranged attacks.

I witnessed a lot of atrocities in this operation. We saw the evidence of the massacres and horrific debauchery which gave us the incentive to go in and bring it to a halt, and administer some punishment. Many whites had been massacred, and if former powers who once controlled the region had intervened earlier, a lot of lives could have been saved. We went storming in, guns blazing, because by then there was no time left for talking.

For me, it was the ultimate – jumping from an aircraft into serious action, in which you never knew if you would come back alive. There were about six days of continuous fighting. Again unbeknown to us, and what French intelligence never told us, was that there were roughly 2,000 Katangan Tigers waiting for us. The element in our favour was that the black soldier, lacking training and discipline, had a particular method of savagery, killing and butchering their foe but having won the battle they stop to have a good time. We advanced on Kolwezi and quickly established our objectives. There was some fierce spasmodic fighting and finally some hand-to-hand, but we overcame the resistance very quickly. We stayed there the night and the next morning. Then, we commandeered the huge lorries that were used to transport ore from the local copper mines and went to the Shaba region which was being overrun by Angolans, backed by the Cubans. We were headed for a mining village where the strength of the opposition was based. We encountered heavy fighting. Four legionnaires were killed and thirty-three injured. The Katangans suffered heavy losses. Half of them were doped up with a local drug which apparently made them feel invincible and certainly it was true that you could hit them with four or five bullets and they would still keep coming at you. Then, they'd just drop. We persevered and secured all our given objectives and spent the remainder of our time there policing the region. Eventually, when the task was done, we were airlifted from Kinshasa and then on to Corsica for a breather.

Meanwhile, the Belgians finally arrived and their paras came the easy way, landing at Kolwezi airport which had been secured by paras of the Zaire army. At the end of the operation, Kolwezi and the surrounding townships were strewn with bodies, over 1,200 killed first by the Katangan raiders and then by the incoming paras.

However, there would be more operations. Later that year, 1REC was back in Chad for the first of a series of expeditions following the assassination of the president. Djibouti also had a few difficult years after its own independence and then the Central African Republic, the former stronghold of France's presence in middle-Africa, came to life in similar fashion. Indeed, across the whole of its former territories, legionnaires were in and out like gadflies.

There were numerous embarrassing moments, but none that could match the French government's own red faces on certain matters, especially in the arrival of Colonel Jean Bokassa who took over as President of the Central African Republic in 1966 and appointed himself Emperor Bokassa in a lavish ceremony in December 1977. Bokassa's regime began to fall apart in January 1979, when an order that school children wear expensive uniforms made in his own factory, prompted widespread protest demonstrations. The army was called in, and many children were put in prison, where they were massacred by the imperial guard. A committee of African judges later concluded that Bokassa had personally participated in the killings. In September 1979 he was overthrown in a French-backed coup.

Arthur's stint in what the legionnaires unaffectionately called 'Bokassaland' led him towards a crossroads – he was heading towards the end of his five-year contract. Time had swept by. He took stock of what had happened since he joined: it had been a tough life, but he had come through it; taken part in two full-on combat operations, served in Africa three times and Guyana once, collected four campaign medals and achieved the rank of corporal, and was still only 23 years old:

I had been formed by the Legion into a different person. They taught you to think for yourself and, more importantly, for other people. When I came in, I was looking to older legionnaires for guidance and the way through it. It hadn't been easy. I'd taken a lot of punishment and a lot of knocks but I'd made it, that's how I saw it. I'd made good and become a fit, strong frontline soldier. I was now getting pleasure from helping the new batch of youngsters coming through. I was a tough bastard, too. That's what the Legion is all about. Constant renewal. There was another aspect that I often pondered. There were very few English legionnaires around at the time. The number in 2REP could almost be counted on one hand. That changed dramatically after the Falklands War when paras and soldiers discharged from British units came looking for action. There was an influx of more than 300 into the REP alone, although I doubt that more than 100 of them stayed more than two years. Quite a few deserted and others transferred out to other regiments for overseas posting. I was proud to have been among a very small number of Brits at the time who had come through the REP and completed five years.

As my contract term came towards its close, I decided that it was time for a change of scenery. Corsica had been terrific. It had given me everything I wanted, it was the ultimate. The social life had been terrific, all the usual requisites of Legion life that have gone down in history were available. The island provided all that serving soldiers ever needed, including a large contingent of pretty girls on holiday from across Europe every summer. Strong lads in smart uniforms were still an attraction. It was time to do other things. I re-enlisted for another five years and in 1982, I was posted to Tahiti, or to be more precise, to the island of Mururoa, where in the midst of these palmy atols they were blowing up nuclear bombs.

21

CHANGING TIMES

'There had been NCOs who were quite clearly sadists – and a sadist in that sort of environment is very distasteful and actively discouraged.'

TADEUSZ MICHNIEWICZ refused to change his name. He is of Polish background. His parents came to Britain just after World War II. His two grandfathers had served in Polish forces fighting for the Allies, after dramatic escapes from Siberian prison camps. Both sides of his family came from eastern Poland, in the region annexed by the Soviet Union in 1939. Tadeusz is British, but in France no one would believe him. To his friends, he accepted the shortened version of 'Mich'. He was a brilliant student when he joined the Legion at 18, much to the chagrin of his mother. It had been his ambition to get a commission with the British army after joining the cadets while at school. From then on, he was heading for a military career which looked set fair with ten O-levels and one A-level at 16, and he was doing three more A-levels. He intended to go for a short service commission in the Royal Marines but failed the eye test, being short-sighted. His next choice was the Parachute Regiment, but there was a two-year waiting list and they suggested he joined the Royal Engineers – which he didn't want to do.

Mich's arrival at the Legion recruiting office (see Prologue) brought his mother to the edge of apoplexy. When Mich first told her he planned to volunteer for the Legion, she tried desperately to talk him out of it, and enlisted the help of relatives and friends to try to persuade him against it. Even when he was accepted, she tried to get him out. He had been in for about six weeks when he was called up to the Regimental Security Officer, and was asked point blank: 'Do you want to be here?'

He said, 'Absolutely.'

'Are you sure?'

'Absolutely.'

'Here's a pen and a piece of paper . . . now write to your mother and tell her that will you!'

She had been on to the French Embassy, the British Embassy and everyone else she could think of, convinced that her teenage son should not be in the Foreign Legion and that he wanted to come out. 'I had already written to her and told her I was fine,' said Mich, 'but as mothers do, she refused to accept that I wanted to say in.'

Mich was a natural candidate for 2REP, which by then had six companies, four combat companies, a recce and support company and a logistics company. It was a big regiment, 1,300 strong. Most of the recruits were sent to 3rd Company which had the reputation of being the toughest in the regiment. It is supplied by a training regiment that still operates on the tried-and-tested system of 'farming' its candidates. Each training platoon is sent to one of them and each 'farm', in the middle of nowhere, is converted into a self-contained training camp within its own grounds. For Mich, the first stages consisted of what he described as 'indoctrination in the ethos of the Legion . . . the traditions and the history'. Language training was also begun, concentrating on commands and terms for weaponry and progressing to very basic military skills. There was a lot of marching and a lot of running with people flaking out left, right and centre and being given a kick and told to get up. He commented:

> One of the things that struck me was that at the time, volunteers renounced all civilian status, which is why your passport and clothes were taken away. You come under French military

law and have no rights as a citizen of France. You are purely and simply a paid soldier. When the French joined, they were given an arbitrary nationality, of another French-speaking country, so that in theory they become non-French nationals and renounce their citizenship as well. All the French had to change their names because they could not keep their original ones. The oddest thing was that even though they were French and could understand the language, they seemed to be the slowest in catching on. In the Legion when you are told to do something, you do it instantly, otherwise it's too late and you feel a heavy hand or boot thudding into some part of your body. Frenchmen seemed to have a tendency towards avoiding instant reaction. Next thing they knew, they were on the ground spitting out a few teeth.

In spite of these incidents of traumatic intrusions upon your anatomy, the first month passed with incredible speed. There was never a free moment from dawn to lights out. We normally averaged four to five hours sleep a night, maximum, and we never seemed to have enough to eat. Breakfast wasn't thought of as a meal. It was generally a bowl of coffee and a croissant. The two main meals were lunch and dinner but during training, before we could go and eat, everyone had to line up at a chin-up bar and a rope; we started by climbing the rope with hands and feet, and then gradually it was made more difficult, like no feet and then hands only with back pack added. If you didn't make the target climb for the day, you didn't eat. The last thing we did in training was a raid march. It lasted three days and two nights over 120 kilometres with full kit. It was designed to cover a lot of distance in a short time carrying a lot of weight. There were certain stands along the way when we were tested on some of the things we had already learned, pretty hard stuff. It was more a test of willpower than anything else and even though we had been toughened up since we joined, a lot of people dropped out with their feet in bits. My training platoon began with seventy-two and ended up with twenty-four. So in all, it was a serious selection process that explodes the myth that the Legion will take anyone. It is simply not true, and I don't think it has been for some considerable time. By the time you reached the end of the process of selection, you were left with a fairly elite bunch of would-be legionnaires.

At the end of the first training period, the Regiment put on a show at the 'farm', with the regimental band and the colonel in attendance. There was a torchlight procession, rousing music and songs and then the rookie legionnaires were authorized to put on their kepis for the first time. After that, they were transported back to the base camp in buses and next day were given their first day off since they joined. It consisted of an organized meal out of camp, a late lunch at a restaurant in town with NCOs and an officer. From mid-afternoon the legionnaires were free until midnight. Two Brits who had met in Colchester military prison before they joined the Legion, emboldened by large quantities of alcohol, chose the occasion to take on the whole of the Castelnaudary rugby fifteen in their own bar and managed to put half a dozen of them in hospital, plus a couple of the MPs who came to pick them up.

Next morning, they were marched from the guardhouse to see the colonel, their heads cut and bloody and none too steady on their feet having been 'calmed down' by the MPs in the regimental jail. The colonel was apparently impressed by their performance against the rugby team, who were old adversaries, but not sufficiently pleased to show any leniency. They were given fifteen days in the guardhouse.

Drunkenness, fighting or other disorderly conduct will never get a legionnaire thrown out, unless he shoots someone while under the influence. A few days in the guardhouse came to virtually everyone at some stage of their Legion career, some visiting more often than others. There was no particular stigma attached to it. In matters military, however, Legion doctrine and discipline stood above all else and, like others before him, Mich in his personal observations of Legion training techniques and the occasional violence, concluded it was a perfectly simple and straightforward philosophy:

When someone did something wrong, as well as that person being hit a few times the whole unit had to do some form

226

of physical exercise which pissed everybody off. Consequently, there was peer pressure on those who were prone to misdemeanour. The standard form of collective punishment was press-ups. We did a lot of press-ups. The interesting thing was, though, that the man who gave the punishment also joined in. If a corporal or sergeant gave the order, he would be down with you, doing the same number of press-ups. There was also a lot of running around with rifles over your heads, but one of the most excruciating forms of punishment in the Legion ever devised was called the 'duck walk', which was squatting down with your hands behind your neck and waddling on your haunches. The worst 'duck walk' I ever had to do was from the firing point on the range to the target and back – a distance of 200 metres. The whole platoon took that one because our shooting wasn't good enough. There was a double edge to punishment. It served to emphasize a point in training and it formed part of the procedures for bringing you to peak fitness and efficiency. NCOs were determined to get your skills up to the highest level, better than anyone else. The fitness level, which was already high anyhow, was constantly topped up.

Those who were flagging were given a kick to help them through the pain barrier. And while some have spoken about the violence in the Legion, something which is ruthlessly applied by NCOs, there is a big difference between brutality and physical discipline. There seemed to be an instinctive knowledge among the NCOs of what was acceptable and what wasn't, or how far they could go with the person who was being beaten. There had been NCOs who were quite clearly sadists – and a sadist in that sort of environment is very distasteful and actively discouraged. However, it was quite often difficult for the senior NCOs and officers to get evidence that something like that was going on.

I had a case like that in my platoon, a French guy who did not like Brits. A heavily built man with a strong presence, he was a corporal and lived with the platoon. He was a nightmare. He was picking off the Brits one by one, hitting them for no reason, or continuing to punish them for something they did the day before yesterday. When it came to my turn, I just lost my temper. I slammed him against the wall and said that if he ever laid a finger on me again for no reason whatsoever, I'd beat the living shit out of him. He knew he had overstepped the mark and he didn't touch me again. I took a risk. If he'd reported me, I'd have got forty days inside. What these people traded on was that junior legionnaires were so scared of upsetting authority. Measured physical discipline for a reason was acceptable; sadistic brutality was not.

Junior soldiers entering an environment where this type of punishment is known to exist expect to get whacked now and again if they have done something wrong or failed to obey a command. When they haven't done anything wrong, then the NCO is exposed for what he is, and they know it.

Old enmities built up during early months among recruits and NCOs were temporarily set aside at the end of basic training, when those who came through the process were taken on an organized night out – only the second time they had been allowed out since they arrived in the Legion. Mich continued:

The tensions over the previous four months were released that night because we all thought that was it, the end of our training. In truth, it was only the preparation for the next stage and for those of us going to the Parachute Regiment it began again instantly. Even the worst of the bullshit we had experienced so far had nothing on what now began to unravel. I was glad we had that night out when we did, because I did not get another minute's free time for the next three months.

They had become legionnaires, and now they were to undergo the rigours of para training, with the emphasis on teamwork. Every one of them was carefully observed, not just in the quality of work but in his attitude to the whole package, particularly, said Mich, 'the bullshit'. If there was a hint of carelessness or lack of interest, life would become so unpleasant that they would either desert or ask for a transfer. Mich believed there was a certain built-in logic to this procedure:

Having made their selections for the Regiment, they could not turn round and ask for the man to be moved out because they had to give a reason, and bureaucracy kicks in. This way, they worked around it. There were a few desertions during those first few months in Corsica but I believe only one, a Frenchman, managed to get off the island. After deserting, whether he gets clear or not, the man is usually transferred out of the Parachute Regiment, because of obvious lack of commitment. In fact, he may even find Legion life more acceptable in another regiment where although the discipline is much the same, the work is less intense and there is a good deal more free time. As a package of man-management techniques, extreme though it may be, it works and those who come out the other side generally have no regrets. They become proficient paratroopers, highly skilled, toughened to well beyond their own perceived capabilities. The blind hatred harboured for your NCOs becomes less and less until finally, you are accepted and they accept you. Very soon you may have aspirations to become one of them.

22

1982: LEBANON ERUPTS

'We arrived two weeks after the
American Embassy had been hit
by a truck bomber.'

BY THE 1980s, the Legion's role as an interven-
tion force, capable of putting substantial numbers of specialized troops
into virtually any volatile situation, was well established. It was sufficiently skilled and equipped to be included in international peace-
keeping actions, pursuing attempts to separate and hold warring
factions apart until diplomacy could be brought to bear. Many situations across Africa and the Middle East developed through the decade
and on into the 1990s. The 'peace' element in the job description was
a variable term, and not one usually applied when legionnaires are in
action – and especially not in the case of 2REP who as a matter of
course generally go in feet first.

One of the first peace-keeping operations for the legion came in
August 1982. They were to form part of an international attempt to
force some kind of calm upon the Lebanon, which was invaded by the
Israelis in June of that year. The Legion's 2REP joined the combined
French–Italian–American effort to end the Israelis' six-week siege of
Beirut which culminated with Yasser Arafat and 7,000 troops of the
Palestine Liberation Organization being forced out of the country that
had been their power base for the previous twelve years. The operation

was called Killer Whale One, and Legion companies had the honour of being first in, as the multi-national force attempted to set up a buffer zone between the Lebanese Christian Militia, the Palestinians and the Israelis.

The Legion paras set off in trucks from Calvi for a three-hour drive across Corsica to the airport for the flight out. They were accompanied part of the way by the girls from the brothels outside the main gates of the camp. They were in cars and jeeps, hanging out of the windows and weaving in and out of the trucks and blowing kisses to their departing clients. Mich was among those photographed loading gear into the aircraft, and the picture appeared in newspapers around the world, including the following day's *Daily Mail* in Britain, which landed him in hot water at home. It was the first his mother knew that he was going on active service. He had thought it best she did not know straightaway, and was unaware he was being photographed. So once again, she was ringing the camp for news.

They flew to Cyprus and spent the night on the tarmac, guarding the stores and equipment before moving on to Beirut. There was a news camera crew there and once again, British relatives of 2REP saw them on the BBC news. They were shipped from Larnaca by French amphibious troop carrier straight into Beirut harbour. In theory, the Israelis should have vacated the harbour before the first of the multi-national troops arrived. They hadn't done so, and were still in total control of the harbour. The para's colonel walked over to the Israeli officer in charge, a major, and made his displeasure known that the Israelis were still there and told them to get the hell out.

Beirut was chaotic and dangerous, the once beautiful city decimated by Israeli attacks and years of local warmongering. The port area became the rear base for the 2REP contingent, which consisted of around 700 men. They were the only Legion regiment involved in the first phase of the operation to give protective cover for the evacuation of the PLO army, led by Yasser Arafat, which was being dispersed across North Africa. Next, they were tasked to secure the port area to enable the free movement of other troops coming in over the next ten days – first the French regulars, followed by the Italians and finally American Marines. They then moved on into the city, drawing the fire of any remaining nests of local militia. Although the Lebanese factions had been separated by the so-called 'green-line', there was still sporadic shellfire and at night the legionnaires watched the coloured tracers shooting across the sky. From the first night, 2REP actively patrolled their designated area in assault and cover formations, demonstrating what was termed a 'robust presence'. This meant if any of their troops were attacked or threatened in any way, they were to respond in kind. The Legion's policy angered the peace-keeping commanders who thought heavy-handed legionnaires would merely antagonize the already fraught situation. Legion section commanders were unrepentant. They were not prepared to allow legionnaires to become sitting ducks for the trigger-happy Arabs.

The first night of patrols was eerie. The troops were warned there would be booby traps and mines, so proceeded with care. They also came under occasional sniper fire which was met with a hail of return fire from their own assault teams. Eventually, they were left alone. The multi-national force began arriving over the next two weeks and the Americans took over the port. Legion units were pushed further out to begin establishing the buffer zone. It became rather more tense during this period, but they suffered only a few light casualties from shell splinters. And then it stopped.

The French government ordered the Legion out of the operation ahead of schedule, on 13 September, as did the Americans following the election of President Gemayal, a non-Muslim, who was promptly assassinated. The powder-keg situation was further aggravated by the massacre of hundreds of men, women and children in a Palestinian refugee camp by Phalangists on 18 September 1982. Yasser Arafat, through King Hussein of Jordan, appealed to France to restore its troops. It did so with a regular French army unit, although the Legion would return the following year when the tension again mounted.

In the meantime, 2REP's mission, though only partially completed, was recognized as an excellent response to a delicate and dangerous situation, and a medal for courageous service was cast. In November, on Armistice Day, 2REP was selected to represent the Legion in a static parade at the Arc de Triomphe, inspected by President Mitterand. Mich was able to get a message to his mother and she hurriedly prepared to make her way to Paris to watch her son on parade. It would be the first time she had seen him since he enlisted. He said:

In the end, I think she was quite proud. There was her son in the midst of these tough legionnaires, medal on chest, but she was only slightly less worried. We had been given permission to roam free in Paris that night, but we were warned to be back at Fort Nugent by midnight, as we were flying back to Corsica at dawn. I arranged to have a meal with my mother afterwards, but I'm afraid I let her down. It was only a brief meeting and I was full of apologies when I explained that this was the first time since I joined the Legion that we had been allowed out. I don't think she really understood how important it was for me to be with the rest of the unit and get out on the town.

My memory of the evening faded into a haze of alcohol and I awoke the next morning in a strange bed, realizing I had missed the midnight deadline by about six hours. I grabbed my clothes and had a hair-raising taxi drive to the airport, to arrive just as the unit was being presented to the colonel prior to boarding the aircraft. The sergeant-major had just reported two missing when I fell out of the cab, dishevelled and half drunk. 'Correction', said the sergeant, 'one missing'. That was another Brit, from Northern Ireland, who joined just before I did. We never saw him again, and I heard later he had returned to England and re-joined the Royal Marines. Virtually the whole of the unit, it transpired, had been late and because there were so many defaulters, the colonel handed out a collective punishment of just one day's restriction of privileges.

The troubles in Lebanon, from which the Legion had been abruptly evacuated in September 1982, flared again and engaged the 2REI and 1REC at various times from the late spring of 1983, once again as part of France's overall contribution to the so-called peace-keeping attempts. The Legion came in as part of 31 Brigade, an armoured force designed to move by air and created specifically for overseas operations in 1980. The situation was calmer but tense when they arrived and, gradually, it heightened as the unidentifiable militias operating in Beirut began to step up the action. Legion operations were hampered first by a sensitive political situation which restricted any aggressive military action, and second in the urban house-to-house warfare which epitomized the unrest.

Gradually, following the relative calm they walked into, Legion units found themselves sheltering from a hail of heavy calibre shellfire. Among those who experienced the illogical and unidentifiable attacks was Phil Meason, who as a communications operator was at the hub of the command centre which tried to make sense of what was going on around them.

Like Mich and the rest, Meason's family was also concerned as to his whereabouts and safety. They had not seen him since Christmas 1980 when he joined the Legion after five years in the Royal Navy. He departed company with the navy with some bitterness after a six month battle of personalities between himself and a petty officer. Meason was kicked out and the officer was busted. He worked in Portsmouth for a while and then when in France, on a hitch-hiking holiday, ended up in Monaco in a bar which by coincidence had a corner dedicated to the Foreign Legion, with posters and souvenirs.

There was a Legion calendar with the address of a recruiting office at Nice. He went along a couple of days later and soon found himself inside. On New Years' Eve 1980, he was taken to Fort Saint Nicholas in Marseille, and from there up to Aubagne. His family knew nothing of his plans. He'd sent them a postcard from France, but they didn't hear from him again until about four months later, when he was accepted into the Legion after his training:

The discipline was not a lot different to the Royal Navy, or probably any other military organization. Same bullshit, different language. We had quite a few Brits coming in at the time and a lot more would follow at the end of the Falklands War. The deserters tended to be those who had not had previous military service and consequently had not experienced the wrath of an excitable sergeant major. There were quite a few like me who hadn't quite made it in life and wanted to redeem themselves elsewhere.

They changed the last letter of my name and my age. The most curious thing about the selection process I found was that they kept trying to talk you out of volunteering. The British corporal who signed me up kept saying, 'Are you sure you want to do this?' We started with forty-two and ended up with twenty-eight. The two Brits who were with me were both dropped. One night after the second guy was sent home I got called out of bed to see the corporal: 'You're the last one, so don't fuck it up.'

With his previous naval experience, Meason had been earmarked for communications, a radio operator, and opted for the infantry, 2REI based in Corsica. The Regiment had six companies on the island, rotationally serving overseas. It was all very chummy. The six who went from the training regiment 2REI were brought before the colonel who asked what they would prefer to do. Meason requested an amphibious company and so he became a radio operator in 5th Company which, sure enough, was an amphibious unit. He arrived in late afternoon and that night went straight out to join the company who were on the rifle ranges. The company commander was a German adjutant. Phil had a couple of days acquainting himself with the routine and that was that: he was fully operational within the week. He was later sent on a radio operations course and on completion was posted to the command platoon as the captain's radio operator.

Before the Lebanon experience, Meason had already become a seasoned Legion traveller, and incidentally to some of the best postings available – the sun, surf and silver beaches of Mayotte in the Indian Ocean, the spice of Madagascar and then the more earthy Senegal. He'd availed himself of some excellent courses and training before he rejoined his old platoon back in Corsica for a mountain skiing course in the alps. If there was a time when soldiering could be classed as enjoyment, Phil Meason appeared to have discovered it, in excess. But it was Beirut next stop:

We arrived two weeks after the American Embassy had been hit by a truck bomber. The Legion had one company deployed in the foothills, engaged in training the Lebanese army with weapons supplied by the Americans. Another company was based at an old swimming pool, battered and bomb scarred. The pool was empty of course, and we bunked in the changing rooms. We ran patrols out in the streets and alleys. Our main task was protection of the French Embassy, liaising with multi-national forces, including the US Seals who were working offshore. The French Green Berets were in a hotel down the road from us. To begin with it was fairly quiet although very tense, the patrols had to operate with extreme caution. There were still a lot of car bombs going off. We spent a brief spell in the mountains, relieving another company, and then we were brought back into Beirut, just as the shit hit the fan.

We were moved on to the eighth floor of a block of flats. We could feel the tension building up. Other platoons were spread out through the area. One night, at around 8 p.m., we were just finishing our coffee when we heard this shouting and screaming. I went out on to the balcony and saw that the block of flats across the street was being emptied of people and the same was happening all along the road. Within minutes the whole street was packed. I yelled to the captain and down we went and grabbed the first guy who passed and he said the militia was coming. It was in fact the first anniversary of the massacre of the Palestinian refugee camp. There were a mass of lights heading down the street towards us, a lot of gunfire followed. The captain ordered a protective ring with what personnel we had available until the Premier REC could get there to back us up. Meanwhile the Lebanese army started blasting their way through the city looking for the militia.

We stayed well past our departure date, stuck between gunfire and shelling all around us. We were eventually evacuated by ship to Cyprus, from where we returned to Corsica. We heard soon afterwards that the building we had used for our command platoon was blown up by a suicide bomber. He drove a truck laden with explosives into the block of flats. Fifteen French paratroopers who had taken over the building from us were killed, which caused a big stink back in France. During our time there, eleven legionnaires were killed and fifteen injured.

TOP Soldiers of the Foreign Legion during an amphibious assault.

BELOW In defensive position in the Saudi desert, 80km from the Iraqi border during the Gulf War, November 1990.

Legionnaires parachuting in training in Corsica in 1989

BELOW The 13th Demi-Brigade marching through London in 1940 before joining de Gaulle and the British in Africa where they fought the Vichy Legion.

Borstal boy made good…Kevin Arthur completed 21½ years in the Legion.

BELOW Needs must: a goat to the slaughter by African-based legionnaires in search of food.

Humanitarian work in Chad: the legionnaires evacuated many wounded locals for treatment after the conflict in 1984.

BELOW In the heat of battle.

Like all volunteers, Meason had not been home since he joined up. In theory, Brits and other nationals were not allowed to travel out of French territory because the Foreign Legion held on to their passports for the duration of their five-year contract, thus making it difficult for deserters to get home. With the move towards the relaxation of border controls under European Union rules, British legionnaires discovered they could get home using their Legion ID card. They were usually just waved through French immigration, and with a bit of sweet-talking at the British end, usually managed to get through. Meason said:

> I had a really good time. The family were all in tears, of course, because not only had I survived the war in the Lebanon but I had finally left the Foreign Legion – at least that's what they thought when I arrived home. I had to explain that I had no regrets at all. Okay, it had been a hard life on occasions but there was no way I was going to desert. As soon as my leave was up . . . I'd be back there reporting for duty.

23

1983: BAD DAYS IN CHAD;
1987: FRENCH GUYANA

'... guys were sneaking under the Jeeps during the night to drain
water from the radiators to make coffee. We were all in a dire
state through thirst: You couldn't sleep, couldn't eat or swallow.'

FRANCE'S THIRD call to aid the government of
Chad, its former colony, began in August 1983 after rebels backed by
Colonel Gadaffi's Libyan army launched a takeover bid for the country. France responded by dispatching hundreds of troops, while in the
US, President Reagan promised to send $25 million worth of military
hardware. Rebel and government forces were fighting see-saw battles
for several towns in northern Chad, and the rebels had recently recaptured the oasis of Faya-Largeau. The Chadian president accused the
Libyans of using 'Soviet tactics' by moving large numbers of planes,
tanks, and artillery against Faya-Largeau. 'It was genocide,' he said.
'We have seen nothing like it except in films of the Second World War.'

Ironically, France was sending in its own ground and air troops to
deter a Libyan air force which itself was flying French Mirage bombers,
recently supplied by France. By the late autumn, France had 3,300
troops in Chad, including the whole of the Legion's 2REP under a
deployment known as Operation Manta. They came to a region whose
infrastructure was totally unprepared for the arrival of a modern army.
The REP mounted a guard for the airport which was receiving incoming

French supplies and military aircraft and setting up a communications network. The operation began to get interesting when a French air force Jaguar was shot down overflying a Libyan incursion column into Chad. A company from 2REP was ordered to jump into the area to recover the pilot's body and the black box flight recorder.

On the day the plane was brought down, rebel forces also attacked across the 15th parallel which had served as the buffer zone. In doing so, the Libyan-backed troops at last prompted France to get even. On 27 January 1984, the French military ordered its commanders in the field to consolidate their positions in the southern half of the country and shift forces sixty miles to the north. France also doubled the number of combat aircraft in Chad which the Chadian government had been pleading with President Mitterand to do for months. It was still, however, what some in the Legion described as a 'pussy-foot operation'.

The REP began deep patrols close to Libyan positions. They were supporting local rebels but at the time were not actively targeting French troops. Consequently, legionnaires were ordered to let the Chadian army fight the rebels while they kept observation on the Libyans. There were many search and record missions into isolated villages, trying to establish weapon storage. If there was good intelligence that one of these encampments was supporting the rebels, a unit would drive in, get the local population together and then systematically search their tiny homes. There were still a lot of camel-borne nomadic tribes around, using large earthenware jars, normally transported by camel, big enough to hide a person. It was not uncommon for the legionnaires to discover mines, AK47s and handguns hidden inside. Village elders would be brought in for questioning by the Chadian army and the weapons confiscated.

Local warfare was incredible. Mich recalled:

One of our guys witnessed a battle between the Chadian Army and the Libyan-backed rebels, and it was like something out of the Middle Ages, only using modern gear. The army unit, in their Toyotas with machine-guns and rocket launchers mounted on the top, lined up on one side and a kilometre or so away, the rebels did the same. Then they began to charge, as if they were on four-legged mounts, firing as they went and the side with the most vehicles and men left standing at the end of it won. The others would turn on their heels and either regroup or disperse. Both sides had had extensive battle training from their respective 'advisers' yet come the moment, they reverted to the battle charges used when they were on camels or horses!

For other units from 2REP the scenes in Chad were more harrowing, and for Terry Newton (not his real name) the posting was a baptism of fire. In his view the experience confirmed why the Legion needed to keep its troops mentally and physically on top. Some of the appalling sights he saw in the aftermath of African battles could have made those with less of a stomach for the horrors of war suicidal. Terry said:

It's only when you see this kind of destruction of human life that you appreciate all the shit we took in training was not just a matter of hard discipline and brutal punishment. I thought back and remembered how it went all the way down the line, to the extent of making sure that when you're walking out or on parade, you leave the barracks looking pristine, with exactly sixteen ironed creases in your shirt. You set that piece of homebodiness against the sheer graft of an anti-tank course, and when you arrive in the middle of a war zone in Africa, you begin to get the picture.

If you didn't have the feelings knocked out of you at the beginning, you'd never stand the pressures when it came to the real-life horrors, and there were plenty of those when we were posted to Chad. Seeing photographs of bodies hacked to pieces is never the same as seeing it for real.

My unit was out on deep patrols for three or four weeks at a time. We had limited water supplies, and none to wash or shave in. We were stinking and bearded and all suffering from dysentry. The only decent food we got was when we shot a few gazelles or brought goats from villagers, always live. Never buy dead meat. We'd slaughter and skin them ourselves. It got to be routine.

Out in the sticks, we saw the evidence of battles between Chadians and rebel troops backed by Libyans. Both sides were heavily armed, but they had little training and poor skills. Many died from misuse of their own weapons or through machine-gunners opening up in panic on their own troops. Hundreds of bodies were lying around, just left to rot, with hyenas stripping them to the bone. We'd see animals running off with pieces of human anatomy in their mouths.

Up on the border with Libya, the Chadians had opened up a prison camp for captured rebels. The conditions were appalling and it's a wonder that any one of us in a half mile radius didn't catch some life-threatening disease. They used the prisoners for working parties, digging latrines and so on. If they did not work fast enough, they'd machine-gun them all down and get another working party in. We were out on patrol all the time and never spent any time at the base. The Libyans and the rebels were on the move into Chad and there were large numbers of French troops on the ground. There was a lot of tension and we received a message that a whole section of French paras had been wiped out in an ambush. Arab voices had been picked up on the radio, or so they thought. The location was not far from our present position and we were assigned to go and collect the bodies and tend the wounded until the choppers came in to take them away. When we got there, it was a terrible mess. But we discovered they hadn't been ambushed, it was an accident.

They had halted at a battle site which was littered with bodies, abandoned weaponry and tanks. The French paras had stopped to investigate and were taking photographs. One of the guys apparently climbed into one of the tanks and pulled the breach. There was a shell still in the spout and it went off and exploded other stuff. There were about thirty casualties. Many of them were dead or dying and some of those still alive had lost legs and arms. There was no shade, the sun was beating down. Some of the wounded were halucinating and dehydrated. They all needed urgent medical attention.

We gave what medical attention we could. When the rescue choppers came in one of them crashed, and in the confusion they started loading the dead bodies first instead of the wounded. It was a total fuck-up.

We used up most of our own water tending the wounded. No one remembered to ask the rescue choppers to come back to resupply us and, consequently, we had none left. We went for about three days without water. Our commanding officer had to post guards on our vehicles when we stopped because guys were sneaking under the Jeeps during the night to drain water from the radiators to make coffee. We were all in a dire state through thirst: you couldn't sleep, couldn't eat or swallow. It was the first real experience many of us had had of how painful thirst can be. You hear stories of people committing suicide through thirst – and now I could understand that.

We all lost several kilos in weight by the time we got back, stinking and choking through lack of water. We were sent straight away on patrols again across the desert, hostile in both senses – climate and enemy. We were dashing about in Jeeps for days on end on some very long hauls in sandstorms, getting endless punctures. We didn't bother with jacks. We just all piled out, manually lifted the vehicles while a couple of the guys took off the wheel and we did on-the-spot repairs, taking the tyre off and patching up the innertube. It was hard going; sand in your face and hair and eyes, even though we had goggles on.

On one occasion, one of the guys actually stopped the Jeep and started crying, said he couldn't go on. The corporal just looked at him and said, 'Fucking get out'. He pulled him out of the driving seat and got in himself and the guy piled in beside him. Our commanding officer came along and looked at me and balled me out for not wearing my weapon. There was no let up in the discipline, and perhaps there couldn't be under those conditions.

In August, the rebels and their Libyan advisers attacked. We were mobilized in the middle of the night. They told us to take whatever we needed. We loaded ammunition and grenades and set off to move 200 vehicles across the mountains towards the border. On the way, we were getting all tensed up for a fight, hyping ourselves up. I made a pact with one of my mates that if I was badly wounded, lost my legs or whatever, he'd shoot me and I'd do the same for him. It was a two-day trek to the frontier to set up an ambush at one of the villages where we knew the rebels were going to come in. The plan was to let them come into the village and then blow the fuck out of the village while they were in there, shoot them like rats – supposedly. But it didn't work out that way. They didn't show. The Libyans, who had very good communications, intercepted our own radio messages and the cheeky bastards started taking the piss and asked us to speak a bit more clearly. Consequently, our section didn't fire a shot in anger on that operation.

After overseas tours of this nature, the thing you look forward to is your leave. After weeks in the desert, the colours of lush countryside hurts your eyes. You've also built up a fair cache of money and you want to spend it – checking into the best hotels and just letting the tap water run and run. We'd buy new clothes and when they got dirty, we threw them away. It was criminal. And the partying – how can you not go for a blast after that kind of experience!

Newton did his corporal's course and then moved on to a mountain troop and more hard graft of a different kind – a month's climbing course until he was proficient enough to tackle sheer rock. He had an exercise which involved all the French airborne services parachuting in for an anti-tank operation and broke the record for that. The Legion unit won the shooting and the backpacking:

It really pissed off the French paras. On the way back, a gang of us went out to celebrate and got into trouble. We all went to the nick for that. There, we did fourteen-hour days digging rock out of the mountain watched over by guards with Alsatians, so you didn't argue with them. We also did eight kilometre runs with full backpack. The problem was that the nick was so packed at the time that at nights you were sleeping so close to the next guy you could hardly move about, and when you heard the bolts going the next morning, everybody clammered to get out. There were so many of us, there was no time for showers so we were all hosed down.

We had two other postings to Africa in the next couple of years, one to Djibouti and then Chad again, although by then it had quietened down. The Djibouti excursions proved to be another horror story. We had to go out to a plane crash; 24 dead. The bodies were hanging out of the trees. The stench was awful. But I tell you what . . . thank goodness for the Legion. We were given the shit jobs in Africa and the French expats knew it. If there was anywhere in the world that typified the need for the toughness of legionnaires, it was this succession of calls into Africa, playing piggy in the middle of warring factions armed to the teeth, with so much manpower. What we witnessed in Chad can hardly be repeated. The most worrying was seeing kids not yet in their teens running around with weapons bigger than they were.

Among Newton's best times were his excursions to French Guyana and the Legion's jungle warfare training programme. 'No one ever had a bad word to say about the place,' said Phil Meason, who went out there with 3REI in 1985 for what was the first of three postings which he thoroughly enjoyed, although a small rebellion in Surinam, backed once again by Libyan advisers, caused a few headaches for the Legion during the mid-1980s.

French Guyana is located in an equatorial forest zone of South America, separated along an indistinguishable frontier from Brazil by the Tumuc-Humac mountain range on the south and by the Oyapock River on the east. The Maroni, Litani and Lawa rivers mark its boundary with Surinam on the west. The land rises from a marshy coastal plateau in the north through the broad central regions covered by dense tropical forest, to the *terres hautes*, or highlands ascending from foothills to the Eureupoucigne and Oroye ranges in the extreme south. The climate of French Guyana is tropical with temperatures of 80°F. The dry season from June to November is succeeded by torrential rains, with an annual rainfall of around 126 inches. Conditions in a country four-fifths of which was covered by forest were ideal for troop training in extreme conditions and consequently the Legion entertained many internationals groups, ranging from Canadian forces to European special forces.

During the late 1980s, French Guyana had a population of fewer than 120,000, mostly Creoles, native American and black Africans. Native Americans, descended from the aboriginal Arawak, Carib and Tupí-Guaraní groups, inhabit the remote interior of French Guyana. Virtually untouched by Western civilization, they have preserved their traditional customs and part of Legion duties was to police these regions and keep out poachers and other mischief makers. Along the waterways are the settlements of the Saramancas, Boeschs, and Bonis, whose forebears were fugitive black slaves.

Phil Meason, fresh from his adventures in Africa, took a two year posting there and enjoyed every second of it, so much so that he would return again and again. He joined the headquarters company of 3REI. The engineers were there building a road from Guyana to Brazil. The Brazilians were supposed to start at the other end. They built about eight kilometres of the road when the money dried up and the company was disbanded. They were moved to Kourou when the main role of the 3rd was the defence of the French Space Centre where the European Space Centre *Ariane* rocket was launched.

There were three stages for the launch which required the attendance of the whole regiment: transfer of the rocket to the launch site, dress rehearsal and the actual launch. By then, there was a launch every six weeks and the first Meason witnessed was the fifteenth. In February 1998, when he recalled these moments in his career, the launch tally had just reached 100.

With the Space Centre already in active mode, another rebellion in the neighbouring former Dutch colony of Surinam was not treated lightly, especially as Colonel Gadaffi was backing the rebel leader, one Ronnie Brunswick. Meason recalls:

> French intelligence had tracked Libyan nationals moving into Surinam, acting as advisers, so the defence of the Space Centre was upgraded. An Air Force unit came in and built a radar

station, the French navy was re-inforced and built a small naval base with small craft operating on the coast side, the gendarmerie was increased in strength and the Legion was bolstered with the addition of an extra company, supplied on rotation every four months from other regiments.

It was not just the defence of the Space Station. We were running border patrols, river patrols and recce patrols to guard against incursions into French Guyana. At the time there were three regiments, Legion and two regular Army units, all doing their own jungle training courses. It was decided to centralize the course and put the whole thing under Legion control. We also had links with the Brazilian jungle training centre, one of the hardest in the world. The course was split into two parts. 1] Technique: river crossings, infiltration, setting up blocks on the river, survival, what you can eat and what you can't, how to build a shelter for six guys in five hours. 2] Tactical: doing it all again only on a real-time basis. It was all excellent stuff, and the only thing that bugs you is the mosquitoes. The river was something else, twice the width of the Thames. We used four-man canoes for our patrols which took us into the reservations where no civilians are allowed.

The rebellion in Surinam led by Ronnie Brunswick and his jungle commandos started out with serious implications, although it degenerated into a farce. He caused big trouble at the beginning, and his running skirmishes with the Surinam forces started a huge refugee problem. Our regiment had three LCMs for moving equipment and a detachment from the Legion was sent with one of these to help rescue refugees. We teamed up with the French river maritime police to set up and maintain a refugee camp for people coming off the river. Being an former Dutch colony, there were quite a lot of Europeans seeking shelter.

We did not have a base as such, just a petrol jetty and a warehouse beside it, but for a lot of the time we lived off the back of the boat – literally for everything. We looked rather like pirates. We were supplied by a French army regiment, staffed by national servicemen. The regiment seemed to have forgotten about us. We spent Christmas there and at the last minute, they sent a lieutenant down with our Christmas presents and booze. But it was a very good experience.

The rebel insurrection dragged on for about four years, although when it first started off we used to sit on our jetty and watch massive gunfights in Albina about two kilometres away from the river. In fact, we were eating our Christmas turkey by tracer-lights. We rescued more than 3,000 refugees in the first two to three weeks. A lot of old communities had been attacked, many were badly wounded or shell-shocked. We converted old leper colony buildings into a refugee camp. We picked up seventy refugees alone after one fire fight during our twelve-hour rotational patrols up and down the river.

One day, four English mercenaries turned up and said they were going to support Brunswick. One of them tried to recruit legionnaires into the cause for big money. One of my mates took exception to this when approached in a local bar and proceeded to tapdance over this guy's windpipe. The legionnaire was arrested by the gendarmerie for assaulting a civilian but then it was discovered that the mercenary he attacked had a load of stolen credit cards on him. So he was booted out of the country and the legionnaire was released. The magazine *Soldier of Fortune* came down to do a piece on us and Ronnie Brunswick. They got him off to a tee, describing him as a 28 year old man with the brain of a 12 year old. He used to flash up and down the river in a ski boat with a large gun mounted on the top. If he ever fired it, the boat would have toppled over backwards.

For the remainder of his service with the Foreign Legion, from 1987 to 1995, Phil Meason would be commuting in triangular fashion between Africa, France and French Guyana, with one diversionary deployment into the Gulf War. The throwbacks from the colonial era were, in the main, providing employment for the Legion, with all the troublespots of the previous two decades erupting every now and again.

In 1988, Phil Meason's outfit was back in Chad in support of a con-bined French Army and Air Force operation with the Legion specifically in defence of the air bases. There was also a good deal of work in and around Epéché, the nearest French air base to the Sudanese border, from which a column of vehicles was reportedly on the move. The Legion was on patrol using camels. Meason was back in French Guyana by the end of the year, from the Sahara to the Amazon with less than three weeks in between the two.

Such postings and the rigours of the Legion's disciplined existence relieved the boredom for many during a time of declining roles of the kind that kept legionnaires on their toes. In 1990, the Legion was back in Africa, this time in the poverty-racked Central African Republic, on a mission that combined stabilizing the political and military scene with attempting to make some sort of contribution to the ruined social services and domestic infrastructure. They were literally building bridges and repairing roads, refurbishing hospitals, including one which had been fully equipped not many years earlier but now had dogs kept in the maternity ward. The Legion began playing a hearts and minds role in some of the most desperate regions of Africa, a contribution that like so many others would be barely noticed in the overall scale of the seemingly insoluble African crisis. It was all very public spirited and a role that increasingly fell to the Legion during the 1980s. It was not, to put it bluntly, what legionnaires joined for. Many were bored and out of sorts because of the lack of the real action that they craved, and there were changes on other fronts too . . .

24

1980s: THE HARD TIMES PERSIST

'Articles on the prison began to surface in the mid-1970s,
alleging torturous beatings on inmates by their guards and
horrendous days chained naked to the wall in a punishment cell.'

THERE WAS a significant change in the Legion
in the mid-1980s, caused partly by the arrival of President Mitterand
in 1981. Many Socialists and certainly the more extreme left-wingers
wanted to get rid of the Foreign Legion and were only persuaded from
doing so by French commanders who made a strong case against losing
what they saw as a very effective and specialist part of French intervention forces. Politicians were not unaware, either, that to sack the
foreigners and send young French men to the war zones and the
troublespots would not win them any votes.

Change was, however, demanded because the general ethos of the
Legion was attracting persistent media coverage of allegations of
extreme brutality – even more so than in the past – much of it generally coming via deserters. Those who stayed were unlikely to complain,
although with much of the Legion being trained on French soil by
then, there was increasing potential for intervention by human rights
lawyers. In 1982, for example, three legionnaires who were French
nationals deserted from Corsica. None had completed even a year in
the Legion. They then went on French national televison complaining
about the brutality of its NCOs, the harshness of the training process,

the severe discipline, the punishment regime and the general lack of human compassion. They presented themselves as evidence. All three had been in trouble for one reason or another. One had tried to desert before and had ended up in a Legion prison in Calvi, one of the few camps that had two forms of incarceration. One was the standard guardhouse for relatively minor misdemeanors. More serious offenders were sent to another place, a Napoleonic fort on high ground, the Legion's disciplinary section on Corsica. It was on a ridge with two peaks. One peak housed the regimental headquarters of the military police and the other was the prison itself. It was the place of harsh discipline for long-term prisoners. The regime there was four to six hours sleep a night, the cells were like those on Devil's Island, set into the ground and open at the top with bars, with a concrete bed and concrete pillow. Inmates may or may not be given a blanket and could only wear underpants in the cell. They were woken early in the morning, washed and shaved, and began physical exercises: running around the fort, usually carrying something very heavy. There was a large rock called Christine painted red and green. Offenders against prison rules had to 'make love' to Christine, which entailed humping the rock around the fort. It was not unknown for persistent deserters to be clamped in leg irons, attached to a ball and chain. Articles on the prison began to surface in the mid-1970s, alleging torturous beatings on inmates by their guards, and horrendous days chained naked to the wall in a punishment cell.

Such brutality had been happening for a long time in various Legion posts, and by now the explanations of legionnaires of its acceptance had been well voiced by those who stayed. They repeatedly said it was part of the hardening process and that, when war or combat arrived, had helped in the process of staying alive. The deserters who got away and spilled the beans were as contemptuous of the men they left behind as their former colleagues were of them for running off. The publicity concerning discipline in the Corsican prison – and the admissions of violence elsewhere – resulted in considerable upheaval. Various government delegations visited Calvi, and Legion camps elsewhere, and demanded changes to the system. The main disciplinary prison on Corsica was closed in 1983 and the whole administration of the Legion began a process of gradual change. The Legion's own penal code was scrapped in favour of the standard disciplinary procedures of the French army. There were continuing inquiries into physical punishment and what some inspectors had described as the 'inhuman brutalization of young men ready to die for France ... it has been going on far too long'.

For quite some time there was a hue and cry over Legion methods and undoubtedly, in an age of political and military correctness, revisions were not only desirable but necessary. *La pelote*, the long-established method of punishment universally hated by legionnaires, was banned in 1984. The following year NCOs were forbidden to mete out press-ups, which had long been part of legion discipline both as a punishment and physical training. NCOs were warned of overstepping the new guidelines, officers began to look over their shoulders, and were very wary of any 'brutal' activity that might be occurring out of their sight in their own companies.

Far from achieving support from legionnaires in general, the reformers actually generated the reverse effect. Morale began to decline as did discipline itself. Cutbacks by the French military in both manpower and its presence in former colonial territories also affected the situation in that there was a decline in operational opportunities abroad, and, for the first time in its history, a large percentage of the Legion's strength was actually based in mainland France.

Arthur, the former Borstal boy from Brentford, had by the mid-1980s come through the mill. He had taken everything the Legion could throw at him and was himself a *caporal-chef* in the Legion's military police. He had a particular view on the subject of violence:

> The plain fact is that the brutality, for want of a better word, was an accepted part of Legion life and the basis of its discipline. Everyone joining the Legion now knew that, and if they didn't they must have been living on Mars. Basically if a man doesn't listen to an order, a smack in the face does tend to wake him up. If he's hurt, he remembers how he got hurt and why. It is necessary sometimes. Let's face it, I didn't graduate from Sunday

School, and nor did they. You are attempting to train and control a certain number of men who may be of a volatile nature. If you have one who is out of line, then you've got to roll your shirtsleeves up and belt him. It's a dual purpose thing; you've got to give him a lesson he won't forget and also it gets the respect of the majority, the men around the one you hit. You need the majority, and once you have their respect then you can command them. Now, unfortunately, in 1983 it started to change. From the time instruction was moved to France, certain elements of Legion discipline were kicked out of the window. Young NCOs coming through found that they were unable to resort to established Legion practices and consequently it affected overall discipline. They could not exercise command and instruction the way it was operated when I first joined. It cut the ground from under the NCOs. Part of the problem arose because by then many French recruits joining the Legion were based on home soil. They could actually go home in their time off, which had never happened in the past. They could exercise their rights. If they were hit, they'd go to see an officer who had to make a formal investigation. This had an disturbing effect, particularly on the longer serving legionnaires and, surprisingly, on younger officers. In the legionnaires' eyes, the officer was God. They wanted someone strong at the helm, a man commanding them who they could trust when they were in a tight corner. The whole premise of Legion discipline was being challenged.

Even so, although the changes evolved in the mid-1980s, they did not totally quash the Legion's traditional treatment of its new recruits or of its offenders against regimental discipline. Far from it. One legionnaire, Jacko, had experience of several Legion 'nicks' in his five-year contract from 1986 to 1991, long after the moderation of treatment had supposedly come into effect. He provided this graphic insight:

Calvi nick wasn't as hard as some other overseas Legion prisons. All those on mainland France were regularly scrutinized, and Calvi especially after the mass of media publicity it received in the early 1980s. That's when they closed down the main nick after a journalist reported on men being chained up on the walls. The chains were still there when I had a look inside. The smaller nick has been used ever since. It wasn't too bad. You'd be up at five in the morning, freezing cold at that time of the day, have your breakfast, such as it was, in the big cell which housed about fourteen people on camp beds. There was hardly enough room to move sometimes. If you'd done something really bad, you'd be in solitary for seven or fourteen days. The guards patrolled with dogs. They were war dogs, nasty bastards, the throwbacks from the litter and in permanent killing mode – Alsatians, Rotweilers and Dobermanns. The dogs had to have training, keep them up to scratch like the rest of us. Every so often, the corporals would come into the cell looking for volunteers. This used to worry me no end. They'd take you down to the training area and put you in a big protective suit and you would start running, fast as you could. Suddenly, you hear the slobbering animal coming up behind you and then it would pounce and you'd hit the deck like a rock. Those animals have got real power. Then, it's ripping your arm apart. You can't feel it because of the protective suit, but believe me you're thinking: 'Jesus, what if the suit rips open?' It has got to be the scariest thing I ever did in my life, listening to that snarling Rotweiler getting closer and closer.

In the nick we ate outside in the courtyard on square tables, whatever the weather. You did the run, eight kilometres every morning with pack, and the dogs would run with you. Then, all you did was gardening and menial tasks. There were so many plants and flowers in the Calvi camp, it could keep a jail full of legionnaires occupied all year round. The days of corporal punishment and rock breaking were long gone when I went in.

Overseas, it was different. Bloody tough . . . out of sight and out of mind, the nick is still hard. An example: in Djibouti in 1987, the French Commando Marines were based with us at the time. One night, one of the 2REP legionnaires was sitting in a bar minding his own business having a quiet drink, with his kepi beside him. A group of Marines came in, started to take the piss and poured beer in his kepi. He got shirty about it; nobody does that to a legionnaire's kepi. The Commando Marines then gave him a good beating and as word spread, other legionnaires and commandos piled in and all hell broke loose. A lot of them were arrested, and the blame seemed to be attached to the Legion, not the Marines who had actually started it. The Legion boys were naturally pretty fed up about this and when nightfall came, those not already locked up took pickaxe handles and anything they could lay their hands on and headed off to town to take their revenge. They smashed up the bars where the Marines drank and gave the Marines themselves a mauling. Back at base, officers were aroused. Since the avenging party had been joined by a number of corporals, the commandant ordered the officer to lead the round-up. Accompanied by MPs with dogs, they drove into town in long range desert patrol vehicles and a couple of old Dodges to pick us up. Eventually order was restored, and about thirty were arrested, piled into the trucks and brought back to camp. There they had us in line and someone called out a song title and we all started singing. There was a definite attitude among us that night. Eventually, we quietened down and all thirty were crammed into an eight-man nick. We spent the night standing up. Next morning, the punishments began that they would not get away with in France: up at 4 a.m. and they started running us around with two sandbags on our backs, followed by sit-ups and press-ups, alternately for an hour. Then we went for breakfast, and because we were the scum of the earth, we were not supplied with cutlery of any description and had to eat with our fingers. After breakfast, we were marched down to the big ammunition depot at the REP base. It was covered in sandbags, thousands of them. The task was to deconstruct the bunker, empty the sandbags, fill them up again and rebuild the bunker. It was a mammoth, tedious task, but there was plenty of time; the sentence was thirty days.

Jacko is a wide, tough Welshman, a warm and friendly guy who welcomes you into his home with a beaming smile. Some things in the Legion may have changed; others have not. He recalls:

I was 29 years old, I had completed twelve years in the British army, first in the infantry and then as a para including service in Germany and five years during the pressure days of Northern Ireland. My marriage had broken down and ended in divorce. I was having difficulty getting access to my son. I had no job and little prospect of getting one. Unemployment in Wales was pretty dire. After all that time in the Army, I found myself in the dole queue with hippies and drop-outs and so I told my mother, 'Mam, I'm going to the Legion.'

She said, 'Don't be so bloody daft, son.'

I said, 'Mam, there's nothing else for it.'

I got the train and ferry to Calais and went straight down to Marseille. I went through all the procedures, told them everything they wanted to know . . . even that my ex-wife had virtually barred me from seeing my own son. So the sergeant who was giving me the third degree began the process of giving me a totally new identity.

He had my real name and then he pulled out a list and picked another beginning with the same initial. Then he found a Christian name. I gave him my birth date and he wrote down something totally different.

Where was I born?

Aberystwyth.

He couldn't even pronounce it but he went over to a map of the world and I showed him where it was. His finger carried on down the coast of Wales and it stopped at Cardigan. He asked my father's name, and changed that too, and my mother's. I ended up with a French father and an English mother. So that was my new identity and all my documents were made out in that name. I would retain that identity for three years, at which time legionnaires have the opportunity of reverting to their real name or keeping the false one.

A little green van came to take us to Aubagne. It looked posh, like a hotel. Then, they showed us to our quarters, three floors up in these little rooms in which you could get about six beds side by side. But they had them stacked three beds high – eighteen beds. I couldn't believe it. I tell you, you had all sorts with you. You were scratching all the time with the things you were picking up. There were people coming in with lice and all sorts! Now I'm a working class lad, me, and I'm not getting at these chaps . . . but, the room stank with them. They'd come from God knows where, hadn't washed for days. No wonder they shaved your heads. Incredible! I was stupid as well, I turned up with two bags of clothes which I never saw again. Had some good stuff in there including my Parachute Regiment jumper and rugby club jumper.

We did all the pre-selection stuff . . . intelligence tests, medical, fitness tests, got our kit from the stores and you are shown your white kepi which is in a plastic bag. You don't see that again until you're in the Legion. Now, they take you to the training camp at Castelnaudary which was the beginning of a nightmare. The first thing they did was run us round and round the square with our bags.

Your kit was dusty and dirty, and all you could do then was wash the whole lot. One of the corporals barked out an instruction in French. I didn't understand a word he was saying. I'm looking at this corporal daft, like. He's just told me to go and get my rifle from the armoury pronto, and I'm still standing there wondering what the hell he said.

Suddenly, bang! I get a punch in the face. And he tells me in French again and then he tells me in English and tells me not to forget it and while I'm still standing wondering what hit me, bang!, another punch in the face and he asks me what I'm waiting for. I can tell you, I've never forgotten that command again and I very quickly learned the rest of the basic commands. You either learn to understand French fast or you get a very fat face. When you've been in for a week or so, you're getting ready to be farmed. The farm is a bit like a school of thought – except that you have no time to think.

It's time to be broken down and built up; it's moulding time. Deprivation of sleep. Deprivation of food. When you come back from the farm you are absolutely mentally and physically shagged. They break you so far, but not so that your spirit is shattered. They want you to have respect. In a way, its good. With a guy like me, who's been in the British army for twelve years, you're probably a bit set in your ways, or the way of the British military. You get moulded into shape the way the Legion wants you. When you think about it, individuality can't work in the Legion.

They don't give a shit for the individual. They don't know the meaning of the word. And I must admit, I thought about upping sticks and pissing off several times. I'd be lying if I said I didn't. I stuck it out, but I'd never do the first two years in the Legion again. It was crazy. Wild . . . If you didn't prove yourself in that time, you'd get your balls broken for the remaining time you were there. But, no, at the end of the day, they didn't give a shit. The Legion didn't ask you to come. You went under your own steam and you walked in and said I want to join. They give you money. They give you clothes. They give you three square meals a day and you've signed a paper which says you'll serve for five years in the French Foreign Legion. It's take it or leave it time.

If you stayed, you had to put up with the shit, and the corporals. It could drive a man crazy. One day one of the corporals slapped me in the face once too often. It was for some trivial misdemeanor like not standing up straight. I just lost it and hit him back, whacked him good, so hard it lifted him off the ground. That night, three corporals came and dragged me out of bed, sprayed CS gas in my face and gave me a right kicking. Even an elephant would go down from CS gas at close range; your respiratory system goes.

A lot of us felt like deserting in those early days of training. You get really low sometimes and that's what they want. So you get slapped and you think: 'What the fuck am I doing here?' But then there were high points: the satisfaction of doing it well, the training, the achievement of doing things you would have previously thought damn-near impossible.

They hit me. So what? I probably deserved it for being so stupid. And would I be able to live with myself if I ran away? No. Only tossers run away. Lazy bastards. One of them was in my unit. He didn't stay for long, deserted while we were in Djibouti and ran home crying. He wrote a book which was so inaccurate and trumped up that everyone who knew him just laughed. It's true that when you look at the stories everyone else tells about the brutality, the obvious question to ask is why on earth would any man who can think for himself even consider volunteering, let alone staying in? It's hard to put into words. I was looking for escape and I found it. There is so much going on, you don't have time to think.

Jacko found the experience of becoming a Legion paratrooper exhilarating:

It was a big day for me, getting to the REP. They threw me into it. Thirteen or fourteen jumps within two weeks and I'd got my wings. No messing around. The drop zone was four miles from the camp, whereas in the British army you have to travel from Aldershot to Brize Norton and mess around for twenty-four hours doing one bloody jump. If the weather was bad in Britain, the jump was called off. In the Legion, you jump whatever the weather. If you went up in an aircraft at Calvi there was no way you'd come down in it. You drop into the back garden of the Calvi base, pick up your parachute when you land, fold it, run to the far end of the drop zone for inspection and hand it in ready to be re-packed, back in the truck and within an hour you're back in the aircraft ready to do another. You could do four jumps in a day; one day we did seven or eight. In my first year I did fifty-seven jumps. Your pay, including your jump pay, more than doubled, and by the third year had tripled.

I went into the 4th Section of the 4th Company, where the adjutant was a German, a Legion veteran. He was a nice guy off-duty, but an animal at all other times. They've got this thing in Corsica, the GR20, which is supposed to be a public footpath which you can follow from the north to the south over the hills. We hadn't been there long before he sent us on this mega-march. There was a corporal there, an English guy who was carrying the adjutant's radio. We had been marching for hours when we stopped for a breather. He was sitting down, pretty near exhausted, and the adjutant called out to him: 'Get up here!'.

Then, when the corporal hadn't moved, the adjutant began kicking him on the hill: 'Get up, get up!' he said: 'I can't go on.' Next thing, the adjutant is shouting for a rope. We all looked on wondering what the fuck was going to happen next. He took the radio off the corporal's back and put it on his own. Then, he tied the rope around him, and he marched off, carrying the radio *and* dragging the corporal behind him. That was the end of him. The adjutant wanted him out after that.

You'll be hard put to find a legionnaire who has completed his five years, or ten or fifteen, who says he wishes he never joined. The answer will always be: 'I have no regrets'. I certainly haven't. I would not say a word against the Legion.

The same sentiment has been expressed time and time again. The brutality is soon forgotten, the hard times put behind them. The result is a camaraderie among those who came together for this journey through dark days, and respect for the Legion as a whole. Which is why this paraxodical organization continues to exist today.

25

1991: THE GULF WAR; 1993: BOSNIA; 1997: REPUBLIC OF CONGO

'The French army and the Legion's own reconnaisance units were
probing Iraqi territory long before the British and American
special forces made their now famous sorties across the border ...'

LEGIONNAIRE Kevin Arthur was coming up to
the completion of fifteen years service when Saddam Hussein began
chaining Western hostages to the public utilities of Iraq. He qualified
for a decent pension and had a tidy sum of money in his Legion bank
account. Arthur was among a declining number of legionnaires with
such a service record. He had served in many of the Legion's global
activities and had been involved in virtually every major combat
operation since he joined. He had jumped with 2REP into Africa,
had been a member of the security team guarding the controversial
French Polynesian nuclear test site at Mururoa atoll, where twenty-one
bombs were exploded at a time when it was under constant harrass-
ment from peace campaigners. He had spent almost eight years as a
caporal-chef in the Legion's military police and was one of fourteen
candidates selected from fifty-six entries for specialist anti-terrorist
training. As such, he had the authority to go out carrying a weapon
and could select his own from the armoury.

In September 1990 he was serving with 2REI based in Nimes and
was about to call it a day when the Iraqi alert went up, and the Legion

was placed on standby for imminent embarkation. Arthur couldn't resist it. Within days, he was among the 4,000 troops who boarded car ferries and other assorted craft en route to the Red Sea, where the Legion's largest deployment of forces since Algeria was being assembled. He said:

I could have retired, but I decided to sign on for the duration. And I'm really glad I did. I was driven by the thrill of another scrap and what could well have been big-time fighting. But what came in as a side issue to all this was that there were many young kids who had barely completed their Legion training among the soldiers going to war. Boys of 18 or 19 who'd never been in any action – blokes we had to look after. That's what gave me as much of a kick as anything, helping young soldiers and giving them tips that might just save their lives. The young legionnaires looked up to the older men. It's one of the traditions they had been learning in their basic training, just as I had. But a lot of things had changed since I joined. Long gone were the days when the Legion was the Cinderella in terms of kit and weaponry. It was now recognized for what it was, an elite fighting force that had units which could compare with the SAS or the US Seals, and in many respects we were a good deal more versatile. As such, the French had given us the right gear; we were extremely well tooled up. These young kids were handling high-powered weapons: semi-automatic 5.56mm machine-guns; 89mm bazookas that could knock out a tank at 600 metres. We all knew, of course, that this was not quite the magnanimous gesture it seemed on the part of the French government. Although there are far more French nationals in the Legion these days, legionnaires are still expendable. No one in France is going to cry over a dead legionnaire. Quite the reverse. Every dead foreign legionnaire means a young French life saved. That's the way it's always been, and it's not likely to change now. The French view of the Legion also remained unchanged: legionnaires weren't asked to join. They came to France to volunteer. Every legionnaire knows that once he signs that contract, if he dies it's his own fault. At the same time, the French military requires us to represent them in exemplary fashion which, these days, means having the ability to perform well in high-tech wars.

The Legion put an initial force of 2,300 men into Saudi Arabia, as part of a French contingent which eventually numbered 10,000 men. The whole of 2REI was mobilized en masse and their base camp at Nimes was closed up and left in the hands of local *gendarmerie*. They were joined by 2REC, based at Orange. Aboard the cramped ferry boats the journey was spent preparing weapons, Nuclear, Biological and Chemical (NBC) protection suits and gas masks for the threatened onslaught of Iraqi chemical and biological weapons. The Legion landed at Yanbu, on the Red Sea coast of Saudi Arabia. There, with superb precision, they prepared to leave for the desert in a 280-vehicle convoy of tanks, armoured personnel carriers and lorries. Although many were too young to have experienced combat, a large percentage of the force was well used to desert conditions, having served on various rotational postings across Africa, in places like Chad and Djibouti. There were enough long service legionnaires who knew the tricks of the trade, which as Arthur explained, made life easier in such conditions:

The Americans, for example, had huge supplies of water, something like fourteen litres per day per man. We used a fraction of that. Now we know that you have to be wary of dehydration, the more straight water you drink, the more you crave for it in the desert. Our intake was considerably less, and we usually mixed it with coffee, sugar and biscuits from our ration packs. That way you get the liquid intake and provide the body with its requirements to fight the heat.

They also looked upon the American Gulf Forces with a touch of envy in regard to their supplies and facilities, but contempt for their overkill in helicopters and logistics support. The Legion focused on necessities, travelling light where possible. They were equipped with thirty per cent more anti-tank weaponry in a platoon and considered themselves better equipped for this type of warfare than a comparable American unit. Nor did they wear flakjackets which they believed would slow them down at times when speed of mobility may have been vital.

They filed out of the warehouse where they had been billeted with their packs weighing more than 70lb and clambered over the vehicles that were to carry them on a 300-mile journey to what would be their base camp in the desert.

There was no doubt that the hype about the prospect of war in the Gulf had given the Legion a new edge. The news media who were scrutinizing the troop arrivals were impressed. Many reports spoke of the Legion's immaculate turn-out in rough conditions, a collection of men who were clearly in prime mental and physical condition and, as one put it, 'possessed by a maturity beyond their average age'.

Many noted that latter point in their reports and said that there was an evident and distinct psychological difference between legionnaires and men of other armies. The point was put to Legion Captain Pierre Chavancy during a visit by the media. His explanation was that the legionnaires 'stay calm in the storm' whereas the American marines, for example, tended to be somewhat 'impetuous'. The impassiveness of legionnaires, he said, came with a maturity learned from the 'heavy and occasionally unpleasant' soldiering that lay behind them. 'A lot of them have seen the rougher side of the world. They simply no longer possess the naivety that is apparent among young American or British soldiers.'

Robert Fisk, writing in Britain's *Independent on Sunday* newspaper, perhaps best caught the mood of the moment in its assessment of the Legion compared with other armies assembling in Saudi. He wrote:

> It may seem uncharitable, especially to the British, who try to ignore them, and the Americans, who sleep in darkness and bitch about the heat and dirt. But the French Foreign Legion are a joy to behold . . . hard as nails, slightly criminal no doubt . . . and while their Anglo-American cousins, lights doused, munch compo rations in the desert night and prepare for war . . . the Legion's encampment, spread across forty miles of sand, is a city of light . . .

when unidentified aircraft fly over at night, they extinguish their lamps and deploy across the desert floor in ten minutes – five minutes less than they believe it would take an Iraqi jet to travel from its airbase to the sky over Hafar al Batin. Thus the Foreign Legion has a deceptive, almost laid back air. Its officers are served ratatouille at high table, drinking from glasses which bear the crest of the Second Infantry Regiment, their voices raised in the Ravel-like chorus of *Au Legionnaire*:

When you've chucked away all your dough
and dirty tricks have laid low your career,
sling your shoes on your back,
for it's time
to hide away in the bottom of a ferryboat and sign
up to become a Legionnaire.

Dirty tricks, of course, are much on the minds of the Americans and British just now. What on Earth are the French doing down here, scarcely thirty miles from the Iraqi frontier, politely refusing to come under US command, pulling back from the border – as they just have – at the very moment Saddam Hussein released the entire contingent of French hostages in Iraq and Kuwait?

The legionnaires and the rest of the French contingent were supposed to be strengthening the multi-national force deployed south-west of Kuwait. Legion units had gone straight to the border, forty miles further forward than the Americans and the British 7th Armoured Brigade. The French army and the Legion's own reconnaisance units were probing Iraqi territory long before the British and American special forces made their now famous sorties across the border once the war had begun. Three French soldiers, not legionnaires, were captured and taken to the Iraqi capital and, unlike British flyers who were captured and tortured, were sent on home to Paris, a move which gave some cause for intrigue and speculation. Journalists at the French press conferences were bluntly warned by General Jean-Charles Mouscardes: 'If you ask about this subject, you will immediately be escorted out of here.'

It was a sensitive time. The French claimed it was an accidental incursion, and that the three soldiers had simply lost their way. The truth was that the recce teams from both Legion and French army units were engaged in long-range intelligence gathering missions almost from the moment of their arrival near the Iraqi frontier. The whole composure of the Legion's desert turn-out was one of rapid movement, utilizing long-held traditions of desert warfare in which their strength was in their mobility rather than firepower. Their long-range desert patrols were capable of travelling fast and light.

When the ground war began on 24 February 1991, the Legion contingent was among the first on the move. They were bombarding Iraqi positions on the west flank of the coalition battle plan, advancing rapidly and efficiently upon their assigned targets in a manner that drew praise from Desert Storm commander General Norman Schwarzkopf. The Legion was part of a manoeuvre to make a wide sweep across the desert and to trap Saddam Hussein's renowned Republican Guard. In fact, the Iraqi troops were in retreat by 26 February, and the war ended the following day. Thereafter, they began rounding up prisoners. The job done, the Legion and the rest of the French contingent returned to France to a rapturous reception from the crowds, followed by parades and medals presentations in which the Legion was well to the fore. Kevin Arthur received a medal for taking out an Iraqi machine-gun nest with five Iraqi soldiers.

Arthur did not retire, as planned, when it was all over. He accepted a two-year posting to French Polynesia, the beautiful sun-drenched, palm-fringed islands scattered over a wide area of the eastern South Pacific Ocean. The principal island is Tahiti with its chief town, Papeete, annexed by France in the 1840s. He joined a mixed Pacific regiment guarding the French nuclear installations around Mururoa atoll. It was to have been by way of a soft option, the wind-down to his retirement from the Legion, and he was engaged for a large part of the time on a hearts and minds operation on one of the remote outer-islands of the Tahitian archipelago which had been badly damaged by an earthquake. With a team of demolition specialists, he was employed on rebuilding some of the island's infrastructure, including six churches. The legionnaires also built a volleyball court for the local youth. The task was interspersed with week-long breaks in the Polynesian capital, which was a very pleasant way of spending his remaining time in the Legion. Or at least, it might have been had all been peaceful and quiet. The problem was that Arthur had arrived at the time of tension in the Pacific surrounding the French nuclear testing programme, eventually halted after protests from the locals and the governments of Australia and New Zealand, as well as some interesting side action from Greenpeace.

For some time, tension had also been running high among the Tahitian independence movement, now seeking to unleash itself from the shackles of French rule. This eventually manifested itself with an outbreak of rioting, initially provoked by France's nuclear test at Muroroa atoll. The riot, which began at the nearby international airport, spread to the city centre. Masked youths threw firebombs at the French Polynesian Territorial Assembly, attacked the French High Commission and went on a rampage of destruction, looting and burning cars, shops, banks, and petrol stations.

Police retaliated with tear-gas, plastic bullets and concussion grenades, but were vastly outnumbered. After a day-long siege of the airport, a force of French paratroops and legionnaires were flown the 750 miles from the Mururoa test site base. Further reinforcements were being sent from New Caledonia and France. In the centre of Papeete, demonstrators gathered at the Place Tarahoi – the site of an anti-nuclear 'Village of Peace' – and attacked government buildings. After firebomb attacks on the Territorial Assembly and the High Commission, police responded with a volley of tear-gas grenades. President Gaston Flosse, appealing for calm, attacked environmental activists, foreign politicians and journalists drawn to Tahiti for the protests against the nuclear tests. The riots were eventually quelled, but the French nuclear programme in the region was scaled down although the Legion's presence was maintained.

When Arthur returned from French Polynesia, he decided to stay on for a further two-and-a-half years to qualify for enhanced pension rights. He joined 1REI when, in the autumn of 1995, he was summoned to a parade ground meeting with thirty other legionnaires, all specialists in anti-terrorist and anti-sniper combat. To conclude what he anticipated would be a peaceful climax to his Legion career, he was bound for Bosnia.

The Legion had been deployed to this unhappy land as part of the international peace-keeping force in early January 1993. It followed the succession of horror stories from the former Yugoslavia, with widespread violations of human rights in the country. The systematic rape of thousands of Muslim women by Serbian soldiers, in the name of so-called ethnic cleansing, was recognized as an unprecedented atrocity. International mediation, however, was able to accomplish very little and all efforts of mediation had failed by mid-1993. The Legion's initial deployment numbered 1,000 men, part of the French contribution to the United Nations protection force, and included many of Serbo-Croat background who had volunteered in the post-communist era, along with a large influx from Eastern Europe. Others chose to stay behind, taking advantage of the Legion tradition of giving legionnaires the option of declining service in their country of birth.

A contingent from 2REP, consisting of its 1st and 4th companies, formed part of the Anglo-French-Dutch Rapid Reaction Force which, with the support of NATO bombers, was credited with relieving the siege of bomb-shattered Sarajevo. Legion positions were under frequent attack, and suffered their first casualty on 11 February 1993, when Legionnaire Ratislav Benko was killed during a mortar attack. The Legion's presence in Bosnia was augmented in May 1993 with the arrival of support companies from 1REC and 2REI, with up to 2,500 legionnaires deployed at any one time. They were confronted with some heavy fighting.

The legionnaires took over the defence of Sarajevo Airport, a task which was not without its problems. Their armoured personnel carriers, more used to desert conditions, did not take kindly to the heavy snow of the Bosnian winters. Further, their presence was not welcomed by the locals, and the legionnaires once again were deployed on hearts and minds operations as well as military strategy. In October 1995, the Dayton Peace Initiative, supported by the Western powers under the NATO alliance, began to set in motion the groundwork for a total cessation of hostilities, although there was still much sporadic fire.

NATO divided Bosnia into three main sectors, with forces of the major allies deployed separately in each. The French sector covered the southern part of the country, with its command headquarters based in Sarajevo which the Bosnian Serbs wanted to remain a divided city. It provided one of the most controversial elements of the Dayton talks and in the meantime, the French had to protect their forces from the continuing sniper fire which had caused such havoc in the city. Arthur was among the anti-sniper specialists moved into the mountains around the capital. They were in teams of four, with two basic tasks – to locate and take out Serbian snipers, and provide intelligence for air and ground reaction. The teams were put out for days at a time, and on occasions they could actually see their enemy in position on the opposite side of the valley, virtually able to wave at them when they clocked on for the watch.

The region was by then swarming with multi-national forces assembled under NATO's Operation Joint Endeavour. The Legion was running top secret operations and patrols that compared with those assigned to US and British special forces, such as the SAS, by NATO's Allied Command Europe Rapid Reaction Force (ARRC) in other regions of Bosnia. ARRC commanders recognized that the Legion's contribution, although attracting some criticism for occasional heavy-handed intervention, was fundamental in helping to meet deadlines set under the Dayton Peace Agreement, thus achieving the separation of the warring factions by D-Day, 18 January 1996.

Arthur, meantime, collected one more campaign medal to add to his collection, totalling eleven in all when he finally retired from the Legion in September 1997 after twenty-one-and-a-half years service.

* * *

The Legion, meanwhile, goes on. In 1997, it fielded a total force of around 9,500 men, a third of the number reached during the peak days of the early 1930s and later during the Algerian troubles. It retains a strong presence in international affairs, increasingly as a force of specialist intervention which fields specialist units that they claim are comparable with the British SAS and SBS. That specialist forces from the US and Canada also train with legionnaires, at their facilities in French Guyana, is some kind of tribute to their expertise in what is today termed 'elite soldiering', the spearhead to virtually every kind of modern-day combat situation, often travelling to a front-line by stealth over land or water, or mob-handed from the air in a style that still retains some of the more traditional arrogant qualities of the Legion.

From time to time, Africa continues to demand the Legion's presence, and the 13th Demi-Brigade remains to this day ensconced in its fort in Djibouti. In the summer of 1997, for example, 600 men of 2REP jumped in full combat gear into Brazzaville, the capital of the new Republic of Congo. In a classic Legion operation, they were sent to bolster 450 legionnaires resident in the Congo since April that year, and who were caught in the middle of the latest in a long line of African civil wars. The paras' most vital task, however, was to help rescue and evacuate hundreds of trapped foreigners. A corporal was killed and five legionnaires were wounded in early exchanges, and the reinforcements arrived as mortars and heavy machine-guns continued to wrack the city.

The paras drove in at dawn in armoured vehicles which had been flown in from French bases in West Africa. They spent days gathering up stranded expatriates. Here, as ever, they were met by the legacy of France's colonialist history in the region, a violent anti-French sentiment which meant they were targets for both sides. Legion commanders issued a stern warning to both sides to leave them alone, and allow them to evacuate those caught up in the fighting. They flung a cordon around the airport and began ferrying the expatriates out. British legionnaire Jim Brown, who was among the invasion force, recalled:

> We had to duck and dive through the artillery to reach two of the main hotels in the city where hundreds of foreigners had taken refuge. They had been there for about six days when we arrived, sleeping in the hallways and on the stairs of the hotels. They had barricaded themselves in with furniture, and covered the windows to prevent injury from flying glass as the bullets and shells hit. As usual, the Legion took the brunt of the attacks as soon as we arrived. There was a good deal of animosity toward us. But we're used to that, aren't we?

It is on that note that these pages draw to a close. We leave the Legion where it began, a group of men most of whom had no particular interest in the politics of the country that employed them, nor even an allegiance to it, fighting for French interests in a faraway place. Soldiers, adventurers, romantics, job-hunters, the slightly criminal and those who simply want to hide away from their world. In that regard, nothing has changed. The call of the Foreign Legion remains unabated.

The feeling is entirely reciprocal. Numbers may have dwindled somewhat compared with past highs, in common with the armies of most European nations now that the Cold War threat has lifted. But still the Legion, with all its own specialised compartments, is a key component in the French military machine and will remain so for the foreseeable future. New recruits will never be turned away.

The French genuinely love them, and that affection is abundantly on display every time the legionnaires perform their arrogant, jaunty 88-paces a minute march in pristine order on major occasions of state. That, in a way, is the ultimate paradox ... the French nation claiming as its own the French Foreign Legion, manned to a large extent by volunteers who have no real affinity with that country or its people.

They are legionnaires. Just that ... and the noisy crowds cheering as they pass by know they owe them a lot.

APPENDIX 1

FOREIGN LEGION REGIMENTS

1RE (1er Régiment Étranger) based at Quartier Viennot, Aubagne, headquarters for the entire Legion and eventual reception centre for all new recruits.

4RE (4ème Régiment Étranger) a military academy regiment, based at Quartier Danjou, Castelnaudary; NCO, and officer schools are here.

1REC (1er Régiment Étranger de Cavalerie) originally a cavalry regiment formed in 1921, based at Quartier Labouche, Orange.

2REI (2ème Régiment Étranger d'Infanterie) a mechanized infantry regiment formed in 1841, based at Quartier Vallongue, Nîmes.

6REG (6ème Régiment Étranger de Genie) formed in 1984, it is the Legion's engineering division, specializing in building projects as well as the clearance of mines and booby traps, based at Camp Ardoise in Avignon.

2REP (2ème Régiment Étranger de Parachutistes) the Legion's airborne elite unit based in Corsica, open to top recruits who must also be volunteers. Most of the Legion's special forces are to be found in specialist units of 2REP such as: CRAP (Commandos de Recherche et d'Action dans la Profondeur), manned almost entirely by NCOs; 1 Company, anti-tank and urban combat; 2 Company, mountain warfare; 3 Company, amphibious; 4 Company, demolition, sabotage and sniping; plus administration, support and logistics companies.

3REI (3ème Régiment Étranger d'Infanterie) formed in 1915 and now stationed in French Guyana, at Quartier Forget.

5RE (5ème Régiment Étranger) was established in Indo-China in 1930, but is now part of the French Mixed Pacific force based in French Polynesia. The primary task is to secure the nuclear test site there, but it also serves as rest and relaxation for long-service legionnaires.

13DBLE (13th Demi-Brigade de Légion Étrangère) established in 1940 in Sidi-bel-Abbès, now based at Quartier Montclar, Djibouti, north-east Africa and the Legion's modern-day desert unit.

DLEM (Détachement de Légion Étrangère de Mayotte) is a small detachment based on Mayotte, in the Comoros archipelago in the Strait of Mozambique. In 1976 the Comoros decided to remain a part of the French Republic. The Legion represents the French presence in the Indian Ocean region and guards communications systems.

APPENDIX 2

CAREER PROSPECTS

At the end of the initial enlistment of five years, the legionnaire can extend his career by signing successive contracts of 6 months, 1 year, 2 years, 3 years, until he reaches 15 years service or more, depending on rank and conduct. After 15 years service he is entitled to a retirement pension payable even in foreign countries. During his career in the Legion he will be regularly posted overseas for which additional bonuses are payable. Many specializations are available to recruits to the Legion, ranging from skills in mortars and missiles to diver, sniper or paratrooper. There are also specialist trades including: signals (radio or mechanic-exchange operator, telephonist); transport (Light vehicle, HGV1 and 2, or tracked vehicle driver); engineers (heavy equipment operator); building trades (bricklayer, plumber, electrician, carpenter, painter); maintenance (mechanic, car electrician, welder, car painter) or miscellaneous, such as musician, medical assistant, cook, photographer, printer, sports instructor, computer operator.

BIBLIOGRAPHY

Aage, Prince of Denmark, *Mes Souvenirs de la Légion Éstrangère*, Paris: Payot, 1936

Beauvoir, Roger de, *Légion Étrangère*, Paris: Firmin-Didot, 1907

Cooper, Adolphus Richard, *March or Bust: Adventures in the Foreign Legion*, London: Hale, 1972

Doty, Bennett J, *The Legion of the Damned*, New York: Century, 1928

Evans, LTC, 'La Légion Étrangère Française', *Army Quarterly and Defence Journal III* (Jan 1981)

Geraghty, Tony, *March or Die: A New History of the French Foreign Legion*, London HarperCollins, 1987

Hart, Adrian Liddell, *Strange Company*, London: Weidenfeld & Nicholson, 1953

Kanitz, Walter, *The White Kepi: A Casual History of the French Foreign Legion*, Chicago: Regnery, 1956

Lapie, Pierre O, *With the Foreign Legion at Narvik*, London: Murray, 1941

Manington, George, *A Soldier of the Legion: An Englishman's Adventures Under the French Flag in Algeria and Tonquin*, London: Murray, 1907

Martyn, Frederic, *Life in the Legion*, London: Everett, 1912

Mercer, Charles, *Legion of Strangers: The Vivid History of a Unique Military Tradition – The French Foreign Legion*, New York: Holt, Rinehart & Winston, 1964

Morel, le Lieutenant-Colonel, *La Légion Étrangère: Recueil de Documents Concernant L'Historique, l'Organisation et la législation Spéciale des Régiments Etrangers*, Paris: Chapelot, 1912

Murray, Simon, *Legionnaire: My Five Years in the French Foreign Legion*, London: Sidgwick & Jackson, 1978

Notes sur la Campagne du 3. Bataillon de la Légion Étrangère au Tonkin, Paris: Charles-Lavauzelle, 1888

O'Ballance, Edgar, *The Story of the French Foreign Legion*, London: Faber & Faber, 1961

Porch, Douglas, *The French Foreign Legion*, London: Macmillan, 1991

Rockwell, Kiffin Yates, *War Letters of Kiffin Yates Rockwell, Foreign Legionnaire and Aviator, France, 1914–1916*, Garden City, New York: Country Life, 1925

Rockwell, Paul Ayres, *American Fighters in the Foreign Legion, 1914–1918*, New York: Houghton Mifflin, 1930

'Whatever Happened to the French Foreign Legion?', *Military Review*, LI (Apr 1971)

INDEX